Roman Britain in Twenty Towns

ALSO AVAILABLE FROM BLOOMSBURY

Hadrian's Wall: Creating Division by Matthew Symonds
Londinium: A Biography by Richard Hingley with illustrations by Christina Unwin
Pompeii: An Archaeological Guide by Paul Wilkinson
Stonehenge: A Brief History by Mike Parker Pearson
Winchester: City of Kings by Susanne Haselgrove and Katherine Barclay

Roman Britain in Twenty Towns

A Visitor's Guide

Richard Hingley

Illustrations by Christina Unwin

BLOOMSBURY ACADEMIC
LONDON • NEW YORK • OXFORD • NEW DELHI • SYDNEY

BLOOMSBURY ACADEMIC

Bloomsbury Publishing Plc, 50 Bedford Square, London, WC1B 3DP, UK
Bloomsbury Publishing Inc, 1359 Broadway, New York, NY 10018, USA
Bloomsbury Publishing Ireland, 29 Earlsfort Terrace, Dublin 2, D02 AY28, Ireland

BLOOMSBURY, BLOOMSBURY ACADEMIC and the Diana logo are
trademarks of Bloomsbury Publishing Plc

First published in Great Britain 2026

Copyright © Richard Hingley, Christina Unwin, 2026

Richard Hingley, Christina Unwin have asserted their right under the Copyright,
Designs and Patents Act, 1988, to be identified as Authors of this work.

Cover design by Jade Barnett
Cover image: Roman Baths © Oliver Taylor/ Adobe Stock

All rights reserved. No part of this publication may be: i) reproduced or
transmitted in any form, electronic or mechanical, including photocopying,
recording or by means of any information storage or retrieval system without
prior permission in writing from the publishers; or ii) used or reproduced in
any way for the training, development or operation of artificial intelligence (AI)
technologies, including generative AI technologies. The rights holders expressly
reserve this publication from the text and data mining exception as per Article
4(3) of the Digital Single Market Directive (EU) 2019/790.

Bloomsbury Publishing Plc does not have any control over, or responsibility for,
any third-party websites referred to or in this book. All internet addresses given
in this book were correct at the time of going to press. The author and publisher
regret any inconvenience caused if addresses have changed or sites have ceased
to exist, but can accept no responsibility for any such changes.

A catalogue record for this book is available from the British Library.

A catalog record for this book is available from the Library of Congress.

ISBN: PB: 978-1-3505-2011-0
ePDF: 978-1-3505-2012-7
eBook: 978-1-3505-2013-4

Typeset by RefineCatch Limited, Bungay, Suffolk
Printed and bound in India

For product safety related questions contact
productsafety@bloomsbury.com.

To find out more about our authors and books visit www.bloomsbury.com
and sign up for our newsletters.

Supplementary resources for this book can be found at:
bloomsbury.pub/Roman-Britain-in-Twenty-Towns

Please type the URL into your web browser
and follow the instructions to access the
Companion Website. If you experience any
problems, please contact Bloomsbury at
onlineresources@bloomsbury.com

To the memory of my brothers Andrew (1960–2023) and Peter (1955–2023).

Contents

List of Illustrations ix
Preface xiii

Towns in Roman Britain 1

1 Aldborough: A Victorian Pleasure Garden 23
2 Bath: Spa of the Goddess Sulis 37
3 Caerwent: Market of the Silures 51
4 Caistor St Edmund: Market of the Iceni 65
5 Canterbury: Sacred Site by the River 75
6 Chichester and King Togidubnus 89
7 Cirencester: Capital of the Dobunni 103
8 Colchester: Fortress of Camulos 117
9 Corbridge: Hosting Place on the Frontier 137
10 Dorchester: A Town with Henges 149
11 Exeter: Riverine Place 163
12 Gloucester: The Bright Place 173

13 Leicester: The Earthen Fort 183

14 Lincoln: Place by the Pool 197

15 London: A Place Frequented by Traders 217

16 Silchester: Place in the Woods 239

17 Verulamium: Dwelling of the Very Greatest One 251

18 Winchester: Market of the Proud Ones 271

19 Wroxeter: The Old Work 283

20 York and Demetrius of Tarsus 299

References 311
Index 319

Illustrations

1	Map of the towns and *civitates* of Roman Britain, showing the twenty towns discussed in this book (in red type)	3
2	Photograph of the sign outside the Camulodunum Inn in Colchester	21
3	Map of Roman Aldborough	24
4	Map of modern Aldborough with locations mentioned in the text marked	25
5	Photograph of the Roman mosaic with the central star decoration from Aldborough	34
6	Map of Roman Bath	38
7	Map of modern Bath with locations mentioned in the text marked	39
8	Photograph of the Roman baths at Bath	44
9	Map of Roman Caerwent	52
10	Map of modern Caerwent with locations mentioned in the text marked	53
11	Photograph of the Roman south gate at Caerwent from inside the walled circuit	63
12	Photograph of a tower/bastion on the southern section of the town wall at Caerwent	63
13	Map of Roman Caistor St Edmund	66
14	Map of modern Caistor St Edmund with locations mentioned in the text marked	67

15	Map of Roman Canterbury	76
16	Map of modern Canterbury with locations mentioned in the text marked	77
17	Map of Roman Chichester	90
18	Map of modern Chichester with locations mentioned in the text marked	91
19	Photograph of the eighteenth-century inscription that commemorates the construction of the Chichester Townhouse	101
20	Map of Roman Cirencester	104
21	Map of modern Cirencester with locations mentioned in the text marked	105
22	Photograph of a detail from the Roman hunting dog mosaic found in a Roman townhouse in Cirencester	114
23	Map of Roman Colchester	118
24	Map of modern Colchester with locations mentioned in the text marked	119
25	Photograph of the Balkerne Gate at Colchester from inside the town defences	129
26	Map of Roman Corbridge	138
27	Map of modern Corbridge with locations mentioned in the text marked	139
28	Photograph of the stone basin supplied with water by an aqueduct at Corbridge	145
29	Map of Roman Dorchester	150
30	Map of modern Dorchester with locations mentioned in the text marked	151
31	Photograph of the Roman amphitheatre at Dorchester from the south	157
32	Photograph of the Roman townhouse at Dorchester from the east	161

33	Map of Roman Exeter	164
34	Map of modern Exeter with locations mentioned in the text marked	165
35	Map of Roman Gloucester	174
36	Map of modern Gloucester with locations mentioned in the text marked	175
37	Map of Roman Leicester	184
38	Map of modern Leicester with locations mentioned in the text marked	185
39	Photograph of the Jewry Wall in Leicester from the south	191
40	Map of Roman Lincoln	198
41	Map of modern Lincoln with locations mentioned in the text marked	199
42	Photograph of the Newport Arch in Lincoln from the south	206
43	Photograph of the inscription to Sacer, son of Brusus, at St Mary le Wigford, Lincoln	214
44	Map of Roman London	218
45	Map of modern London with locations mentioned in the text marked	219
46	Photograph of the London city wall just south of Tower Hill Underground Station	233
47	Photograph of the London Mithraeum	236
48	Map of ancient Silchester	240
49	Map of modern Silchester with locations mentioned in the text marked	241
50	Aerial photograph of Silchester under excavation in 2018	244
51	Map of Roman Verulamium	252
52	Map of modern Verulamium with locations mentioned in the text marked	253
53	Photograph of the Roman theatre at Verulamium from the air	263

54	Map of ancient Winchester	272
55	Map of modern Winchester with locations mentioned in the text marked	273
56	Photograph of a Roman column built into a modern roadside wall in Winchester	279
57	Map of Roman Wroxeter	284
58	Map of modern Wroxeter with locations mentioned in the text marked	285
59	Photograph of the centre of Roman Wroxeter, showing the bathhouse, including the Old Work in the foreground and the reconstructed townhouse beyond	292
60	Map of Roman York	300
61	Map of modern York with locations mentioned in the text marked	301

Preface

This book develops my lifelong fascination with exploring Iron Age and Roman monuments in countryside and town. It arises, in part, from the deep interest that I developed in the Iron Age and Roman periods of the British past during the many visits that my mother organized to archaeological sites across Britain in the 1970s and early 80s. I have developed this interest while working as a specialist on Roman Britain at Durham University and this has enabled me to explore these sites and delve into their history.

I am particularly grateful to Christina Unwin for advice and input into the theme of the book and for her excellent work on the maps and also to Paul Booth for his very careful reading of a full draft of the book. I am also deeply grateful to my brothers and sisters for their support and love, especially during our early visits to prehistoric and Roman sites across Britain. Thank you to Dr Martha Stewart for her inspired editorial comments on a draft of the text. I am also deeply in debt to the following friends and colleagues for their generous and helpful comments on a draft of the text for each of the following towns: Professor William Bowden (Caistor St Edmund), Richard Brewer (Caerwent), Dr Nick Cooper (Leicester), Frank Hargrave (Colchester), Dr Nick Hodgson (Corbridge), Neil Holbrook (Cirencester), Dr Anthony Lee (Lincoln), Dr Kris Lockyear (Verulamium), Dr Frances McIntosh (Corbridge), Professor Martin Millett (Aldborough), Dr Rebecca Redfern (London),

Dr Jake Weekes (Canterbury), Dr Roger White (Wroxeter) and Dr Steve Willis (Canterbury). I am grateful to Professor David Mattingly, Helen Hingley, Martin Hingley, David Jones, Christina Unwin and Dr Steve Willis for accompanying me on some of my visits. Finally, my thanks to the editing and production team at Bloomsbury, including Lily Mahon, Sophie Beardsworth and Merv Honeywood.

Richard Hingley
Holly Tree Lodge, Shincliffe
April 2025

Towns in Roman Britain

Introduction

This book provides an illustrated guide to twenty of the Roman towns in Britain. Whether you are local to one of these urban sites or visiting from elsewhere in Britain or overseas, it will help you to explore the archaeological remains in each place. There is a great deal to see at most of these locations, but visitors often need to research on the internet before or during visits to find relevant information. This book fills this gap by providing an accessible introduction. With an up-to-date summary of the history and context of each town, I aim to guide you to what is to be seen at each of the sites.

The focus here is on what the visitor can see, and the main emphasis of each chapter is on the surviving (the uncovered and displayed) physical features. Particular attention is paid to the walled circuits and visible ancient monuments. We also explore the histories of these urban communities. One of the main aims is to encourage you to visit other sites you may not have explored or to look again at locations already visited. Visitors are often fascinated to find even the vaguest traces of archaeological structures and this book aims to encourage this approach.

This introductory chapter considers why these urban centres were significant innovations, their origins, and their main physical and cultural characteristics. The subsequent chapters address each town individually by exploring the history of the urban centre and explaining what you can see. Each chapter has two maps, one showing the Roman-period urban landscape and the other depicting the modern topography with the archaeological features emphasized. The maps showing the Roman infrastructure of each town include buildings and structures from all phases. All these maps are reproduced at the same scale, apart from London (where the Roman remains are very extensive). This enables comparison of the extent and layout of all of the towns. It is not possible to mark all the details of the Roman urban topography on these maps. Information provided at each town will enable the visitor to gain a fuller understanding of the layout of individual Roman buildings. Photographs of some significant remains are included. At the end of every chapter is a guide to further reading, and the book is accompanied by a website to provide additional information (for instructions on accessing the website, type the following URL into your web browser: *bloomsbury.pub/Roman-Britain-in-Twenty-Towns*). For each town, a table is provided which lists the main Roman features that can be visited. These are graded on the table from most (***) to least (*) significant.

Which towns are included?

This book addresses the colonies, most of the *civitas* capitals, and three other important urban centres. I have used the modern names of these places in the chapters below, except in the case of Verulamium, where the Roman town is usually referred to by this name. Apart from Verulamium, I refer to the Roman-period names of the towns in italics.

The colonies were defined in legal terms as settlements of Roman citizens. The *civitas* capitals were the political centres of the many peoples (often known as 'tribes') of Britain. These colonies and *civitas*

Figure 1 *Map of the towns and civitates of Roman Britain, showing the twenty towns discussed in this book (in red type) (after Mattingly 2006: Figure 10).*

The three civitas capitals not discussed are in smaller black type. Drawn by Christina Unwin.

capitals were formal foundations and part of the administrative system of the province. Since there is little trace of Roman structures to explore at three of the places usually thought to have been *civitas* capitals (Brough on Humber, Carmarthen and Carlisle), they are omitted. A summary of the archaeology of these three towns is provided on the accompanying website.

Three additional towns are included in the book because they are popular sites for visitors and have substantial visible remains (below) – their inclusion gives some impression of the variability of the urban centres of Britain. This book does not include the substantial group of other settlements sometimes titled 'small towns'. There were hundreds of these settlements. Some of these smaller centres have impressive archaeological remains and were important in their own right, but there is not enough space to address them here.

The names of the towns used in the chapter titles

We know the Roman-period names of all the towns addressed in this book and many of the titles of the chapters below derive from translations of these names. I have been creative in developing some of the other chapter titles since not all recorded place names are straightforwardly translatable (as explained in each chapter). Recorded in ancient documents and inscriptions, the meaning attributed to these names is often subject to considerable discussion. Some names are descriptive of the topography of the place that they named ('place by the pool', 'place in the woods'), while others refer to individuals ('dwelling of the very greatest one') and occasionally divinities (Camulos, Sulis). Most derive from Celtic, the language spoken in pre-Roman Britain, and were used to denominate the towns which developed during the first century of Roman rule. The only exception to using Celtic terms for these towns is the Roman-period name *Aquae Sulis* for the settlement at Bath. This name combines the Latin word for water with the name of the goddess Sulis.

Urban origins

It is often stated that towns were the crux of civilization in Roman terms. To count as 'çivilized' in the minds of the Roman ruling classes, the Britons had to adopt urban living. Without towns, people were considered 'barbarians'. One fundamental reason for this is that the Roman administration depended on local government to control the provinces they incorporated into their empire. Rome had, in ancient terms, a highly efficient military but only a limited number of civil administrators. As a result, the provincial administrators actively encouraged the development of urban centres across the empire, and the ruling classes of the peoples they incorporated were tasked with keeping order over the population and taxing them. The highest status administrators in Britain were the provincial governor and the procurator. These men, members of the Roman ruling elite, were appointed to serve in Britain for a term of a few years at a time by the reigning emperor. They directed any military campaigning, controlled the system of taxation, and ensured the stability of the province. They depended upon the ruling elites of the individual British peoples (or 'tribes') to manage and tax their own communities on Rome's behalf, however. For information on the Roman conquest of Britain, see the suggested further reading at the end of this chapter.

Iron Age *oppida*

Before the arrival of Rome, many of the rulers of the Iron Age peoples across southern Britain ruled from *oppida*, which were not urban in form. In pre-Roman times, Britain was populated by multiple peoples, each occupying a relatively small territory. Well-known peoples across the south included the Catuvellauni, the Trinovantes and the Atrebates. The *oppida* constituted meeting places to which each ruler's clients were summoned at certain times of year. These *oppida* were characterized by extensive dykes (earthworks) which may have served a defensive purpose, and sometimes by small areas of settlement and high-status burials. Examples included Canterbury, Colchester, Silchester, Verulamium and Bagendon (near Cirencester). After the conquest, people settled more permanently at many of these *oppida*, and towns gradually developed. In some instances, towns also appear to have developed at locations which, though not the sites of *oppida*, had been places of significance before the conquest (below).

Roman colonies

In a famous quote, the classical author Tacitus explains that the colony of *Camulodunum* (Colchester) was founded in the seventh year of the invasion of Britain (49 CE) to act as a bastion against rebellion and to form a model of urban living for people to draw upon. Colchester was the first of the towns in Britain, a colony constructed and occupied by veteran legionary soldiers. Since only men with Roman citizenship could serve in the legions, all legionary veterans held this status. As a consequence, colonies were high-status towns in cultural and political terms since they had many Roman citizens among the population. Colchester was founded on the site of a decommissioned legionary fortress, reusing many of the military barracks and administrative buildings. This fortress and the later colony were built to control the territory of a powerful people, and the soldiers and colonists deprived at least some of the local elite families of their land during the conquest of the *oppidum*.

The other two colonies established in the first century – at Lincoln and Gloucester – were also founded when a legion moved on from its former base. The urban settlers reused the roads and the fortifications of the decommissioned legionary fortresses. At all three colonies, the urban communities swiftly commissioned the construction of the public buildings that were a hallmark of urbanism, particularly the forum. London and York were probably promoted to the status of colonies later in the Roman period, although their histories differed significantly from those of the first-century colonies.

Civitas capitals

During the early years of the conquest, other settlements began to develop into the *civitas* capitals that formed the focus for many of the peoples of Britain. These urban settlements did not have quite the same status as the colonies and would have been home to fewer citizens. There are thought to have been fifteen *civitas* capitals in Britain, although there may have been more. Roman administrators worked with the ruling families during the decades following the conquest and incorporation of their people, to ensure that they each established a *civitas* capital.

These towns, including Canterbury, Chichester, Silchester and Verulamium, often developed on or close to the sites of the *oppidum* of the pre-Roman rulers. The process of conquest enabled the leading families of the peoples of southern Britain to acquire more wealth and power over their clients and neighbours. These local elite families were left to rule over their people in exchange for their support of the Roman military conquest of less friendly neighbours. Based on information in the writings of Tacitus, the *oppidum* at Verulamium is thought to have been granted special rights as a *municipium*. As a result, certain magistrates who ruled at Verulamium became Roman citizens because of their civic roles.

This urbanization process proved more challenging across the centre and west of Britain, probably because these communities, including their leading families, had different social structures and the concept of urbanization was initially completely alien. This explains the late creation of several *civitas* capitals (including

Caerwent and Caistor). The direct role played by the military in establishing towns in other locations illustrates that these communities were at least in part imposed upon the local populations (Corbridge, Exeter and Wroxeter).

Three other towns

The additional towns described below have notable archaeological remains and are popular with visitors. Despite an impressive monumental centre and walls, the spa at Bath never achieved the status of a colony or *civitas* capital. Established as a trading centre in the first decade of the conquest, London, meanwhile, became the largest town in Britain and may have been designated a colony in the late first or second century. Unlike the other towns addressed here (with the exception of York) Corbridge was as much a military as a civil community. It was also the most northerly town in Britain.

Balancing a Roman urban bias

From the late sixteenth century onwards classically educated people picked up the concept that urbanization was a central element of how ancient Britons were taught public order and became civil. As a result, it has long been supposed that these towns constituted centres of civilization. The towns can easily be seen this way since the system that Rome exploited and developed created relative peace, and the urban centres included market buildings, law courts, bathhouses, sewers and sources of fresh water. The concept of 'What the Romans did for us', prominent in school education in England in recent times, sees all these things in entirely favourable terms.

Since Roman rule was imposed on many of the peoples of Britain, there is another side to the Roman conquest. Even where provincial administrators befriended certain rulers, such as Togidubnus, these individuals had little option but to subjugate themselves and their people. The military fought and defeated many of the peoples who continued to resist Rome, killing and enslaving such opponents.

The biased and pro-Roman perspective on the conquest as enabling new ways of life is also emphasized by what you can see at these towns. The ancient monuments uncovered and displayed by past generations mainly include the monumental public buildings and the defences. Antiquaries and archaeologists from the sixteenth century to the present have uncovered the infrastructure of urban administration – the forums, bathhouses and places of meeting and display (including amphitheatres and theatres). These types of monumental buildings are prominent among those available to visit and inspect because previous generations viewed them as particularly significant and because they have often survived and were visible. Even among urban houses, attention tended to focus on high-status residences with mosaics and hypocausts.

From the 1960s onwards, however, archaeologists began to excavate the houses and shops of lower-status residents. Excavations in cities which have seen large-scale redevelopment have provided considerable insights into the lives of these less wealthy people. Archaeological excavation in London has played a prominent role here. As a result of this, over the past two decades several museums have communicated the enabling aspects of urbanization to their visitors. This approach emphasizes the idea that Rome fostered the conditions in which relatively lowly and marginalized people could make a new life through trading and industry. This is an important perspective, and museum displays consequently focus on the life and death of various individuals and their communities. Nevertheless, we should not lose sight of the fact that Roman society was run by and in the interests of the elite, and that the conquest benefited those in Britain who were already the richest and most influential. The lives of many ordinary people, whether enslaved or free, in countryside or town, will have been highly unpleasant and often relatively short.

Important new information about the prevalence of enslaved people is provided by the Vine Street excavations at Leicester, where a curse tablet from a townhouse records slave quarters. Household slaves living in these towns will usually have lived less awful lives than those working industrially. Such inequalities within society need to be acknowledged, however, when touring these places. 'What the Romans did for us' gives a very biased picture of life in Britain. The museums featuring life at these urban sites understandably emphasize the positive aspects of Roman rule since they cater for school groups, and aim to enthuse and inform their visitors. At Cirencester and Verulamium, new museum displays emphasize the lives of less wealthy urban occupants. We might keep in mind, as we explore these places, that many people were killed, enslaved and marginalized during the conquest and incorporation of southern and central Britain into the empire. Many of the families occupying the timber-built commercial and industrial properties will also not have been at all wealthy and will have lived unhealthy lives in squalid conditions.

Ten urban characteristics

The origins of the towns were highly variable, but there was nevertheless something of a blueprint which many urban centres adopted.

1. Civil and military origins

Many Roman towns developed on Iron Age sites, as exemplified by those where *oppida* can be identified (above). That *oppida* were not the only locations of significance before the arrival of the Romans is demonstrated by the Iron Age forts that preceded the towns of Dorchester and Winchester. Place names also sometimes indicate the potential significance of a location prior to the Roman conquest. Examples include the use of the Celtic names *Venta* (Caerwent, Caistor and Winchester) and *Coria* (Corbridge). The use of these terms as the name of the towns suggests that in each case the urban centre grew up at a significant pre-Roman meeting place.

Other towns had clear military origins, as we have seen for the colonies at Colchester, Lincoln and Gloucester which replaced legionary fortresses. At Wroxeter and Exeter, the decommissioned fortresses were succeeded by *civitas* capitals, while at York the colony developed next to the fortress. Corbridge developed on a fort site, which may have been the case at several other towns considered below. Current evidence suggests, however, that sites where a town was preceded by a fort are few, and recent work at Silchester may indicate that Roman soldiers were housed in buildings in the *oppidum* during the conquest period. Soldiers will have visited the towns and often settled in these communities as veterans (see the chapters on Aldborough, Leicester and Wroxeter). By the end of the first century the urban communities of many towns in southern Britain included retired auxiliary soldiers who had seen service in the military. They will have brought their knowledge, skills and contacts with them to these places.

2. Population centres

Most towns represented significant concentrations of people. Before the Roman invasion, some settlements and hillforts served as population centres, but most Roman towns had larger populations than these earlier sites. We do not know the exact population of any town. We can provide a rough estimate, however, by examining the extent of urban settlements and estimating how many houses were occupied at any given time. London was the largest urban centre in Britain, possibly reaching a peak population of 35,000 by the end of the second century. While this number may seem small by modern standards, this was the largest concentration of people ever to settle in one place in Britain, and it was not until medieval times that London's population surpassed this figure.

Other towns had populations in the thousands. For instance, the *civitas* capital at Silchester during the second century may have had about 7,000 residents. Some towns had smaller populations. Excavations at Bath, for example, indicate that the settlement did not in fact feature many houses. Bath was primarily a destination for visitors to its spa and temple, which raises questions about whether it can truly be classified as a town. Nevertheless, Bath had defensive walls – typically an urban feature – along with a classical temple and a significant bathing complex.

3. Waterlogged locations

A significant point that is difficult to appreciate when visiting Roman towns today is the extent to which the rivers and wetlands that characterized many of these urban sites were drained and occupied during the Roman period. Many towns occupied low-lying and marshy locations, as considered below, and from the first settlement of these sites strenuous efforts were made to control rivers, build up their banks, and drain wetlands. At several towns, archaeological work has mapped the approximate extent of the rivers and marshy areas (see Exeter, Lincoln, London and Leicester). The riverine character of these settlements is emphasized in the chapters below.

4. Established street systems

Most of these towns featured relatively regular networks of metalled roads. The introduction of paved streets was a significant innovation because, while tracks are known from Iron Age *oppida*, there is little evidence of metalled road construction before the Roman conquest. A century of archaeological research has, however, shown that the street systems were often less regular than previously believed (see Caistor). Those who established these urban street grids drew upon knowledge of the street systems of Continental towns and also the layout of the forts established during the conquest of Britain. At the three first-century colonies, street systems were established early on. At Colchester, for instance, the road system of the legionary fortress was reused when the colony was founded in the early 50s CE. By contrast, several of the *civitas* capitals did not have a regular metalled road system until the late first or early second century. At Bath, a consistent system of streets was never developed.

5. Public buildings

The construction of monumental 'public' buildings is a defining characteristic of all the towns considered here. The term 'public' is a misnomer since access to many of these buildings was restricted in several ways. As Roman social relations operated on a system of patronage, the grander private houses also served a public purpose as they were places where patrons regularly met their clients. Nevertheless, the term 'public' cannot easily be avoided when discussing structures such as the forum and the amphitheatre.

The key building, often at the centre of the town, was the **forum**. Apart from Bath, all the towns considered here had such buildings. These courtyard complexes, which included the forum and a basilica (an aisled hall), acted as the centre of local self-government. The basilica was also where the inequalities in status in the urban community were acted out (see Caerwent). Justice was dispensed (or imposed) there, and since the market traders paid a fee to the urban authorities the markets held at the forum were a significant source of revenue. The scale and monumentality of the forum buildings of many of the towns indicate their central role in the lives of the people of the *civitas*.

In many places the **amphitheatre** was another type of public structure constructed during the early phases of development, and possibly before the building of the forum. Usually considered to have played host to gladiatorial games, some archaeologists now think that the primary purpose of the amphitheatres was to act as a venue where the urban population and country dwellers from the surrounding area would come together. The unexpected discovery of Britain's only circus monument (for horse racing) at Colchester in 2004 suggests that amphitheatres are yet to be discovered at several towns.

All the towns must have had suites of **public baths**, which could also sometimes be grand and monumental (see Leicester and Wroxeter). Often, the first substantial bathhouse at each *civitas* capital was constructed around the time of the building of the forum and the establishment of the street system. This raises the question of how local authorities paid for the construction of the baths, and how they afforded to run these facilities. Specialist builders would have had to be brought in to the urban community. The bathhouse and other urban features such as fountains also required a water supply as did the aqueducts, or engineered leats that enabled water to be transported into the towns from local springs. The control of water helps to explain how the urban facilities were funded. The urban elite of each town would have charged for access to fresh water (see Lincoln). They also charged for access to public spaces such as the baths, and perhaps for people to attend meetings at the amphitheatres and theatres.

6. Religious centres

A significant urban characteristic is the presence of religious structures, temples and sacred spaces. All the towns included multiple structures related to the rituals and beliefs of their inhabitants. Some of these ritual spaces originated from the Iron Age and were reconstructed as monumental shrines (see Canterbury and Verulamium). At Bath, the **baths** were next to a grand classical temple and served a religious purpose. Indeed, all the bath buildings in these towns had ritual and religious associations in addition to their social roles and function as bathing places.

There were two types of **temples**. The most common were 'Romano-Celtic' temples, such as the example displayed at Caerwent. These consisted of a small sacred room (*cella*), which housed the statue of the divinity worshipped at the shrine. An ambulatory, or walkway, surrounded the *cella*. The monumental classical temples at Bath and Colchester were instead based on the traditional Greek and Roman temple model. A sacred enclosure (*temenos*) surrounded each temple. Several towns also had **theatres**, often positioned next to temple sites because they served as places for religious gatherings. Evidence for the spread of other cults throughout the empire include important monuments such as the London Mithraeum and the small building, possibly a church, displayed at Colchester.

Religious beliefs were deeply embedded in the mindset of these people, influencing all the buildings and structures within their towns. Many domestic houses included shrines dedicated to gods sacred to the family. The forum also held sacred associations, often featuring statues of deceased emperors who had been deified. In this way the towns served as sacred sites as well as economic and cultural centres.

7. Defended centres

These towns are characterized by their urban defences, often the most notable features visible to modern visitors. The three early colonies of Colchester, Lincoln and Gloucester were supplied with walled circuits during the first century, and several other prominent *civitas* capitals also had earthwork defences. From their earliest origins, all towns probably had some form of boundary marked by shallow ditches and banks. Understanding the extent and location of early defensive circuits can be challenging. At Caistor, Exeter and Verulamium, early boundaries were replaced by new defensive circuits that encompassed larger areas. By the early third century, many towns had circuits of ditches and ramparts, which were often later reinforced with masonry walls. At some towns, the masonry wall was a key component from the outset of the earthwork defences, though Wroxeter did not have a stone wall at any point. The decision to build these defences was primarily initiated by the urban community, although provincial governors may occasionally have provided support.

In the past, these urban 'defences' were usually interpreted as protective measures for the community. Colchester was burnt to the ground by Boudica's followers in 60 CE partly because (according to Tacitus) the defences of the legionary fortress had not been maintained by the colonists. It should be recognized, however, that these 'defences' were a sign of status for the town and also held considerable ritual significance. At Bath the walls defined the area sacred to Sulis Minerva, and all the circuits of town defences had ritual associations. The need for defence will certainly have been the case during the fourth century as the political situation across the province deteriorated. At this time, towers (often known as bastions) were added to the outer face of the walls of several towns, strengthening the defences by providing firing platforms to drive away potential attackers.

8. Commercial centres

The presence of shops and houses is another characteristic. A common type of building in early London was the strip house, which had a shop or workshop at the end facing onto the street and a living area for the family at the back. These buildings also became common in many, perhaps all, of the towns. At the colonies of Colchester and Gloucester, the barrack buildings of the preceding fortresses were reused to provide houses for the colonists.

Although relatively simple timber buildings continued to be a common form of housing in later times, more elaborate houses equipped with hypocausts (underfloor heating systems), mosaics and painted plaster also began to be constructed. The townhouse at Dorchester provides a good example, while the well-preserved Billingsgate bathhouse in London was probably the bathing facility of a private dwelling. The remains of several houses and shops of different levels of status are displayed at Caerwent, Canterbury, Corbridge and Verulamium. One of the excavated houses at Wroxeter was used as the basis for a full-scale reconstruction to present this aspect of urban life. Several museums address the nature of urban houses and shops and the lives of their occupants.

9. Boundary zones

Each town had a boundary zone outside the limits of its defences. Most towns possessed areas of extramural settlement, often located outside the gates through the walls. In many cases, the defences were constructed at least a century after the initial establishment of these towns, which means that some of the areas of extramural occupation were left out of the defended circuit when the decision was made to build these limits. Industrial activities such as metalworking and pottery production were regular activities in the extramural areas. As some houses excavated in these marginal urban areas were elaborate masonry structures, however, we cannot assume that poor people were always pushed to the margin of the settlement.

The boundaries of each town were also where the deceased members of the urban community were cremated and interred. While our knowledge of how the dead were treated in earlier Roman times is limited, by the later period cemeteries began to develop around most towns. Some individuals were cremated before burial while others were buried unburnt, and certain towns featured streets lined with masonry mausolea. Unfortunately, none of these cemeteries are displayed to the public. To fully appreciate the various ways the dead were commemorated, visit the London Museum (reopening in 2026), the Gloucester Museum and the Yorkshire Museum (York). These institutions offer extensive information on death and burial practices. Additionally, many museums display tombstones that once marked the burial sites of the deceased.

10. Diverse populations

Archaeological work on urban cemeteries has documented a final key characteristic of these communities by indicating the diversity of their inhabitants. Scientific research on the remains of the dead from towns, including London, York and Winchester, shows that these urban communities drew populations from across the Roman world, including areas south and east of the Mediterranean. The best way to discover more about this aspect of urban living is to visit the London Museum and the displays at the Yorkshire Museum (York). These museums highlight the origins and identities of some of the people that archaeological research has uncovered. Information about members of the urban population is included below, although it is impossible to explore this issue thoroughly in this book.

Urban afterlives

Although *Britannia* was initially a single province it was divided into two during the early third century, and later into four. Under this reorganization, London, York and Lincoln became the capitals of individual provinces, and Cirencester may have been the fourth such centre. By the fourth century, life in the provinces of Britain had become unsettled and the trading function of towns declined. Instead, they took on greater relevance as defended foci from which order could be maintained. The defensive circuits were strengthened, and many towns remained significant during the fourth century.

The adoption of Christianity as the official state religion in the fourth century had a significant impact upon the urban authorities. Christianity was present in Britain before this time. St Alban, one of the British martyrs, was executed at Verulamium during the mid-third century. Several towns sent bishops to attend the Council of Arles in 314. Some temples may have been closed during the fourth century, and churches were probably established in many towns. These have proved difficult to locate, however, although one possible example is displayed at Colchester. The site of another possible late Roman church can be visited at Lincoln.

Late Roman structures have been uncovered in several of the towns. Urban life may have continued in several places beyond the early fifth century when the provinces of *Britannia* ceased to form part of the empire (see Canterbury and Wroxeter). Many of these towns may also have become dangerous to visit as the masonry buildings will swiftly have become unstable when they ceased to be maintained.

These ruined towns lived on into the post-Roman ages since their walled circuits remained as monumental features. The stone walls of many provided the defensive circuits of the medieval towns that succeeded them. Early examples include the reuse of Roman defences at the eighth-century burgh at Winchester and the ninth-century burgh at London. Many impressive defensive circuits survive today. In medieval times, myths developed to explain the surviving remains, and several such tales are mentioned below, including the role of the mythical kings Lud and Bladud in the establishment of London and Bath.

During the eleventh century Roman buildings were uncovered at Verulamium on the orders of the abbot of St Alban's. The Renaissance of the sixteenth century led antiquaries to identify and study the Roman towns, and knowledge of their past was accumulated through uncovering buried remains. The discovery of the Togidubnus inscription from Chichester provides an interesting example of the impact of one such discovery on an eighteenth-century urban community. The excavation and display of remains at many of these towns commenced during the nineteenth century. The earliest example which can still be explored was the uncovering during the 1830s and 40s of two mosaic floors at Aldborough. Some towns have seen extensive excavations that have provided considerable insight into life in Roman Britain. During the early twentieth century the remaining structures of significant Roman buildings were often consolidated and displayed. This has continued, as exemplified by the recent displays of the Mithraeum and the City Wall at Vine Street in London.

The wealth of ancient monuments displayed in Roman towns and the exhibits in many museums testify to the significance attributed to these early phases of urban history. Another aspect of the

Figure 2 *Photograph of the sign outside the Camulodunum Inn in Colchester. This Inn has closed since this photograph was taken in 2019 and the sign has been removed.* © Richard Hingley.

commemoration of the Iron Age and Roman past in these urban communities is the use of the names of ancient people as titles for streets, venues and properties. My favourite example from my tour around these twenty places is the sign for the Camulodunum Inn in Colchester.

Further reading

For a general background to the Roman conquest and settlement of Britain, see Mattingly (2006) and Hingley (2022). Wacher (1995) remains a useful and detailed account of Roman town walls since relatively little recent work has been undertaken on these structures. Fulford and Holbrook (2015) provides a detailed account of the results of recent developer-funded excavations. Revell (2016) and

Rogers (2016) provide accessible accounts of urbanism in Roman Britain and urban monumentality.

The fullest account of the Roman-period names of the towns is Rivet and Smith (1979). Where there has been a more up-to-date discussion of the place names, the reference is given in the further reading for each chapter. For a guide to the ethnic diversity of Roman Britain, see Eckardt and Müldner (2016). For discussion of problems with the concept of 'What the Romans did for us', see Hingley (2019) and Hingley, Sharpe and Yarrow (2025).

1
Aldborough: A Victorian Pleasure Garden

Introduction

Aldborough was the *civitas* capital of the Brigantes. The town developed during the 70s CE close to a Roman fort and retained a connection with the military throughout its history. The visible archaeological remains include two mosaics from a townhouse and a short section of the town walls. These were excavated and displayed in the Victorian period within the landscape garden of a country house and can still be explored. The English Heritage Museum features archaeological finds from the Roman town.

Aldborough provides a pleasant location to wander over the buried remains of Roman urban buildings and structures. Recent geophysical survey and excavations have provided considerable insights into the topography and history of Roman Aldborough and led to the thorough updating of the information available for visitors.

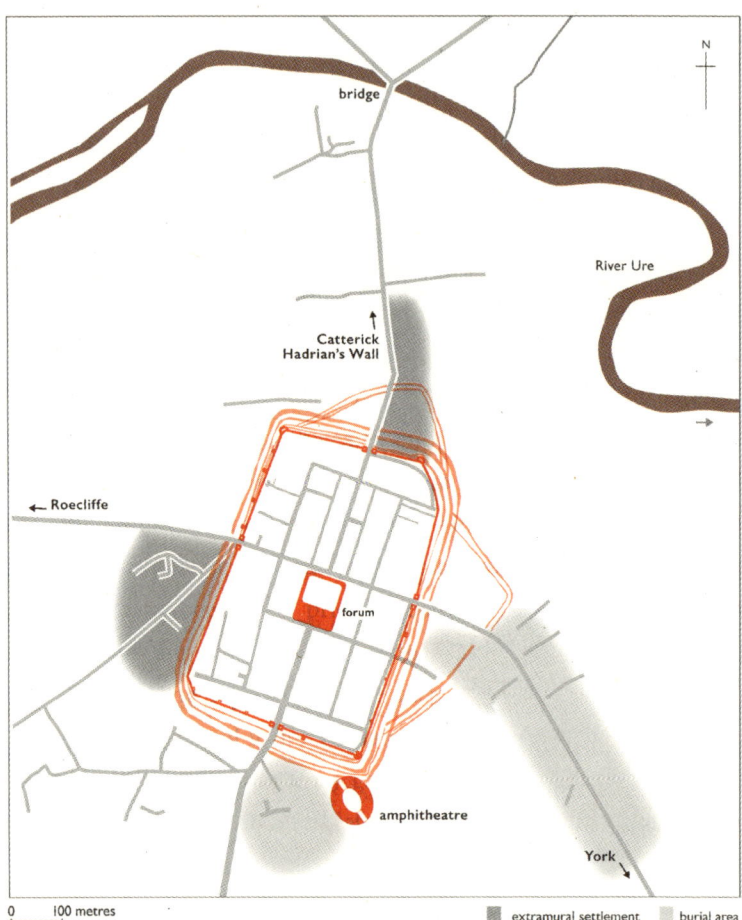

Figure 3 *Map of Roman Aldborough (after Ferraby and Millett 2020: Figures 4.11 and 4.12). Drawn by Christina Unwin.*

Main visible archaeological features with grading

	Star rating
Forum-basilica	*
Townhouses	**
Town walls	**
Museum	**

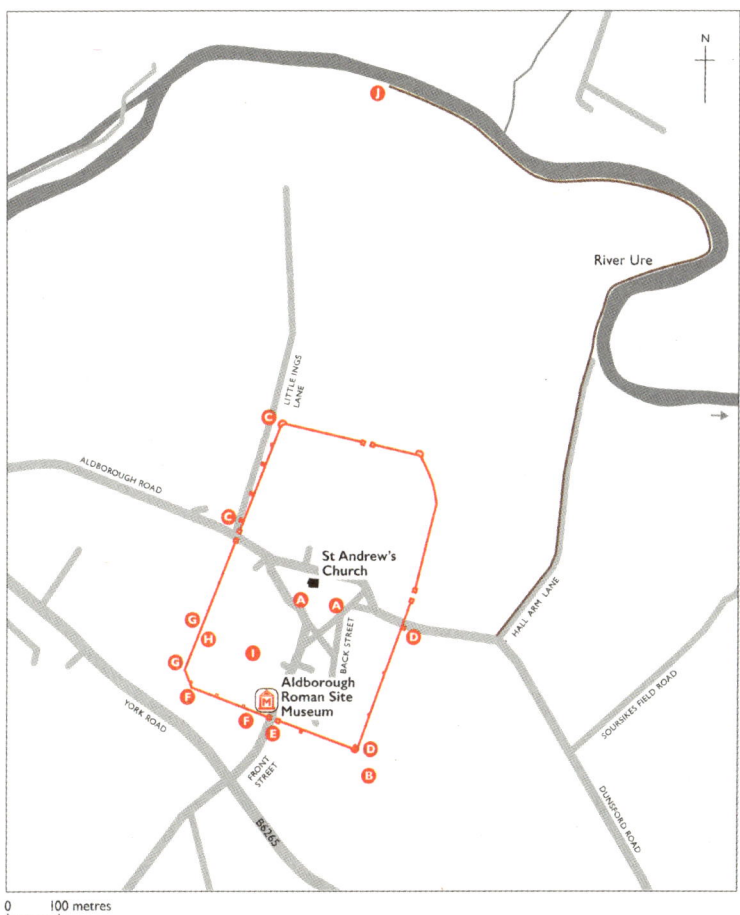

Figure 4 *Map of modern Aldborough with locations mentioned in the text marked. Drawn by Christina Unwin using information from Google Maps.*

Getting there

The village of Aldborough is located 1 kilometre east of the market town of Boroughbridge. You can usually park in the village or use the public car park in Boroughbridge and walk to the site. A bus service provides access to the village, and the surrounding countryside is very popular with cyclists.

Exploring Aldborough

Walking around the Roman remains is a pleasant experience on a warm, sunny day. It took me 2½ hours to explore the site of the Roman town, although you could easily spend longer in the surrounding countryside. The Ordnance Survey maps for exploring the outskirts of the town are OS *Explorer* 299 and OS *Landranger* 99. The best way to appreciate Roman Aldborough is to visit the English Heritage site and museum, which is open from Friday to Sunday from April to the end of September. The village itself has no shop. The Ship Inn serves meals, but as it is not open every day check the website before setting out. Boroughbridge has accommodation, meals and a good range of shops.

Historical summary

Aldborough was the most northerly of the first-century *civitas* capitals. There was no Iron Age occupation here, and the town was a Roman foundation that grew up during the 70s CE when a community of incomers and local people settled here. There was a Roman fort 2 kilometres to the west of Aldborough. The town originated as a trading post associated with the annexation of the surrounding area and was located where a road crosses the River Ure, close to the highest navigable point. The street system and forum were probably constructed during the 120s. Although the area enclosed by the town defences is small compared to many other *civitas* capitals, extensive extramural areas of occupation indicate that this was a highly successful town. The strengthening of the town walls in the late Roman period by the addition of bastions and multiple external ditches indicates that Aldborough remained a thriving town (Figure 3).

The rediscovery of Roman Aldborough

Aldborough was abandoned after the Roman period, although the walls of the masonry buildings and the defences survived in a ruined condition for centuries. Roman remains were uncovered and recorded from the late seventeenth and early eighteenth centuries. Excavations during the nineteenth century uncovered some of the town's buildings and the enclosing walls. The owner of the manor, Andrew Lawson, laid out an ornamental garden to display the remains and opened a museum. Excavations also occurred during the early twentieth century. The most recent research – including geophysical surveys, field walking and some limited excavation – has been undertaken by Cambridge University (since 2009). This has helped inform the complete redisplay of the Roman town, the updating of the display in the museum, and the production of the informative English Heritage guidebook.

A Roman fort at Roecliffe

A Roman fort was constructed at Roecliffe (NGR SE386667) during the late 60s CE, close to the location of three ancient (Neolithic or early Bronze Age) standing stones known today as 'The Devil's Arrows'. Roecliffe fort, which has been partially excavated, was the base for *c.* 500 auxiliary soldiers. Today, the fort lies in agricultural fields just west of the A1(M) motorway, and there is nothing to see on the ground. It was probably decommissioned by the late 70s CE when the unit moved north. This area was subdued by this time, and a settlement had begun to develop at Aldborough, 2 kilometres east of the fort.

The early town

This town was named *Isurium*, which is believed to mean 'place in the region on this side of the River Uria'. The name Uria is preserved in the present-day name of the River Ure, which flows north of the village. The ancient name of this river probably refers to 'the clean one', highlighting the purity of the river water. Knowledge of the earliest phases is limited due to the restricted extent and early dates of many excavations. Coins found at the site suggest that occupation began c. 70 CE, while the neighbouring fort was still in use. By the end of the first century, an extensive settlement had developed, covering at least 10 hectares in the northern part of the area later occupied by the town. The pottery discovered during excavations indicates the trading connections of this urban community. Stamped tiles bearing the names of the Ninth Legion Hispana and the Sixth Legion Victrix suggest that some building materials were sourced from military suppliers.

Isurium is one of several places referenced in the Vindolanda Tablets, demonstrating the involvement of soldiers in life here at the end of the first century. The settlement at Aldborough was supplying accommodation, food and drink to passing soldiers. Campaigning to the north would have meant a constant flow of military personnel and traders throughout the centuries of Roman rule.

Nothing of the early phases of settlement at Aldborough is visible today. This settlement would have included shops and houses arranged along tracks or roads. It lay at the point of intersection of roads running east–west and north–south. The early buildings were constructed of timber and earth, although some were roofed with tiles. Their occupants had access to imported pottery, local wares and Roman coins. There may have been a gravel marketplace within the developing settlement. It was decided to rebuild the town on a monumental scale early in the second century.

The *civitas* capital

Aldborough became the capital of the Brigantes, a people inhabiting a vast area of central Britain at the time of the Roman conquest. It is unlikely, however, that the entire area attributed to the Brigantes was ruled and taxed from Aldborough. It is more likely that the Roman administration (provincial governor or procurator) decided to establish this *civitas* capital to serve part of the area occupied by the Brigantes during the early second century. The developing settlement had already attracted traders and settlers from outside the region, although local people would also have settled here to exploit trading opportunities.

The town was formally established probably *c.* 120 CE, involving the total replanning of the settlement with an unusually regular street grid and the laying out and building of the forum (Figure 3). The town's street grid was aligned on the forum. At some point, a stone bridge was constructed over the River Ure 700 metres north of the Roman town. At this time, the course of Dere Street was diverted from its former route, crossing the river at Roecliffe, to run through Aldborough instead.

The new town covered an area of *c.* 20 hectares. Several terraces created level ground for building on the hill-slope site. The amphitheatre, to the south-east of the town, was probably built during the early second century. Little of this phase of urban development is visible today. Elements of the line of the main north–south and the east–west roads survive in the streets of the modern village (compare Figures 3 and 4), although the grid layout has been lost. Traces of the substantial terraces constructed across the hill slope can be viewed by wandering around the village streets.

The forum

Information about the forum derives from an eighteenth-century excavation and a small recent trial trench. The approach to the forum was from the north, and a colonnade fronted the building. The basilica lay to the south of the courtyard. A terrace cut into the hill slope created a level area for the forum. The churchyard of St Andrew's Church exploits this Roman terrace and, if you go to the south entrance of the church and look away from the church building, you can see a distinct change in level between the churchyard and the houses facing you (Figure 4, A–A). This change in level appears to be the dividing line between the forum courtyard on the lower ground, now partly occupied by the churchyard, and the basilica, on the higher terrace under modern houses, gardens and roads.

St Andrew's Church also contains an eroded sculpture of Mercury, which can be found inside the church at its western end, just north of the tower. It is not known exactly where in Aldborough this statue was found.

The amphitheatre

A geophysical survey has identified an ampitheatre on the prominent hill south-east of Aldborough (B). It has not been excavated and is not publicly accessible. A substantial structure with an arena of *c.* 60 metres by 40 metres surrounded by banks of seating, the amphitheatre had entrances to the south-east and north-west.

The town walls

A substantial set of defences was built during the late second or early third century, defining an area of *c.* 21 hectares. The gates stood at the midpoint of each of the four sides of the town wall, which enclosed an approximately rectangular area. The earth bank, or rampart, was fronted with at least one substantial ditch, forming the first phase of the urban defences. A stone wall was added to the outer face of the earthen rampart and is probably the same date as the bank. The addition of bastions to the outside of at least part of the town wall strengthened the defences during the fourth century. The geophysical surveys have also indicated the addition of several circuits of ditches outside the walls in the late fourth or early fifth century.

Traces of the defences have survived centuries of intensive cultivation in the fields surrounding Aldborough village. The earthwork remains of the ramparts (on private land) can be viewed from the roads entering the village from the east and west. Where the road from Boroughbridge crosses the rampart is the site of the west gate. To the west of the defensive circuit, a public right of way follows a private road called Little Ings Lane (marked by an information board at the edge of the road; Figure 4, C–C). This allows access along the outside of the northern part of the western defences of the town, from the site of the west gate to the north-western corner. The increased height of the ground to the east of this road marks the location of the town rampart with the ditch in front.

To the east of Roman Aldborough, the boundaries of the gardens of the houses at the village margin mark the line of the rampart and can be viewed by walking up Dunsford Road and looking south (D–D). There is no public access to these earthworks. On top of the rise of the hill viewed from the road, the prominent earthwork visible against the skyline is the amphitheatre (B).

The location of the south gate is close to where you enter the English Heritage site from the village road (E). A section of the town defences has been excavated and is visible for visitors to inspect just beyond the museum (F–F). These fragments of the town wall, displayed in a landscape garden by the Victorian landowner, are interpreted by the information boards on site. Traces of the stone rampart with the foundation layers of internal towers are visible. The fragmentary remains of the earth rampart can also be understood by reading the information boards.

Through an agreement with the current landowner, visitors can also walk further along the southern section of the western defences (G–G). Various pieces of Roman masonry are displayed in this landscape garden area, including an altar and several sections of columns.

Other public buildings

The geophysical survey located two temple buildings. Traces of monumental masonry, including foliage columns and Tuscan capitals, also indicate that elaborate buildings once ornamented the town. Seven altars have been found, one dedicated to Jupiter Optimus Maximus and the Matres (the Mother Goddesses).

Houses

The town was built up with domestic dwellings, as recent geophysical surveys indicate. Traces of two townhouses are displayed. Within the landscape garden area, close to the displayed remains of Roman sculptures, the slight traces of the foundations of some rooms from a substantial Roman house are visible (H). The geophysical survey indicates that this was the west wing of a courtyard house, one of several monumental private houses within the walled circuit. An information board provides some additional information.

The path beyond this structure turns right and crosses a field from which it is possible to appreciate the subtle evidence of the Roman terracing of the slope across which the town was built. Since it stands on the site of the forum, the tower of St Andrew's Church also gives us an idea of the scale of the terracing.

Continuing to the east brings you to the displayed remains of two of the mosaics of a courtyard house (I). The front of this house was on a Roman street on the line of the modern road (beyond the houses further to the east). Part of the house was uncovered in 1823, with additional excavation in 2016. The mosaics are protected from the weather by two small buildings dating from 1832 and 1848. These are among the earliest surviving examples of structures built to display ancient monuments in Britain. One of these mosaics, which features the fragmentary figure of a lion, has been dated to the later second century on stylistic grounds. The second mosaic, which is less damaged, has a simpler geometric design (Figure 5).

On the way back to the site museum a grassed area with a metal plaque records the original location of the so-called Helicon Mosaic, which once graced the dining room floor of another opulent townhouse. The surviving fragment of this mosaic, which featured the nine classical muses, is displayed in the site museum.

The nineteenth-century excavators of the town focused their attention on high-quality mosaics. Records indicate that twenty-two mosaics were discovered, and more are likely to survive buried under houses and green spaces in the village. The recent geophysical surveys indicated that strip houses – relatively simple buildings with a shop or workshop at one end and living area at the other – were far more common than grander townhouses.

Extramural occupation, cemeteries and a bridge

The recent geophysical survey has provided an excellent understanding of the area surrounding the town (Figure 3), although no traces of these features are visible today. Occupation and industrial areas were sited outside all four gates, and the houses to the west suggest that the walls did not enclose the entirety of the early-second-century town. There were cemeteries to the north, east and south of the town. A cemetery with several masonry mausolea lay alongside Dunsford Road (outside the east gate). One gravestone, found in the nineteenth

Figure 5 *Photograph of the Roman mosaic with the central star decoration from Aldborough.* © *https://www.gettyimages.co.uk/detail/news-photo/mosaic-floor-with-central-star-decoration-aldborough-roman-news-photo/1022863746?adppopup=true.*

century, records a woman named Felicula, the wife of a Roman citizen whose name survives only in part. There is no additional information on other urban residents.

The geophysical survey has shown that a masonry bridge carried the Roman road running north from Aldborough over the Rive Ure (Figure 4, J). Today, there is nothing visible to indicate the location of the bridge. The site can be visited by walking east from the village along Dunsford Road before turning left up Hall Arm Lane and following the footpath alongside the river towards Boroughbridge. The public right of way up Little Ings Lane also allows access to the river and the site of the bridge.

An early church?

St Andrew's Church lies at the centre of the area formerly occupied by the Roman forum. Although the present church dates to the fourteenth century, there was probably an earlier church here. It is even possible, as suggested for Lincoln, that there was a late Roman church at Aldborough, and that this has remained a site of Christian worship ever since.

Further reading

Millett and Ferraby (2016) is an excellent short guide to the Roman town for visitors. The fullest and most up-to-date detailed account is Ferraby and Millett (2020). For an account of Roecliffe Roman fort, see Bishop (2005). For relevant web links, see the website connected with this book.

2

Bath: Spa of the Goddess Sulis

Introduction

Bath is unusual among the Roman towns in this book since it was a spa centre, not a colony or *civitas* capital. Famous for its baths, this was a significant sanctuary in Roman times, attracting visitors from overseas. This World Heritage Site is extremely popular with visitors, reflecting the significance of the Roman baths and the evocative archaeological remains displayed here.

Early in the Roman period, the baths and the temple of Sulis Minerva were constructed to exploit one of the three thermal springs at this sacred location in a bend of the River Avon. The shrine was dedicated to the goddess Sulis, illustrating that this was already a sacred site in pre-Roman times. The cult of this local goddess was twinned with the classical goddess Minerva. Several other temples and sanctuaries developed around the Roman baths. This cult centre was later enclosed with a defensive circuit, a feature of many Roman towns in Britain. The town lacked a forum or regular street system, however, and most of the population probably resided outside the defences.

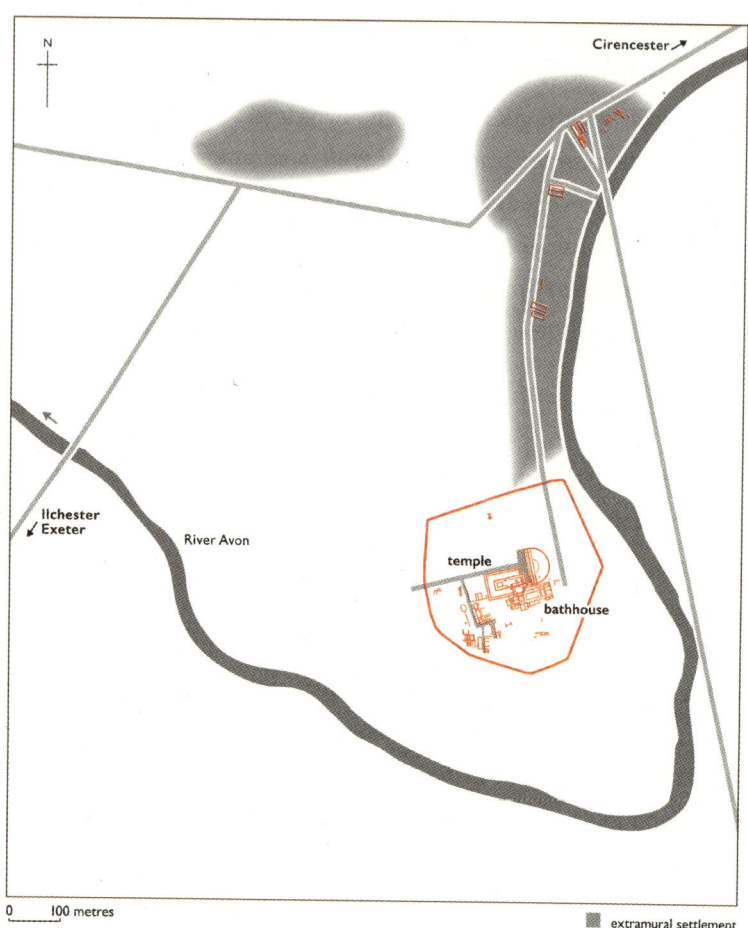

Figure 6 *Map of Roman Bath (after Davenport 2021: Figures 59 and 66). Drawn by Christina Unwin.*

Main visible archaeological features with grading

	Star rating
Baths	***
Town defences	*
Museum	***

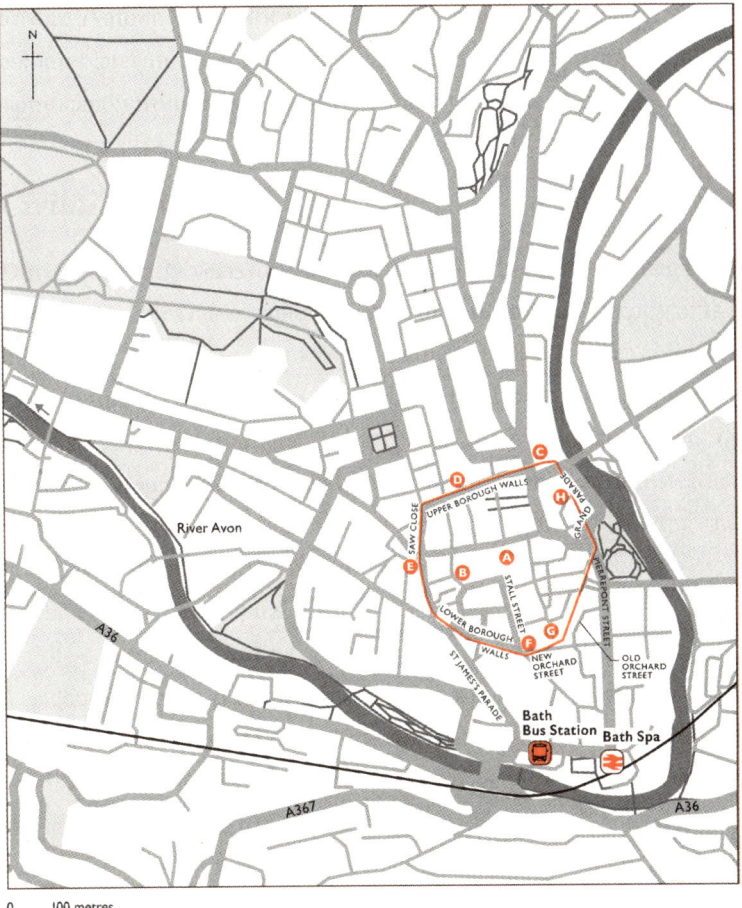

Figure 7 *Map of modern Bath with locations mentioned in the text marked. Drawn by Christina Unwin using information from Google Maps.*

Exploring Roman Bath

This city is a popular tourist destination and parking in the city is difficult. I used one of three Park and Ride services situated on the outskirts of Bath. The Bath Spa railway and bus stations, just south of the town centre, provide easy access to the Roman baths. As it is busy throughout the year, advance booking to visit the baths is imperative.

There are many places to stay and to eat in the city. At the baths the excavated remains of this large Roman bathing complex and the associated temple of Sulis Minerva are displayed. This heritage centre also contains a wealth of artefacts and architectural details uncovered during the excavation. The baths took me 2 hours to explore, but more time could be spent here. It took me 1 hour to investigate the course of the former town walls. There is much more to Bath than the Roman past, and you could easily spend several days visiting the city.

Historical summary

A significant junction in the Roman road system less than 1 kilometre north of Bath (Figure 6) may have been the location of a fort in the conquest period, *c.* 48 CE. The bath complex, including a substantial classical temple, and probably a theatre, was built *c.* 60–70. Streets and buildings close to the Roman baths were constructed during the middle of the second century, while an earth rampart and ditch defined the sacred area. During the third century, the town defences were supplemented with a masonry wall. The baths and temple continued to be maintained and visited until at least the early fifth century.

The rediscovery of Roman Bath

Significant Roman discoveries were made during the eighteenth century when the fashion for bathing resulted in the construction of elaborate new buildings. This led to the notable discovery of the remains of the Roman baths and temple of Sulis and Minerva, including evocative sculptures which fascinated antiquaries. Additional discoveries during the subsequent 200 years included the uncovering of the Great Bath during the 1880s. The large-scale excavation of the 1970s and 1980s directed by Professor Barry Cunliffe led to the excavation of the Sacred Spring, the redisplay of the baths themselves, and the finds from this site in the site museum (part of the Roman baths). Excavations at other locations within the city since the 1970s have revealed additional Roman structures in and around the walled town.

Origins

Three thermal springs bubble up from underground. These are Britain's only true hot springs, and ancient people would have found them fascinating. The dedication of the main spring to Sulis indicates that these waters must have been considered sacred before the arrival of the Romans. The Roman-period name of the town, *Aquae Sulis*, the Waters of Sulis, commemorates the goddess's sacred place.

During the early first century CE a causeway of gravel and stone was built at the edge of the largest spring pool, the Sacred Spring (Figure 7, A). Along with the Roman coins and other votive objects, eighteen Iron Age coins were found in this spring which in early Roman times came to form a central feature of the sanctuary of Sulis Minerva. Iron Age coins continued to be deposited, however, well into the Roman period, and these finds may have been offered to the goddess after the Roman military conquered the area.

Although several roads were constructed to the north of the sacred site, unlike in many other locations that developed as towns, Bath was not at the hub of this communication network and did not have a street grid (Figure 6). A small military unit may have been based at Bath, as indicated by the discovery of the tombstone of an auxiliary soldier, Lucius Vitellius Tancinus, displayed in the museum. To the north of Bath, gravel roads and buildings were constructed around Walcot, as shown on Figure 6. This may have been a civil settlement built outside the north gate of a Roman fort, but no indications of a fort were uncovered during excavations in and around the town.

Another possibility is that the buildings were constructed to serve the needs of travellers attracted to the sacred springs. It has long been supposed that the thermal and mineral springs developed as a healing sanctuary in the Roman period. Although this idea has recently been disputed, it could explain the presence of the soldiers attested by several tombstones. These auxiliary soldiers and civilian visitors, attested by tombstones, probably came here to be cured of their ailments but died during their visit.

The baths and temple of Sulis Minerva

The construction of the baths and the temple of Sulis Minerva dates to 60–75 CE (Figure 7, A), remarkably early in the Roman conquest of this area. It is entirely unclear who was responsible for this significant building project since the dedicatory inscription from the temple has not been found. The scale of the construction suggests the involvement of the provincial governor as a patron or a very wealthy individual, possibly from Gaul. The Great Bath has been heavily restored, but much of the substantial remains of the other elements of the Roman baths are displayed.

Work on the site of the Roman baths began with the consolidation of the unstable ground around the spring, which was then enclosed with a stone wall lined with lead sheets. This reservoir formed a head of water to feed the baths. Although the pool had a practical function, it also played a sacred function throughout the life of the building. Many offerings, including coins, jewellery and lead curses, were found when excavating the deposits in the pool. These curses are of considerable interest, forming requests to the divinities to punish people who had stolen items from their owners. Early in the Roman period, the local goddess Sulis was twinned with the classical divinity Minerva. These curses are mainly dedicated to Sulis and/or Minerva and request the goddess to take revenge on thieves.

The scale of the Roman baths suggests either the involvement of military engineers or architects from the Continent. The original baths had a spacious entrance hall overlooking the Sacred Spring to the north, a suite of steam rooms heated from beneath by hypocausts, and three thermal swimming baths to the east. The Great Bath was the largest of these pools and formed the heart of the complex. It was a large, roofed swimming bath surrounded by a broad walkway paved with stone slabs. The walls were decorated with painted plaster, and patterned mosaics decorated the floors, although these do not survive. Much of the original Roman masonry is visible in the footings of the walls and the paving. The superstructure above ground level was constructed in neoclassical style after the excavation of the Great Bath in the 1880s (Figure 8).

For 300 years after their construction the baths were modified and supplemented, and visitors today can explore the Great Bath, the East Baths, the West Baths and the hot spring, in addition to an area of the temple courtyard. The museum contains impressive finds from the site.

The temple of Sulis Minerva was constructed just north of the Sacred Spring and was integral to the bathing complex. The remains of this temple lie mainly under the Pump Room, just to the north of the baths. After the temple of Claudius in Colchester, this monumental building was the second classical temple to be constructed in Britain, demonstrating the considerable significance of the sanctuary. The building was set on a high podium reached by a flight of steps. Over its entry to the east was an ornate pediment supported by four massive Corinthian columns. Behind the facade was the *cella*, where a life-sized statue of Sulis Minerva was displayed. Much of the pediment was recovered and can be seen in the museum, along with the head from the cult statue and monumental masonry from the temple. The

Figure 8 *Photograph of the Roman baths at Bath.* © *https://www.gettyimages.co.uk/detail/photo/ancient-baths-royalty-free-image/182484374?searchscope=image%2Cfilm&adppopup=true.*

famous bust, known as the Gorgon, displays a fearsome male head with flowing hair and beard, held aloft by two winged victories.

In front of the eastern facade of the temple was a sacrificial altar. The temple was set centrally in a walled *temenos*, or sacred enclosure, with an eastern porched entry and colonnades along its north, south and western sides. The close connection between the baths and the temple is indicated by the inclusion of the Sacred Spring, the source of water for the baths, in the south-eastern corner of the *temenos*. This enclosure, comparable to the portico surrounding the temple of Claudius at Colchester, was completed during the mid-second century.

A tombstone commemorates Gaius Calpurnius Receptus, a priest of Sulis. Another inscription records an offering to Sulis by Lucius

Marcius Memor, who describes himself as a *haruspex*, or soothsayer. The role of a *haruspex* was to interpret animal sacrifices, and it is unclear whether Memor was based at Bath or visiting the spa with an important official. Memor is the only *haruspex* recorded in Britain.

The town

Bath was unusual among the Roman towns of Britain as it was not a substantial population centre and had no forum. The baths and temple formed the ceremonial centre of this town. Indeed, relatively few houses have been found within the earthwork enclosure, which defined a sacred rather than defended area, strictly speaking. Bath was a destination for pilgrims, and inscriptions in the museum record soldiers and civilians, men, women and children among the visitors. Two travellers from Germany were a man called Peregrinus from Trier and a woman named Rusonia Aventina from Metz. Many visitors were more local, including those who left curses in the Sacred Spring.

Additional buildings were constructed during the late first and second centuries, including shrines at the two smaller springs and an unusual circular monument on the site now occupied by Bath Abbey. Carvings from the circular structure, located east of the temple *temenos*, are particularly ornate, and this was an architecturally elaborate monument, presumably another temple. Streets have also been discovered, although Bath did not have a street grid comparable to other towns. A second sacred area developed around the Cross Bath Springs (Figure 7, B), and a substantial masonry courtyard house just to the south-east had a connected bathhouse. Perhaps this was where the priests lived or was a hotel for important pilgrims visiting the spa. There was probably also a theatre to house religious events at festivals.

Walking the walls

The earthwork defences and town walls enclosed an area of 10 hectares centred on the baths and the temple of Sulis Minerva. These defences were constructed during the later second century to define a sacred area around the sanctuary. The initial phase probably took the form of an earth rampart with an external ditch. A stone wall was added to the front of the rampart, probably during the third century. The Roman sanctuary/town may have had two gateways, on the north and west, but even this is uncertain, as there has been so little excavation.

The few surviving fragments of town defences are medieval (or later), representing the refortification of Bath centuries after the abandonment of the Roman town. No trace of the Roman defences can be seen, although some buried sections have been uncovered and recorded. The circuit, which provides an insight into the layout of Georgian and modern Bath, is difficult to follow unless you have a map.

I started exploring at the site of the north gate at the top of High Street, which was probably the site of one of the Roman gates (Figure 7, C). The course can be followed by turning left into Upper Borough Walls. One section of the crenellated wall has been identified as a fragment of the medieval town, as recorded by a metal plaque (D). This wall has been rebuilt on the line of the earlier town wall (it is less than 1 metre thick). Since the ground level drops by about 2 metres outside the line of the town defences, by walking north to Trim Street it is possible to appreciate something of the substantial earthwork which once existed. You should then return to Upper Borough Walls, and when you reach New Theatre Royal, turn left down Saw Close to the former location of the west gate, with Westgate Street on your left (E). This was probably the site of the other Roman gate, which may have been located just to the south of the junction of the roads.

Carry straight on down Saw Close following the course of the defences. Turn left down St James Parade before forking left into

Lower Borough Walls. The original location of the medieval south gate is where you cross Stall Street on your left and Southgate Street on your right (F). This is not thought to have been the site of a Roman gate. Follow New Orchard Street and turn left into Old Orchard Street. If you turn left immediately on reaching Old Orchard Street, you can see a heavily restored section of the medieval town wall behind Manvers Gospel Hall, again marked by a metal plaque (G).

The original line of the wall is obscured by development beyond this point. If you follow Old Orchard Street, however, and turn left onto Pierpoint Street and then the Grand Parade, you can locate the medieval east gate. This survives in an area below the street level in Boat Stalls Lane (H). Again, this medieval gate was probably not preceded by a Roman gate. From here, the course of the wall is lost in the urban development. Walking along Grand Parade and turning left with Pultney Bridge to your right brings you back to the location of the Roman north gate (C).

Occupation outside the defences

An extensive area of extramural settlement lined the road running north of the spa for over 1 kilometre (Figure 6). The first buildings in this area date to the earliest phase of Roman activity, and the settlement continued to develop in subsequent centuries. This extramural settlement was probably home to the people who supplied the visiting pilgrims with food and other services. Burials have also been found alongside this road and elsewhere on the outskirts of the Roman town. Some of the tombstones are displayed at the Roman baths.

Late Roman Bath

The baths and temple were maintained well into the fourth century, and coins continued to be deposited as offerings. Worship of the spring and its goddess even continued for decades after the decline of Roman power. As visitors to the spa gradually reduced, the level of drainage of the bath complex site declined. The condition of the masonry buildings became unstable before the site was abandoned and slowly fell into ruins. The eight-century poem *The Ruin* is thought to refer to the ruined remains of these grand buildings.

King Bladud and Georgian Bath

In the centuries that followed, stories were told to explain the origins of Bath. One tale concerning the legendary founder of the city, King Bladud, featured in Geoffrey of Monmouth's medieval account of the history of Britain, was later taken up by the famous eighteenth-century architect John Wood the Elder. Wood designed many of the impressive Georgian buildings in Bath and drew on the tale of Bladud as inspiration for the buildings he constructed. Wood also published an account of the city's origins, describing Bladud as its founder in the ninth century BCE. In the mind of Wood, this imagined pre-Roman history of Bath provided ancient origins to its existence as a fashionable Georgian spa.

A sculpture of King Bladud is displayed in the Roman baths. The accompanying inscription dates the sculpture to 1699 and describes Bladud's role in founding the city and the baths. Judging by postings on the internet, some people continue to believe that Bladud was an actual historical figure!

Further reading

The key excavation report is Cunliffe and Davenport (1995). An accessible and up-to-date account of Roman Bath is Davenport

(2021). A guide to the baths briefly addresses the archaeological remains and museum (Bird and Cunliffe 2019). La Trobe-Bateman and Niblett (2016) provide a more detailed account of the archaeology of Bath. Cousins (2020) explores the imperial context of the baths. For inscriptions: Lucius Vitellius Tancinus (RIB 159), Gaius Calpurnius Receptus (RIB 155), Lucius Marcius Memor (RIB 3049), Peregrinus (RIB 139) and Rusonia Aventina (RIB 162). Hingley (2008: 198–201) provides an account of Bladud. For relevant web links, see the website connected with this book.

3

Caerwent: Market of the Silures

Introduction

The impressive Roman remains in this attractive village include the best-preserved Roman town walls in Britain. Early excavations at the site uncovered much of the layout of the Roman town, and the foundations of the forum-basilica, shops, houses and a temple are available to explore.

Caerwent was the *civitas* capital of a people known as the Silures, who occupied what is now south-east Wales. There was a protracted conflict between Rome and the Silures during the early years of the conquest of western Britain, and the town took some time to develop from its origin in the later first century CE. The forum was constructed *c.* 120, probably when the developing urban settlement became a *civitas* capital.

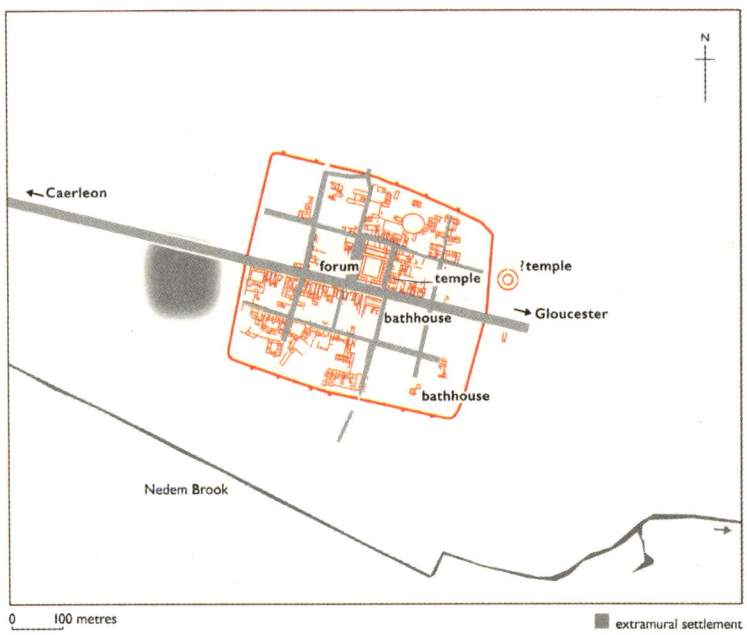

Figure 9 *Map of Roman Caerwent (after a map produced by Cadw, reproduced at Guest 2020: Figure 2). Drawn by Christina Unwin.*

Main visible archaeological features with grading

	Star rating
Forum-basilica	***
Temple	***
Townhouses	**
Town walls	***
Inscriptions	**

Getting there

There is a large public car park to the west of the modern village. Cadw maintains and displays the monument. Entry to all

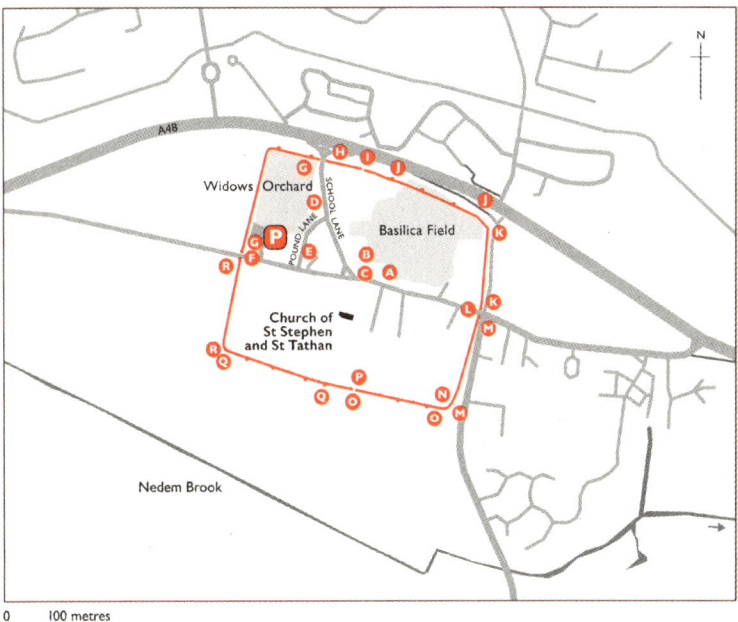

Figure 10 *Map of modern Caerwent with locations mentioned in the text marked. Drawn by Christina Unwin using information from Google Maps.*

parts of the site is free, and the car park is open from 10.00 a.m. to 4.00 p.m. throughout the year. At other times, visitors can park in the village. The area around the Roman town is popular with cyclists. Cadw's website explains how to get to the site by bike, bus or car.

Exploring Caerwent

The remains are displayed in an attractive rural setting, with the village partly overlying the Roman town. You can wander around the archaeology, and walking on top of the ramparts provides a prospect over the site and surrounding landscape. It took me 4 hours to explore all the Roman remains, which involved much walking. Although the village has a post office and pub, neither was open when I visited. The village is 6½ kilometres west of Chepstow, with its fine castle, shops, pubs and cafes. It is also possible to add on a visit to the impressive remains of the legionary fortress of Caerleon, 16 kilometres to the west. Some of the finds from Caerwent are displayed at Newport Museum and Art Gallery.

Historical summary

Excavation has revealed that there was a small settlement at Caerwent c. 70–85 CE, consisting of earth and timber houses. The forum is believed to date to c. 120, probably when the town's new status was established. During the later second century, a series of earth defences were constructed, followed in the late third century by the addition of a stone wall to the rampart. By the middle of the fourth century substantial towers (bastions) were incorporated into the walls on the south and north sides, indicating the town's continued importance.

The rediscovery of Roman Caerwent

Much of the layout of the late Roman town is well-documented as a result of extensive excavations by Thomas Ashby and Alfred Hudd between 1899 and 1913 (see Figure 9). Approximately two-thirds of the town's interior was explored over fourteen excavation seasons. The information gathered primarily pertains to the late Roman masonry phases, however, while little attention was given to the earlier timber buildings, which are buried more deeply. Subsequent excavations revealed the public baths and several shops located west of the forum. The town's defences were also explored. From 1981 to 1995 substantial excavations were carried out by the Museum of Wales under the direction of Richard Brewer. These uncovered much of the basilica, the temple located east of the forum, and one of the townhouses. They provided valuable insights into the town's origins and the timber structures preceding the later masonry buildings. Recent work has included excavations of additional buildings and a geophysical survey of the walled area and locations outside the town's defences.

Origins

It is unclear when occupation commenced, although this area of south Wales is known to have been the focus of Roman campaigning in the mid-50s CE. First established c. 70 and 85 as a trading settlement, Caerwent developed alongside the road connecting the Roman fortresses of Gloucester and Caerleon. The town was known as *Venta*, a name which probably means 'marketplace' or 'field' (as at Winchester and Caistor). The designation may signify that these towns were established at sites with a previous history as meeting places for their surrounding communities.

The earliest timber buildings were discovered beneath the stone temple to the east of the forum (Figure 10, A). A roadside strip building, comparable to examples in other early Roman urban contexts in Britain, was found. It is unclear how extensive the settlement was at this early stage or if there were any early public buildings before the construction of the forum.

The *civitas* capital

This town was the *civitas* capital of the Silures, a people who resisted Roman conquest from the late 40s CE to c. 74/5. A decision was made, probably around the time of the construction of the forum in c. 120, to establish Caerwent as the capital of the Silures. By then, this area of Wales had been pacified. Although the development must have been planned with the support of the local elite, this may still have required some forceful persuasion. The main streets were possibly also laid out at this time, although the town grid was probably not completed until the later third century.

The excavations during the early twentieth century uncovered considerable information about the buildings in the town (Figure 9). Later excavations have provided additional chronological information. The excavated foundations of several buildings are on public display, with information boards offering interpretation. These include part of the basilica attached to the forum, a temple complex, and two groups of houses. The town walls are preserved around almost the entire circuit. Several streets in the modern village follow the courses of Roman streets.

The forum

Since the excavations uncovered much of the building, we are confident about the forum's plan. The foundations of the northern end of the building – including most of the basilica, part of the forum courtyard, and a small section of the forum's east wing – are displayed within a fenced enclosure in the south-western corner of Basilica Field (Figure 10, B). The buried remains of the forum's west, south and east wings lie under the gardens of the two properties to the south of the displayed remains. The line of the outer face of the forum's eastern wing is preserved by the modern property boundary of the house (just to the west of the Roman temple).

To the south, the forum was fronted by the main east–west road. Excavations alongside this road uncovered a monumental gateway to the forum, but this is no longer visible (C). The forum's open piazza (courtyard) was flanked on three sides by colonnaded porticos sheltering ranges of small shops. This courtyard has been buried, and the only remains visible within the displayed area are one of the shops (in the north-east corner) and part of the stone paving of the courtyard. The basilica, much of which is uncovered and displayed, formed the fourth (north) side.

The open courtyard of the forum was where merchants set up their stalls on market days. Statues of emperors and other significant men connected with the *civitas* capital would have adorned this space. One of the statues likely to have been in the forum commemorated a senior Roman called Tiberius Claudius Paulinus, a patron of the town during the early third century. The base for this statue, with its Latin inscription, is displayed in the porch of the village church (below). Paulinus had served as *praetor*, an elected magistrate, in Rome before governing the province of *Narbonensis* (southern Gaul). He was then appointed legionary commander of the fortress at Caerleon, and this must be when he became a patron of the urban community at Caerwent. He later became a *consul* (chief magistrate) in Rome before taking command of the Sixth Legion at their fortress in York. The urban elite who ruled from Caerwent dedicated the statue in honour of their influential patron.

Raised above the forum, the basilica was accessed from the courtyard by steps which are heavily worn. The basilica consisted of a hall with a range of seven rooms on its northern side. The eastern two-thirds of the aisled hall and all the rooms to its north are displayed. A colonnade formed from Corinthian columns separated the nave of the basilica from the aisles to the north and south. At the east and west ends of the nave were two *tribunals*, only the eastern one being within the displayed area. The *tribunals* were rooms where the local magistrates heard legal cases. The second (and largest) of the rooms from the western end of the basilica, the *curia* (council chamber), had a mosaic floor, although no trace of the mosaic survives. The town's ruling elite had access to this room for meetings to discuss the government of the *civitas*. The next room east of the *curia* in the centre of the range housed a shrine, possibly dedicated to the imperial cult. Several of the rooms in the basilica had decorated wall plaster.

After a fourth-century restoration of the building, the forum may have remained in use into the early fifth century, suggesting the continuation of civic life over three centuries.

The temple

Just east of the forum, the foundations of a Romano-Celtic temple are displayed (Figure 10, A). One of the few such temples on public display at a Roman town in Britain, this building and its surrounding enclosure were excavated from 1984 to 1988. The temple was constructed *c.* 330 CE on a previously occupied site. The entrance to the temple building was from the main road to the south, which passed through a long entrance hall with an apsidal east end and a tessellated floor. The temple itself took the form of a small square *cella*, the residence of the god, with an outer rectangular ambulatory. It had the unusual feature of an apse on the northern face of the *cella*. The temple and entrance hall were enclosed within a masonry boundary wall.

Houses and shops

The Edwardian excavations uncovered the plans of many masonry houses, of which at least seventeen were substantial residences. At least one of the courtyard houses uncovered by Ashby and Hudd had a private bathing suite, and quite a few had mosaic floors. The areas of housing on public display include the remains of three courtyard houses belonging to the wealthier families of the late Roman town.

The foundations of one of these dwellings were uncovered during excavations in 1981–4, at a site identified by Cadw on the information board as the 'Courtyard House' (north of Pound Lane; Figure 10, D). The excavations revealed a sequence of buildings, the earliest of which was a timber building on stone foundations dated to the late second or early third century. This building was replaced by a much more substantial winged-corridor house during the late third century. In the early fourth century, the house was extended with rooms ranging around two courtyards. The residential rooms, decorated with painted plaster, lay around the northern courtyard. Two of these rooms had hypocausts, and the supporting columns are visible onsite. The rooms around the southern courtyard were much plainer and included a large storeroom and a corn-dryer, which may indicate that this property was a farm.

You can visit a second area of housing along the eastern side of Pound Lane (E). Pound Lane and the main east–west road through the village follow the approximate course of Roman roads. Excavations in 1946–8 uncovered the foundations of a range of shops fronting the street at the south end of Pound Lane, where it meets the east–west road. The masonry shops were constructed in the early or middle of the second century, and archaeological finds indicate that one was a blacksmith's workshop. During the earlier fourth century, a large courtyard house (only partly within the displayed area) replaced these commercial premises. Another courtyard house to the north was further away from the town's main road. Only part was excavated and displayed, but this included a hypocaust with a mosaic floor (not visible).

Archaeological finds at Caerwent church

Another location that includes significant Roman artefacts is St Stephen and St Tathan's Church. The commemorative stone that mentions Tiberius Claudius Paulinus (above) is in the church porch alongside an altar dedicated to the deity Mars Ocelus. When I visited, a conservator was working on the Paulinus stone. He told me that when this inscription was found in 1903 the British Museum wished to acquire it for their collection, but the villagers would not allow this. Also on display is a fragment of a mosaic floor derived from one of the houses excavated in the western area of the town in 1910, together with carved stones found during building works in 1900 and 1911. Four of these blocks of stone depict floral motifs and may have come from a free-standing monument, possibly connected with the public bathhouse. This bathhouse lies beneath the fields east of the church. The cinerary urn displayed in a stone alcove beside the sculpted stones is one of several cremation burials found within the town.

Walking the walls

Caerwent's town walls were not rebuilt in post-Roman times and retain their original form. They define a relatively small area of 18 hectares, and there is little to indicate any extensive extramural settlement outside the gates. A geophysical survey to the west of the walled circuit has located traces of anomalies alongside the Roman road, probably signalling the presence of buildings. An octagonal temple, or perhaps a high-status mausoleum, was sited outside the walls to the east of the town, just north of the eastern gate (Figure 9). Little is known about this apart from its plan, and it may pre- or post-date the construction of the defences. Although a geophysical survey to the south of the walls failed to find any sign of extramural occupation, it is still possible that there were areas of occupation outside the east and north gates.

The dating of the sequence of the defences was determined by a series of excavations. These indicated that they originated in the later second century, developing from an earth rampart with one or two external ditches. The four stone gatehouses may have been constructed at the same time. During the late third century a substantial stone wall, *c.* 7 metres high including parapets, was added to the outer face of the rampart. The two ditches were retained. Mid-fourth-century modifications included the addition of substantial stone towers (often called bastions) to the north and south lines of the wall, requiring the infilling of the inner town ditch. Some of these polygonal towers are well preserved.

I started my exploration of the town defences at the west gate (Figure 10, F), just west of the car park. The only fragment of masonry of this gate visible today is part of the south tower (to the south of the road). The road beyond the gateway, which probably had twin carriageways, led to the legionary fortress of Caerleon. If time is short, you may wish to turn south to explore the well-preserved southern defences before walking back through the village from the east gate. I walked northwards from the west gate along the top of the rampart by following the western and northern boundary of the meadow known as Widows Orchard (G–G). This offers an elevated prospect from which you can see the level of the ground outside the line of the defences. Private land fronts this section of the wall and is not accessible. When you reach the north-eastern corner of Widows Orchard, turn right and walk past the Courtyard House (D) until your reach the junction of School Lane and Pound Lane. To return to the walls, walk north up School Lane and follow the road as it bends to the right until you reach the A48.

From this point, you can walk along the path beside the road: the wall survives behind the houses and gardens on the south (right) side of the A48 (H). The substantial remains of much of the north gate, only missing the arch, are visible on private land behind the approach to one of the houses (I). This was a single-carriageway gate that was blocked during the later Roman period. Beyond the point at which the row of houses ends, the physical remains of the wall have mostly disappeared. The earthwork remains of the defences can be spotted to the right of the footpath until you reach the north-east corner, however (J–J).

Turning right at the end of this path brings you along the east side of the defences (on your right), which are well-preserved and impressive (K–K). The octagonal temple mentioned above lay just to your left, under the almshouses and gardens. When you reach the east gate (L), at the junction with the main east–west village street, you can see the remains of part of the southern section of the gateway tower (look in front of you, to the right). This gateway, like the west gateway, had twin carriageways. The road running east from here eventually reached the colony at Gloucester. Continuing the walk south along the lane in front, a well-preserved length of town wall runs to the south-east corner of the walled circuit (M–M). The massive earth mound on top of the corner of the defences is the remains of a medieval castle mound (motte) (N).

The southern section is exceptionally well-preserved as far as the south gate and beyond (O–O). The foundations of two towers are visible along the course, but better-preserved towers lie further west. Just beyond the later break in the town wall is the site of the south gate (P). The northern (inner) face of this gateway is well-preserved. The late Roman blocking of the gateway with masonry has helped protect some architectural details, including the two piers, the imposts on either side of the entrance, and several voussoirs (Figure 11). Since it was partially demolished when the gate was blocked, the gate's southern (outer) face is far less impressive. Geophysical survey in the field to the south of the gate has located the Roman road running away from the town south towards the coast. Much of the land visible to the south of the urban defences was a coastal marsh in Roman times.

Further to the west along the wall are the remains of four unusually well-preserved towers (Figure 10, Q–Q; Figure 12). Since they are not bonded into the masonry, you can see that these polygonal projecting towers were added to the pre-existing wall. It is then possible to follow the line of the wall around the west defences and back to the west gate (Figure 10, R–R).

Figure 11 *Photograph of the Roman south gate at Caerwent from inside the walled circuit.* © *Richard Hingley.*

Figure 12 *Photograph of a tower/bastion on the southern section of the town wall at Caerwent.* © *Richard Hingley.*

The dead of the town

Little is known about the town's cemeteries, probably located outside one or more of the gateways. The archaeological work has focused almost entirely on the defences and the area inside the walls. Only two funerary inscriptions have been found, both reused in later buildings within Caerwent, and further work would be required to explore the location and character of these burial grounds.

The end of the town

Occupation of the town continued into the late fourth and, perhaps, the early fifth century. As the military situation in southern Wales deteriorated, the circuit of walls would have given the townsfolk a sense of security. People may have continued to live here into the early medieval period, although traces of buildings have yet to be found. A medieval story gives an account of St Tatheus who is commemorated in the name of Caerwent's church. This tale suggests that during the sixth century he founded a monastic settlement within the walls, possibly on the site of the present church.

Further reading

Brewer (2006) offers a thorough account of the archaeology and the various elements of the Roman town. Guest (2022) provides an up-to-date summary of the archaeology and a detailed discussion on the forum-basilica. The inscription mentioning Tiberius Claudius Paulinus is RIB 311 (see Tomlin 2018: 243–4). The altar dedicated to Mars Ocelus is RIB 310. For relevant web links, see the website connected with this book.

4

Caistor St Edmund: Market of the Iceni

Introduction

This Roman town is in a rural setting, *c.* 6 kilometres south of Norwich. The impressive urban defences, set in fields and woodland alongside the floodplain of the River Tas, are a popular area for walking. The only building within the Roman defences is the medieval church of St Edmund, after which the neighbouring hamlet is named. This town was the *civitas* capital of the Iceni, a people famous for their uprising against the Romans under Boudica. Their *civitas* capital was established several decades after the suppression of the uprising. Roman Caistor covered a larger area than its comparatively small walled circuit, and excavation, geophysical survey and aerial photography have revealed the plan of the roads and buildings in and around the walls. Caistor is a pleasant location to explore, and the defences are well-preserved, especially around the eastern half of the circuit.

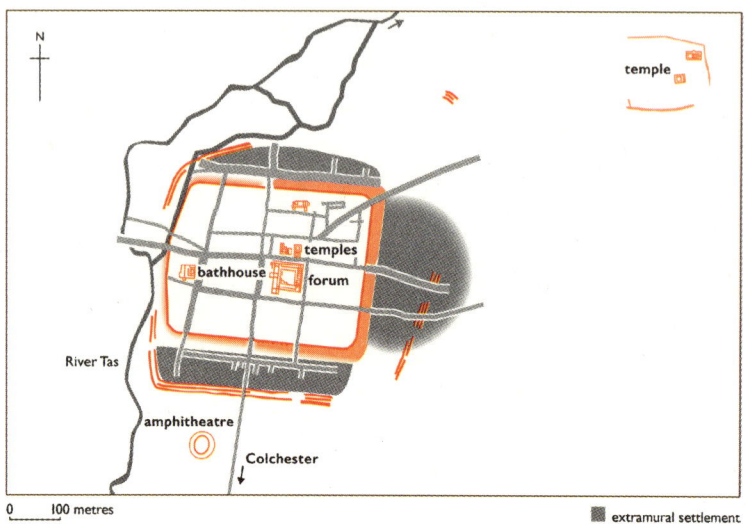

Figure 13 *Map of Roman Caistor St Edmund (after Bowden 2020: Figure 26). Drawn by Christina Unwin.*

Main visible archaeological features with grading

	Star rating
Town defences	***

Exploring Roman Caistor

Caistor is simplest to reach by car or bicycle. There is a car park on the road just outside the south-east corner of the town defences. It took me 2 hours to walk around the walls, explore the field to the south of the town, and visit the site of the Roman temple (almost 1 kilometre north-east of the car park). There are no shops or services at Caistor.

The Norfolk Archaeological Trust looks after the site, and the areas of open-access land maintained to the south and east of the town

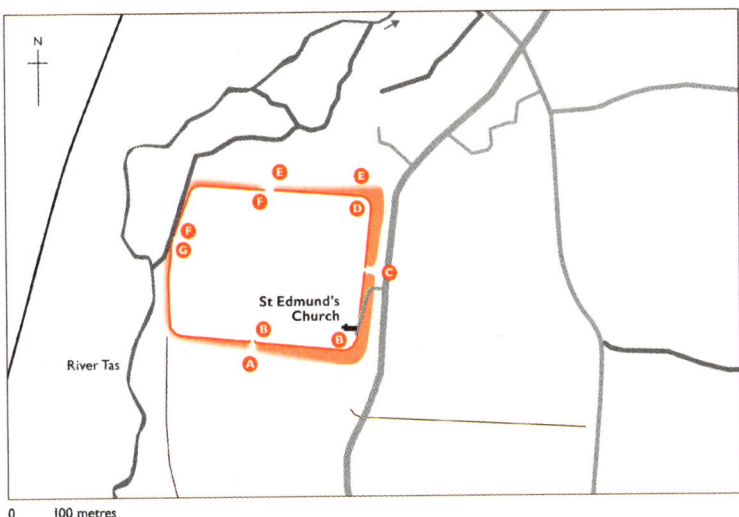

Figure 14 *Map of modern Caistor St Edmund with locations mentioned in the text marked. Drawn by Christina Unwin using information from Google Maps.*

allow visitors to wander at will. There are information boards on site, and some finds from the excavation are displayed at Norwich Castle Museum.

Historical summary

Although it may have had earlier origins, the earliest known settlement began to develop during the final decades of the first century CE. The buildings were of timber and earth, and the town may have had defensive earthworks. The construction of streets within the town started *c.* 100 CE, and the masonry forum was built around the middle of the second century. The substantial defences may have been built in one go, perhaps during the later third century. The external masonry towers, or bastions, were probably added to the stone wall during the fourth century.

The rediscovery of Roman Caistor

Recognized as a Roman foundation during the later sixteenth century, the town was initially considered a military camp. In 1928, aerial photography revealed much of the street system and some Roman buildings. Aerial reconnaissance was in its early stages then, and these dramatic results led to a series of excavations within the walled circuit, directed by Donald Atkinson between 1929 and 1937. He uncovered the forum, two temples, a bathhouse and the south gate. The site has been investigated since 2007 by a community project in collaboration with the University of Nottingham, which has provided additional information about the town's surroundings.

Origins

The excavations and artefacts from the site suggest that the earliest settlement began to develop after the Boudican uprising, *c.* 70–90 CE. Although no evidence of Iron Age settlement has been found at the Roman town, its original name of *Venta Icenorum* may suggest that Caistor was established in a location that had long been a significant Iron Age meeting place. The term *Venta* may denote a pre-existing meeting place or a market, as at Winchester and Caerwent.

During the late first century, a Romano-Celtic temple was constructed about 1 kilometre north-east of the town (Figure 13). This temple site, of which there are no visible remains, was located just east of the Caistor St Edmund village, along Caistor Lane. Recent excavations have uncovered Iron Age finds, suggesting that this site may have been sacred prior to Roman occupation. The original Roman temple was built of timber on stone foundations, and replaced by a larger stone temple during the mid-second century. This substantial structure was situated within a *temenos* (sacred enclosure) and accompanied by another building. The temple was connected to the developing town by a gravel road. When the urban street grid was established in the second century, this road was retained, despite its awkward angle to the urban streets.

The buildings on the site later occupied by the town were of timber and clay on flint foundations. As large quantities of painted plaster and the burnt traces of a timber structure were found in layers underlying the later forum building, the earlier buildings may have included a forum. Little is known about these structures because of the early date of the excavations, and even the extent of the settlement is unclear. An extensive series of ditches surrounded a large kite-shaped area centred on the town (Figure 13). Located through aerial photography and geophysical surveys, limited excavations across these ditches suggest they were constructed *c.* 100 CE. They probably served to demarcate the area rather than having a direct defensive purpose. Indeed, as they appear discontinuous, it is even unclear whether these ditches formed a single enclosure.

The *civitas* capital

The gravel streets began to take shape across the urban area around the start of the second century. While there appears to have been a fairly regular system of streets defining the *insulae*, individual roads continued to be constructed throughout the second century. Will Bowden, who led recent archaeological work at Caistor, has noted that the street system was not as regular as suggested by Edwardian archaeologists, who often overstated the regularity of Roman towns. These streets extend well beyond the area that was later enclosed by the defences (Figure 13).

The fields within the walled circuit, as well as the area to the south, are maintained as openly accessible land, allowing visitors to walk freely across the sites of several public buildings. The forum, excavated by Atkinson, resembles other examples from Roman towns in Britain. It is believed that the forum was constructed *c.* 150 CE, abandoned by the third century, and reconstructed during the fourth century. A substantial public bathhouse was built in the west part of the town around this time or later. Atkinson also excavated two Romano-Celtic temples of late-second-century date, which were located just north of the forum. These temples were connected to the other temple mentioned above by a gravel road running to the north-east of the town. To the south, aerial photography has identified an amphitheatre, although it has not yet been excavated.

Walking the walls

The walls enclose 14 hectares, one of the smallest circuits of urban defences for a *civitas* capital. The construction of these works was an immense undertaking that must have disrupted life in Caistor. Considering the extent of the street system, it is not known why such a small area was enclosed. The defences cut across and put several of the urban streets out of use. These included the road that ran to the temple north-east of Caistor. It is unclear how many houses lay outside the enclosed town, as the settlement may have contracted during the third century.

Little is known about the sequence of activities undertaken to construct the defences. The early excavations suggested that the rear bank was contemporary with the stone wall, but based on many other towns, the sequence may have been more complex. These defences are remarkably well-preserved and were not reused in post-Roman times. The ditch surrounding the wall is particularly notable since this feature rarely survives at other towns.

I started my exploration by walking from the car park to the site of the south gate (Figure 14, A). Atkinson excavated this gate and found a simple opening through the stone rampart, with guard chambers flanking the gate. A path leads you to the top of the rampart. I turned right and walked to the south-eastern corner of the defences and then to the site of St Edmund's Church (B–B). The ramparts in this part of the circuit are covered in trees. The earliest documentary reference to a church here dates to the late eleventh century, although excavations on the foundations of the building in 2009 suggested an earlier origin. The church fabric incorporates Roman tile.

I left the church by walking through the (private) church car park just to the north, but if you prefer you can also walk outside the ramparts to view the scale of the town defences from below. The east gate was located where the road into the car park cuts through the defences (C). From this point, you can walk along the top of the rampart as far as the north-east corner (D). I then walked down the bank of the rampart to study the northern defences from outside their course (E–E). The section of the stone wall as far as the north gate is very well-preserved, if fragmentary, and stands, in part, at its full height. The path then goes through the site of the gate and continues to the right along the top of the rampart. Sections of the stone wall protrude from the surviving bank to your right (F–F).

Walking along the rampart brings you to the site of the west gate (G). The road running beyond the ramparts, which has been located through aerial photography, led down to a ford or possibly a bridge over the river. Just before you arrive at this gate, a substantial stump of masonry protruding from the long vegetation marks the remains of one of the external towers (bastions) that were added to the outer face of the town wall. You can walk along the top of the defences from this location until you arrive back at the south gate (A).

Houses and people

The 1930s excavations uncovered traces of timber buildings, some stone houses, and evidence of industry. The recent geophysical survey of the walled area shows that a dense distribution of masonry houses occupied much of the interior.

A lead curse dedicated to Neptune, which was found on the west bank of the River Tas, may well have been deposited in the river or on its banks to request the assistance of the water god. It contains part of the dedicator's name, mentions the theft from the dedicator of a range of items, and promises a pair of leggings to Neptune if the god punishes the thief. The lack of tombstones means there is no information on other townspeople. Burials have been located on all sides of the town, although there have been no significant recent excavations of the cemeteries. One extensive cemetery outside the east gate, uncovered during the 1930s, included many early medieval graves. It was probably a Roman burial ground originally.

The end of the Roman town

Like many other towns, occupation probably continued until the early fifth century, when the walled area was deserted. The many early medieval burials immediately around the town indicate that Caistor nevertheless remained a significant location. Some early Germanic settlers may have been brought in to help defend the settlement in the fourth century and continued living at the town or nearby. In the seventh and eighth centuries there was also an extensive settlement to the west of the River Tas.

Further reading

Bowden (2020) is an excellent general guide to the Roman town and its surroundings. For the date and nature of the street system and the early Roman enclosure ditches, see Bowden and Bescoby (2008). Bowden (2013a) includes additional information on geophysical surveys in and around Caistor, while Bowden (2013b) summarizes the information from the early excavations and the results of some of the more recent excavations. Frere (1971) addresses what can be reconstructed of the forum from the early excavations. For discussion of the excavation of the temple north-east of Caistor, see Hilts and Bowden (2021) and Hilts (2022). Some information on the buildings and defences is included in Wacher (1995), although the description of the historical context of the town is out of date. For Boudica and the Iceni, see Hingley and Unwin (2005). For relevant web links, see the website connected with this book.

5

Canterbury: Sacred Site by the River

Introduction

This attractive city was the site of a Late Iron Age *oppidum* and a Roman *civitas* capital. Although the survival of the city's historic buildings has limited the amount of archaeological excavation, we have important information about the Iron Age and Roman past. The visible Roman remains include part of a townhouse, displayed in the Canterbury Roman Museum, and the town defences. The museum displays archaeological finds from the city. Three kilometres west is the Iron Age hillfort of Bigbury Camp.

Main archaeological features with grading

	Star rating
Townhouse	**
Town walls	**
Museum	**

Figure 15 *Map of Roman Canterbury (after Millett 2007: Figure 5.15, and Historic Towns Trust 2021). Drawn by Christina Unwin.*

Getting there

There are two railway stations, Canterbury East and Canterbury West, both of which are close to the city centre and convenient for exploring the Roman town. There is also a bus station in the city and several car parks. If you wish to visit Bigbury Camp, it is worth obtaining the local Ordnance Survey maps (OS *Explorer* 150 and OS *Landranger* 179). There is no parking close to this hillfort nor any facilities. If travelling by car, I would suggest leaving the car at Harbledown and proceeding by foot. If you walk to Bigbury from the city and back, as I did, you will need to allow several hours for your visit.

Canterbury: Sacred Site by the River

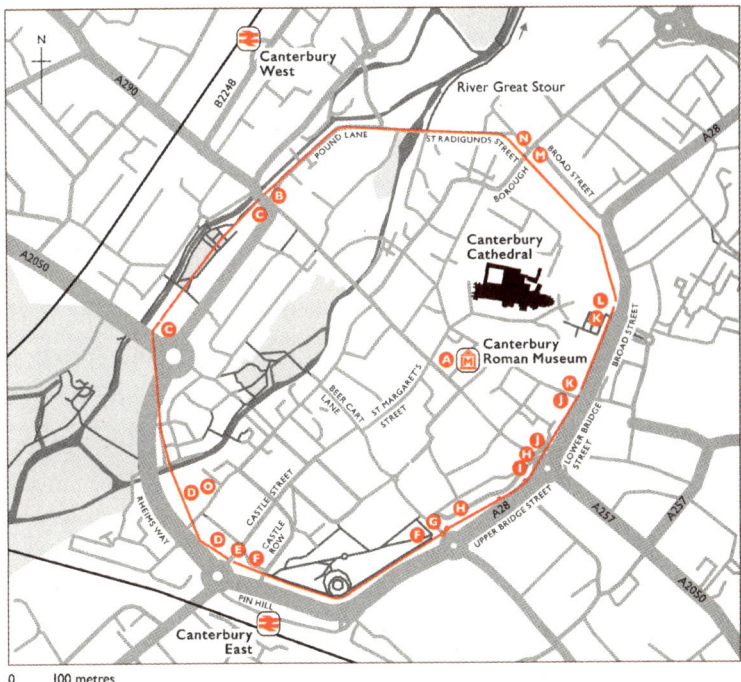

Figure 16 *Map of modern Canterbury with locations mentioned in the text marked. Drawn by Christina Unwin using information from Google Maps.*

Exploring ancient Canterbury

In addition to the Roman remains, the city also has impressive medieval buildings, including the cathedral. There are many restaurants, cafes and places to stay. I took 4 hours to explore the Roman archaeological sites and visit the museum, but it would be well worth staying longer to visit the medieval buildings and shops.

Historical summary

The area around Canterbury includes many Iron Age sites, and although the exact character of settlement and activity is unclear, this may have been an *oppidum*. An extensive series of Iron Age earthworks to the west of the city may have been the core of the *oppidum*, with the activity at the valley-bottom site at Canterbury an outlier to the main site. Traces of occupation have been found here, and the excavations have uncovered plentiful evidence of trade with the Continent.

Several decades after the Roman conquest, a settlement with timber buildings started to develop. The construction of a theatre during the late first century CE was a significant feature of the town's early development. The street system was created during the early second century, and other monumental buildings, including a classical temple, were constructed as Canterbury became the *civitas* capital of the Cantiaci. The defences date to the late third century, and occupation continued until the early fifth century.

The rediscovery of ancient Canterbury

Canterbury was long known to have been a Roman settlement. It was the excavation of bomb-damaged sites after the Second World War, however, that resulted in a detailed knowledge of its Iron Age and Roman past. More recently, information has emerged from a series of excavations undertaken by the Canterbury Archaeological Trust in advance of development in the city. These excavations have produced a detailed understanding of the layout and development of Iron Age and Roman Canterbury.

Iron Age *oppidum*

It appears possible that the Late Iron Age occupation on the site of the later Roman town at Canterbury was part of an extensive *oppidum*, of which we know relatively little. Excavations have uncovered evidence of Iron Age activity beneath a large area of the modern city, including roundhouses and part of a triple-ditched enclosure of uncertain function. This site developed on both sides of a braided river course, which must have flooded regularly. Finds include Iron Age coins and coin moulds, which suggest the production of coins at the site. Imported amphorae and other pottery have been uncovered, along with an imported bronze bowl from Italy which accompanied the burial of an important individual who probably died in the early first century BCE.

Three kilometres to the west are the remains of one of Kent's few hillforts at Bigbury Camp (NGR TR 117 577). The earthworks of the hillfort are part of a wildlife reserve that is open to the public. A footpath skirts the west side of the hillfort and passes through the so-called annexe of the fort defined by surviving earthworks; an ascent to the flat summit can be made here. Tree growth and the steepness of the incline make the better-preserved earthworks, on the north side, more difficult to access. This hillfort may have been the place attacked by Julius Caesar during his second invasion of Britain in 54 BCE. Although this identification is uncertain, Bigbury was evidently part of a much more extensive series of enclosures and linear earthworks on the hills west of Canterbury. On display in the Roman Museum is the Bridge Helmet, a significant archaeological artefact found just south-east of Canterbury which dates to around the time of Caesar's incursions.

A sacred site

Little appears to have changed at Canterbury for around four decades after the Roman invasion. One excavation suggested that in the early years of the conquest a Roman fortlet was located close to Canterbury Castle. The information to indicate a military presence is far from conclusive, however. The first significant changes date to the final two decades of the first century CE, when a theatre, built of timber and earth, was constructed on rising ground to the east of a ford over the River Stour (Figure 15). When the Roman town was laid out, it effectively fossilized a cluster of earlier enclosures and buildings in the centre of Canterbury, as indicated by the alignment of the theatre and bathhouse and of the road that divided these two buildings from the temple precinct. These buildings and boundaries were aligned differently from the main street grid, which, in turn, is thought to date to the early second century. The boundaries of the sacred precinct that developed at the centre of Canterbury probably pre-dated the establishment of the main street system by several decades.

In Britain and Gaul, theatres were often associated with temples, as at Bath, Verulamium and Gosbecks (Colchester). Baths were also often associated with sanctuaries, and the bathhouse at Canterbury may have also been part of the sacred complex. The excavations suggest that this bathhouse was constructed during the early second century and, as at Silchester, there may have been an earlier bathhouse on this site. A classical temple, probably constructed during the early second century (below), was built on the site of an earlier sanctuary. At Canterbury, as at Verulamium, the sacred topography of the Iron Age *oppidum* influenced the development of the Roman town.

Excavation indicates that houses and industry clustered around this complex of sacred structures, although the population of Canterbury was probably not very substantial during the later first century.

The *civitas* capital

The replanning of the town *c*. 100 CE may signal the foundation of the *civitas* capital. The new streets and property divisions had a different alignment from the earlier roads and boundaries defining the sacred focus at the centre of the developing town. We know relatively little about the chronology and sequence of the public buildings. The classical temple was probably constructed during the early second century, with a colonnaded portico. This portico constructed around the temple during the late second or early third century is comparable to similar structures at Bath and Colchester. The temple building has not been excavated, but the many fragments of Italian marble found in this area indicate its high status. It was probably comparable in opulence to the classical temples at Colchester and Bath. Architectural fragments include several Corinthian capitals.

Although we know the forum was located just north of the temple, there is very little information about the dating and construction sequence. The original timber-and-earth theatre was reconstructed as a substantial and ornate stone structure during the late second or early third century, located where three modern (largely pedestrianized) roads meet: Castle Street, Beer Cart Lane and St Margaret's Street. If you stand at this junction, you are in the orchestra area (*platea*) of the former theatre.

Excavations have uncovered the courses of roads on both sides of the River Great Stour. A low-lying floodplain ran through the centre of the urban area, and bridges probably carried two of the streets over the river. Excavations have located several townhouses. As at other towns, the first-century buildings were timber-built, and the later Roman houses were masonry. Some of these masonry houses had hypocausts, mosaics and painted wall plaster. The Roman Museum was constructed around, and displays the remains of, one of these townhouses *in situ*.

The townhouse at the museum

Workers digging trenches for new drains in 1868 uncovered a Roman mosaic. Further work after bomb damage during the Second

World War revealed other parts of a late Roman house, including more mosaics and a room with a hypocaust, which is displayed onsite (Figure 16, A). The eastern arm of this courtyard house, constructed in the second century, had a dark grey tessellated pavement with three rectangular mosaic panels. The house, which also featured a connected bathhouse, was abandoned by the mid-fourth century.

Walking the walls

The town was defined by a stone wall with an accompanying bank and external ditch enclosing *c.* 53 hectares of land, including some areas only partly occupied. Excavations across its line suggest that these defences were constructed as a single operation during the late third century, somewhat later than the urban defences of many *civitas* capitals. Since it was rebuilt and modified in the medieval period, the course of the Roman wall has survived. The walled area enclosed the valley bottom of the River Great Stour and rising ground to both sides. Although all traces of the western half of the circuit have been lost, from just west of Northgate to Worth Gate, the physical remains of much of the rest of the defences can be followed.

The wall was almost 2½ metres wide and built of coursed flint and mortar. A substantial bank lay to the rear, and excavations suggest a single sizeable external ditch. At least five gates gave access to the town, and there may have been two more. Square towers were later added to the inner face of the wall, and there are some indications from the excavations of towers (bastions) added to the outer face. The bastions visible around the east of the defensive circuit are medieval. Although the Roman wall was substantially rebuilt between the eleventh and sixteenth centuries, fragments of the original structure survive in several places, as noted below.

I started my exploration at the West Gate (B) and walked anticlockwise. The substantial medieval Westgate probably reused the site of a Roman gate. From this point, the defences ran along the south-eastern bank of the western stream of the River Great Stour and you can follow the course of the wall by turning into the Westgate Garden River Walk (C–C). The Tower House in the park reused the structure of one of the medieval bastions, which lay on the course of the Roman and medieval walls. When you reach the end of Westgate Gardens, you are close to the site of the London Gate. The excavation of this narrow gate showed that it was single-arched and probably surmounted by a tower. The gate lay on Watling Street and gave access towards London.

To follow the line of the walls from here it is best to walk back to the path through Westgate Gardens and turn right down St Peter's Place until you reach the St Peter's Roundabout. This lies within the course of the former city wall, which is lost under the road system for several hundred metres beyond this point. I followed the approximate course of the ramparts by walking from the roundabout down Old Watling Street, turning right into Creine Mill Lane, then right again down The Rope Walk. Turn left onto the footbridge over the river and follow the footpath to Rheims Way (A290), past the remains of Canterbury Castle on your left. This route takes you past a surviving section of the medieval city wall, which follows the course of the Roman defences (D–D). Where you reach Castle Street, with the Wincheap Roundabout on your right, you are at the site of a Roman gate at Worth Gate (E). Travellers would journey from here towards Lympne on the Kent coast.

The section of the wall to the east of Castle Street is no longer visible, but if you walk a short way up Pin Hill and turn up Castle Row to the left, you can view the next surviving section. If you return to Pin Hill, by walking on the grass verge along this busy road you can follow the outside of a long section of the medieval city wall with impressive bastions. Once again, this reused the remains of the Roman defence. A more pleasant walk is to turn right off Castle Row and walk along the top of the city wall through Dane John Gardens (F–F). This route takes you past the prominent mound of a medieval motte with a modern monument on top. Walking through the park takes you to the former Riding Gate (G), where a modern walkway takes the walltop walk across Watling Street. Excavation of this Roman gate showed that it was a twin portal gate, which gave access to the port at Dover.

Crossing over Watling Street leads to another section of the walls running alongside Upper Bridge Street as far as St George's Gate (H–H). There is no evidence that a Roman gate preceded the medieval gate once sited here. If you turn left into St George's Street, then left again into St George's Terrace, you will find the remains of one of the Roman internal towers that were built into the back of the wall. This is displayed in a covered area to the right (west) of the cycle shop (I).

The damaged remains of the medieval wall run alongside Lower Bridge Street to a street named Burgate (J–J). To examine this section of wall, you will need to walk along Lower Bridge Street. Burgate was the site of another of the Roman gates, which gave access to the town and fort at Richborough. The wall remains are better preserved in Queningate Car Park (K–K), where trace remains of the Quening Gate (L) are visible just to the south-west of the most northerly of the medieval bastions. You can see the jambs and the right-hand return of this Roman single-arched gateway in the outer face of the wall. Quening Gate was blocked during the fifteenth century.

Walking down Broad Street towards Borough, the remains of the wall survive behind the houses fronting the street to your left. If you turn left onto Borough for a short distance, you reach St Radigunds Street on your right. Immediately facing you (towards the city centre) is the site of the medieval North Gate (M), demolished in the nineteenth century. A Roman gate probably preceded the medieval gate.

The turn from Borough into St Radigunds Street follows the outer course of the Roman and medieval defences. A substantial section of masonry wall survives in the gardens south of St Radigunds Street, to your left (N). This is the surviving section of the north wall of St Mary's Church at the Northgate. Deconsecrated over a century ago, this medieval church is now St Mary's Northgate Hall, but when it was originally built it used a section of Canterbury's walled circuit. This section of medieval city wall reused a substantial section of the masonry of the Roman town wall. The stone facing of the Roman wall survives to a height of $c.$ 5 metres, and there are also faint traces of crenellations. These are considered to be features of the medieval rebuilding, however, rather than part of the original Roman structure. There is a helpful information board at this location.

Just to the right (west) of the north wall of St Mary's Northgate, the foundations of the medieval city wall are preserved. If you continue along St Radigunds Street to the west, you follow the outer line of the Roman and medieval defences. After 30 metres, St Radigunds Street curves to the left, again following the outer line of the former defences. After crossing the River Great Stour, you reach Pound Lane, which follows the former course of the defences until you reach Westgate (B).

Suburbs and cemeteries

Recent excavations have uncovered an area of extramural settlement outside the Worth Gate to the south. Findings from outside the other six gates suggest that there may have been extensive occupation in the vicinity of the walled town. Cemeteries also ringed the town, including a substantial example to the north-west. Several large burial mounds to the south-east of Canterbury may date to the early Roman period.

The end of Roman Canterbury

Although Bede (*Ecclesiastical History*, II.1) tells us of the reuse of Roman churches in Canterbury in the seventh century, we know little more about the religious beliefs of the townspeople. The location of these buildings is uncertain, and the town's later Roman and immediate post-Roman history is very poorly known. As elsewhere, the fourth century seems to have been a time of decline as buildings ceased to be maintained.

During road construction in 1962, a hoard of late Roman silver was found buried just to the south-west of the location of the London Gate on the western side of the town. This significant find, which is displayed in the museum, was deposited in the second decade of the fifth century or perhaps later. It included several coins, four silver ingots, and sixteen silver spoons, one bearing a Christian Chi-Rho symbol. The ingots, which were probably imperial donatives to a senior soldier, may suggest that state business continued at Canterbury around the time when Roman rule was ending in Britain.

Excavations have uncovered the remains of sunken floored dwellings within the Roman town. These buildings may have been the homes of German mercenary soldiers settled here to provide a garrison. There was occupation in and around the town during the fifth century, although what happened thereafter is unclear. A Christian mission to Britain led by St Augustine in 597 resulted in a bishopric being established at Canterbury. Perhaps this led to the reuse of at least one of the Christian churches in the Roman town, but this is speculation. The walls of the Church of St Mildred with St Mary de Castro, established during the eighth century, contain substantial quantities of Roman building material, including stone and tile (Figure 16, O).

Further reading

Sparey-Green (2021) discusses the Iron Age earthworks around Bigbury Camp. Weekes (in preparation) is a detailed account of Roman Canterbury. I am very grateful to Jake Weekes for providing me with a draft of this paper before publication. The Historic Towns Trust has created a handy historical map including substantial information about the Iron Age and Roman settlements (Historic Towns Trust 2021). For the classical temple, see Blagg (1984). The section on Roman Canterbury in Wacher (1995: 189–207) gives an account of the walls. The chapters on Prehistoric Kent, Roman Kent and Anglo-Saxon Kent by Champion (2007), Millett (2007) and Welch (2007) are helpful and informative. For the Late Roman hoard, see Johns and Potter (1985). For other articles on recent excavations, see the journal *Archaeologia Cantiana*. For relevant web links, see the website connected with this book.

6

Chichester and King Togidubnus

Introduction

Chichester is a rewarding city to visit, as much of the historic centre is well-preserved. There is plenty to explore besides the Roman remains, including the impressive medieval cathedral. This was the site of a significant Iron Age *oppidum*. An inscription from Chichester records the name of Togidubnus, a king friendly to the Romans, suggesting that the region in which the town developed played a significant role in the early phases of the Roman conquest. Chichester is also famous as the location of Fishbourne Palace, which may have been Togidubnus' lavish home. The town began to develop during the 60s CE and, after his death, became the *civitas* capital of a people known as the Regni.

Sites on display include the Togidubnus inscription, the remains of the public bathhouse, the earthworks of the amphitheatre, and an impressive circuit of walls. The modern street system also preserves part of the course of the main Roman roads. The Novium Museum features a display of Iron Age and Roman Chichester.

Figure 17 *Map of Roman Chichester (after Wacher 1995: Figure 117, and Dawkes and Hart 2017: Figure 3). Drawn by Christina Unwin.*

Main visible archaeological features with grading

	Star rating
Togidubnus inscription	***
Bathhouse	**
Town walls	***
Amphitheatre	*
Museum	**
Fishbourne Roman Palace	***

Chichester and King Togidubnus

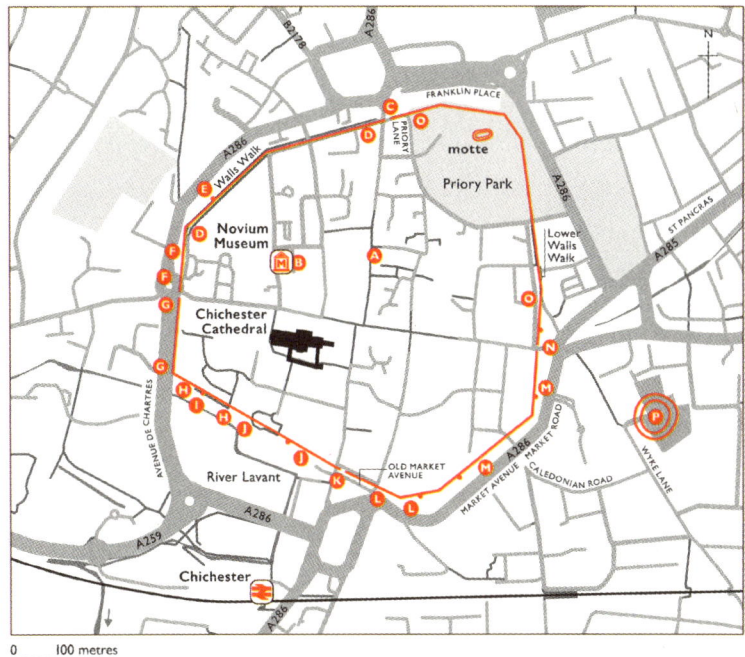

Figure 18 *Map of modern Chichester with locations mentioned in the text marked. Drawn by Christina Unwin using information from Google Maps.*

Getting there

The Roman remains are in the city centre, easily accessible from Chichester railway station. Fishbourne Roman Palace can also be reached by rail. The town has a bus station, and there are many small car parks, including several located just outside the city wall. Traffic within the older part of the city is heavy, and during my visit Chichester did not seem good for cycling.

Exploring ancient Chichester

The best way to explore the Roman sites and the museum is on foot. Fishbourne Place is located *c.* 2½ kilometres west of Chichester and can be reached from the town centre by train. It is also possible to drive to Fishbourne and park there. Although the remains of the palace are a major heritage attraction and can get very busy, especially with school parties, they are not to be missed. It is also possible to inspect the sites of some sections of the Iron Age dykes that surrounded the *oppidum*. Several distinct sections of dyke are marked on the Ordnance Survey map (*Landranger* 197). They can be reached by car and examined from the roadside (but are not discussed further below). It took me 4 hours to explore all the Roman attractions, and you should allow another 2 hours, in addition to journey time, to visit Fishbourne Palace. Chichester has many places to eat and stay overnight.

Historical summary

The earth dykes of the Iron Age *oppidum* define an extensive territory on an area of coastal plain within which the Roman town and palace later developed. The dykes are not very well-dated, and although excavations have uncovered several burial sites (see below), there is little indication of a nucleated pre-Roman settlement anywhere in this area. Fishbourne may have been a centre of occupation before the conquest, and was probably the location of a port. There is no clear indication that the site at which the town later developed had any particular significance at this time.

The inscription that records Togidubnus' name suggests that this *oppidum* was the king's capital during the early period of Roman rule. The palace, which originated as an elaborate villa *c.* 20 years after the conquest and swiftly developed into a luxurious Mediterranean-style courtyard house, is an outstanding feature of this urban settlement.

After Togidubnus, Chichester became the capital of a people known as the Regni, which may have meant 'the people of the kingdom'. The Roman name for Chichester, however, was *Noviomagus* or 'New Place'. This name suggests the town was founded on a new site within Togidubnus' *oppidum*.

The rediscovery of Iron Age and Roman Chichester

Antiquarian interest in the site, beginning in the seventeenth and eighteenth centuries, resulted in discoveries including the Togidubnus inscription. Excavation increased in scale during the 1960s and 1970s with the creation of the Chichester District Archaeological Unit, much of its work directed by Alec Down. A major spur to work in the city was the excavation (by Barry Cunliffe) of Fishbourne Palace in the 1960s. More recent excavations have uncovered additional information.

Iron Age *oppidum*

Although the Iron Age history of the Chichester region is poorly understood, the Chichester dykes define an extensive area of coastal plain across which settlement and burial sites were scattered. Small-scale excavations of the dykes support the idea that they date to the Late Iron Age. The Novium Museum includes a display exploring a high-status warrior burial from North Bersted, 4 kilometres south-east of Chichester. This is one of several such warrior burials found across southern Britain that date to the second half of the first century BCE. Buried with a selection of weapons including the unusual offering of a Roman helmet, this warrior may have served as a Roman cavalry soldier on the Continent before travelling to Britain.

Excavations of early phases underlying Fishbourne Palace found evidence of occupation in the Late Iron Age, including several buildings associated with amphorae and other pottery imported from the Continent. Although there has been some silting in this area,

Fishbourne is close to the sea, and it is likely that this was a significant harbour before and during the Roman conquest of 43 CE. An item of military equipment in an earlier layer of occupation raises the possibility that there were Roman soldiers here several decades before this date. Certainly, there was significant occupation here before the construction of the first phase of the palace.

Togidubnus

We know about this king because of comments written by the classical author Tacitus, who records that Togidubnus had stayed loyal to the Romans almost until the present time (the 90s CE) and that he was a friendly ruler in Britain. There is a dispute about whether this king's name started with a T or a C, and you may know him as Cogidubnus, but the spelling adopted here is probably more accurate. This ancient king is likely to have remained loyal to the Romans during the rebellion of Boudica in 60 CE when three Roman towns were sacked.

During building works in 1723, a substantial fragment of the Togidubnus inscription was uncovered at the junction of Lion Street with North Street (Figure 18, A). The discovery of this remarkable inscription fascinated the antiquarian community because it mentioned a British king who had become a Roman citizen, as indicated by the formula of his name, Tiberius Claudius Togidubnus. Roman citizens usually had three names (the *tria nomina*). The inscription also records a guild of smiths and describes Togidubnus as 'great king of Britain'. It is thought that he ruled over three peoples, including the Regni. This inscription, usually dated to the 60s or 70s CE, formed the dedication of a temple to Neptune and Minerva set up early in the town's history. It is not entirely clear that the great king ruled from Chichester, but this seems likely. The inscription is housed in a glass-panelled display case under the portico at the front of the Council House, close to its original findspot. On both my visits, the few people looking at the display appeared to have had little knowledge of its significance.

We know nothing more about Togidubnus, and he could have been given his kingdoms after the Romans had conquered southern Britain. At least one more monumental building was constructed within the proto-town in 57–8 CE, as indicated by a second dedicatory stone mentioning the emperor Nero. Some timber buildings of early Roman date found during excavations indicate that people were moving to this location. It has been supposed that there was a significant military phase during the early stages of the foundation of the town, although there is no definitive evidence for this. The excavations at Silchester suggest that Roman soldiers were settled in houses in the *oppidum*, and the same may have been the case at Chichester.

Fishbourne Palace

The early phases of the palace, which has seen extensive excavation, have been interpreted as related to the Roman military invasion of southern Britain in 43 CE, although other explanations are possible. What is clear is that the early timber buildings were replaced at an early date, possibly during the 60s, by a substantial masonry building known to archaeologists as the 'proto-Palace'. In *c.* 75, a monumental palace of courtyard design was constructed on a raised platform. It was formed of four large wings fronted by colonnades and ranged around a central garden. Substantial parts of the excavated foundations of this building are displayed, particularly the north wing with its many mosaic-floored rooms. Protected from the weather by a covered timber structure, this building also houses the onsite museum. Broadly comparable to several imperial palaces in Rome and Italy, Fishbourne Palace must have belonged to a wealthy individual. This may well have been the home of Togidubnus or, perhaps, one of his offspring.

The *civitas* capital

The main roads in the modern city preserve the courses of the Roman north–south and east–west roads (Figures 17 and 18). It is not entirely clear when the town's road grid was established, although the earliest streets in the north-eastern quadrant appear to date to the later first century. Little is known of the forum or when this building was constructed. The Togidubnus inscription indicates the location of a classical temple dedicated to Neptune and Minerva (Figure 18, A). These divinities in Britain are commonly associated in Roman mythology with water, as exemplified by the twinning of Minerva with the local spring spirit Sulis at Bath. This suggests that Chichester had a particular association with water deities, reflecting its location close to a significant port.

Several domestic buildings have been uncovered through excavation, and there appears to have been the usual urban progression from houses constructed in timber and earth to building in stone during the third century. Traces of substantial masonry houses were uncovered north of the bathhouse during excavations, but nothing is visible on the ground. Some indications of trade and industry have also been found.

The bathhouse

The remains of the public bathhouse, probably initially constructed in the 70s or 80s CE, have been excavated and are displayed *in situ* in the Novium Museum (B). The excavations revealed part of this bath building, and the remains, well-displayed in a basement in the museum, include an apsed room and two hypocausts. The bathhouse was less well maintained by the early fourth century and was disused by the middle of the century.

Walking the walls

These walls, which enclose an area of c. 40 hectares, are the most impressive remains of Roman Chichester. Excavation has indicated that the defences were constructed during the later third century, rather later than at many Roman towns in Britain. Unlike several other towns, the defences consisted of a stone wall from the start, with a bank of earth to the rear. There will also have been at least one deep ditch outside the wall. As a result of lack of excavation, little is known about the city gates. The east gate nevertheless survived until the eighteenth century, and an engraving depicts the main arch and a second passenger arch comparable to the surviving Newport Arch at Lincoln. Projecting towers (bastions) were added to the outer face of the wall during the fourth century, several of which survive.

The walls were rebuilt in the ninth century and again during the eleventh, reflecting Chichester's later significance. Turned into a promenaded walk for the urban population during the eighteenth century, the wall survives around much of its circuit. Although heavily restored in post-Roman times, the masonry wall retains its Roman character. The walls are particularly impressive to the north of town.

I walked from the site of the north gate (C), designed to give travellers access to the road to Silchester. Modern houses are built outside the city wall along its north-western circuit, all the way to the former site of the west gate, with the ends of their back gardens formed by the stone face. To view this section of the defences, you must walk along the top of the wall, following the lane called Walls Walk (D–D). The impressive scale of the defences is visible from here. At one point, a detached segment of masonry in a private garden marks the site of one of the bastions (E). You come down off the walltop just before reaching the Westgate Roundabout, and if you turn right at the roundabout, you can see the outside of a heavily restored section of the city wall in the Orchard Street Car Park (F–F).

The site of the west gate is partly buried under the Westgate Roundabout. From here, the Roman road ran towards Fishbourne Palace and the Roman settlement at Bitterne. From just to the south of the location of the former west gate, a substantial brick wall has replaced the stone wall (G–G), and you can walk along the top of the wall by going into the Bishop's Palace Garden. I walked down the outer line of the wall along the Avenue De Chartres. After just over 100 metres, a footpath to the left gives you access to the outer face of a well-preserved section of the southern wall. Turning left down the footpath with the River Lavant on your right, this section of stone curtain wall is on your left (H–H). This heavily restored section of the wall features an impressive bastion (I). Slightly further on, the footpath turns right into the fields of the Prebendal School, leaving the course of the city wall. The wall and another bastion are visible through the trees, however (J–J). You then walk past another car park just outside the walls, and another heavily restored section of the city wall can be seen.

Crossing South Street, you reach the former location of the south gate (K). This road gave access to the coastal plain south of the town. From this point, walk down Old Market Avenue, where the wall remains are lost, and you will recognize the heavily rebuilt city wall in Market Avenue Car Park (L–L). Continuing down Market Avenue, the wall has been demolished for some distance but reappears again in St John's Street Car Park. It is then visible at times through the houses and gardens further to the north (M–M). The brick structure built on top of one of the bastions and visible from the road is a modern garden feature. Continuing down Market Road brings you to the former location of the east gate, where you meet East Street (N). Walking another 10 metres, you reach the road to London, forking off to the right. Known by the medieval title of Stane Street, it ran north-east from this gate along the course of St Pancras Road.

Turn left along the pedestrian lane with St Pancras Church to your right and onto Lower Walls Walk. This path takes you along the top of the city wall and into the beautiful parkland in Priory Park, providing a fine view to the south-west across the city, including the substantial earthwork mound (motte) of Chichester's medieval castle (O-O). At the end of Priory Park, turn right into Priory Lane and return to the site of the north gate (C).

The amphitheatre

I visited the amphitheatre while walking the town walls by turning right down Caledonian Road then left up Whyke Lane. You can see slight traces of the remains in a public park just to the right of Whyke Lane (P). It is possible to identify the oval of the arena with its surrounding banks, partially encroached upon by housing. This amphitheatre was discovered in 1934 and excavated on a small scale. It was quite a large oval structure, broadly comparable in plan and scale to the amphitheatre in London. Probably constructed in the second half of the first century, it consisted of a gravel bank with a masonry arena wall. The material for the bank was derived from the earth excavated from the arena, and also from quarries close to the monument. It is likely that the masonry arena wall replaced an earlier timber arena wall, as at Silchester. The masonry arena wall was decorated internally with painted plaster. It is unclear whether this was once a much more substantial earthwork – comparable to the amphitheatres at Dorchester, Silchester and Cirencester.

The outskirts of the town

There has not been much study of extramural settlement areas if these existed. Although there has been comparatively little excavation there, we know that the town's cemeteries lay outside the walls (Figure 17).

Reinventing Togidubnus in Georgian Chichester

The Roman origins of Chichester fascinated the urban elite, and the Togidubnus inscription was one of the most significant finds. After the inscription was unearthed in 1723, it was transported to Goodwood House, the country residence of the second Duke of Richmond. Within eight years of the inscription's discovery, the urban elite built a new Council House close to the find spot (Figure 18, A). At the top of the front facade of this building is an inscription dating the building to 1731 that includes the acronym SPQC, standing for the 'The Senate and People of Chichester' (Figure 19). The iconic SPQR, meaning 'The Senate and People of Rome', was adopted by the Georgian elite of Chichester.

The Togidubnus inscription has since been returned to the city and is displayed under the portico at the front of the Council House. Pride in Chichester's Roman origin also led, during the eighteenth century, to the conversion of the ruins of the city walls into a promenade for the population.

Further reading

Garland (2020) provides an up-to-date summary of the archaeology of Iron Age Chichester. The history of research and recent

Figure 19 *Photograph of the eighteenth-century inscription that commemorates the construction of the Chichester Townhouse.* © *Richard Hingley.*

archaeological work is summarized in Walton and Kenny (2022). For the discovery, significance and later history of the Togidubnus inscription (RIB 91), see Bogaers (1979). For the bathhouse at the Novium Museum, see Dawkes and Hart (2017). Recent excavations are discussed in Fulford and Holbrook (2015). For the Chichester dykes and the town walls, see Magilton (2003). For the excavation of the amphitheatre, see White (1934). For relevant web links, see the website connected with this book.

7
Cirencester: Capital of the Dobunni

Introduction

The buildings of this attractive town, a lovely place to visit, overlie the remains of one of the *civitas* capitals. Cirencester was the capital of a people known as the Dobunni. The town's origins date back to the Late Iron Age when there was an *oppidum* at Bagendon, a few kilometres north of where the Roman town was to develop. Although there is no trace of Iron Age occupation on the site that was to become the Roman town, Tar Barrow (just to the north-east of Cirencester) may have been a high-status burial site.

During the mid-first century CE, people gradually shifted from Bagendon to the low-lying riverside location where the town then developed. Excavations have uncovered part of what may have been a Roman fort. Cirencester developed further in the early second century and became one of the largest towns of Roman Britain. You can follow the course of the defences around much of its circuit, and the amphitheatre earthworks are substantial and well-preserved. The collection in the Corinium Museum has been recently redisplayed, providing an excellent introduction to Cirencester's ancient past.

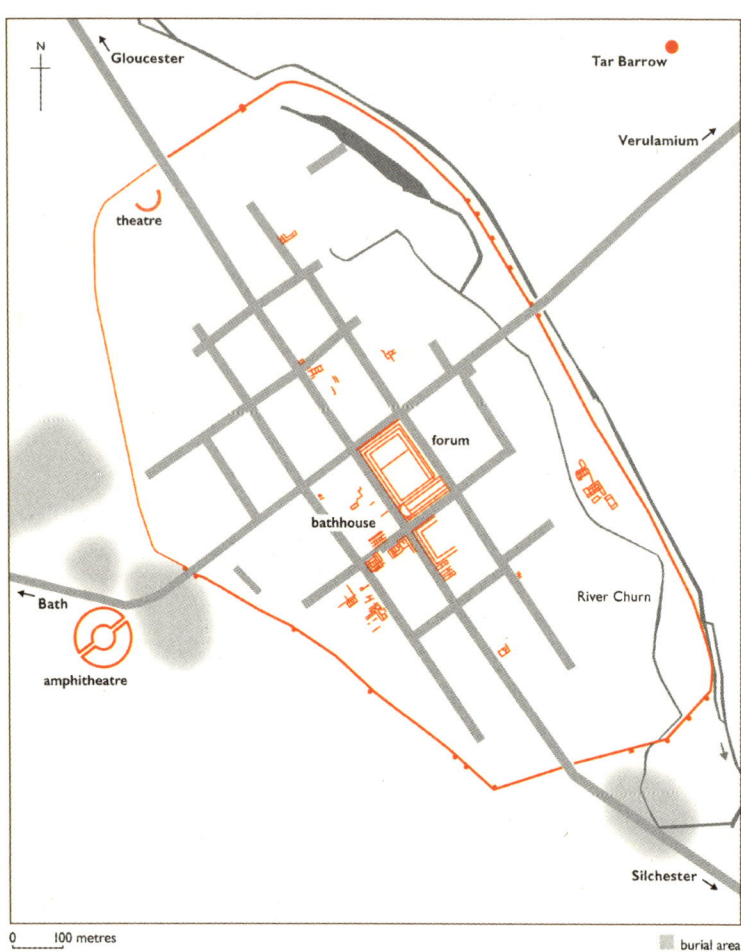

Figure 20 *Map of Roman Cirencester (after Holbrook 2008a: Figure 18). Drawn by Christina Unwin.*

Main visible archaeological features with grading

	Star rating
Town walls	**
Amphitheatre	***
Museum	***

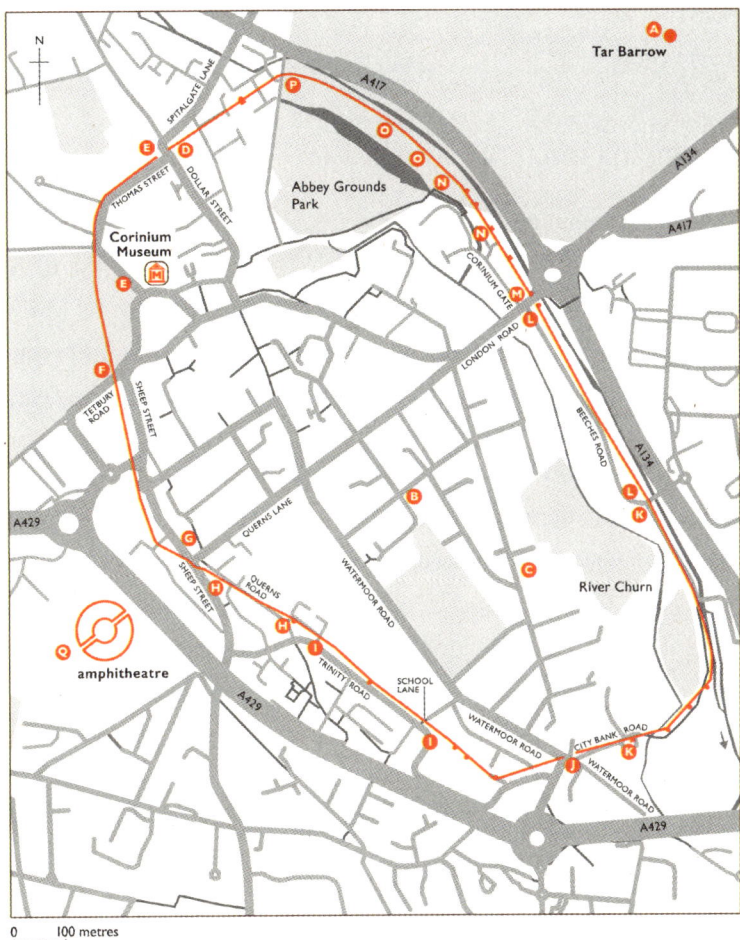

Figure 21 *Map of modern Cirencester with locations mentioned in the text marked. Drawn by Christina Unwin using information from Google Maps.*

Getting there

The nearest railway station is at Kemble, *c.* 11 kilometres from Cirencester. A regular bus carries passengers to Cirencester from London, and there are several substantial car parks within the town centre. It is also possible to cycle into and around the town, and the surrounding countryside is popular with cyclists. A range of high-quality cafes and eating places is available, and accommodation is easy to find. The Ordnance Survey *Explorer* Map 169 will help you locate and explore the Iron Age *oppidum* at Bagendon.

Exploring ancient Cirencester

Visiting the amphitheatre and the Corinium Museum is recommended if you only have a few hours to spare. The museum is in the town centre, and there is a small car park close to the amphitheatre, which lies to the west of the modern (and Roman) town. The museum contains excellent and up-to-date displays of information derived from the excavations. You can walk to the amphitheatre from the town centre if you wish via a bridge across the bypass. You can also walk the circuit of the walls. It took me 6 hours to explore the defences and the amphitheatre, and visit the museum.

If more time is available, a visit to the Iron Age *oppidum* at Bagendon is recommended. Another attractive possibility is to travel to Chedworth Villa, one of Britain's most impressive Roman country houses. Located fourteen kilometres north of Cirencester, this is in the care of the National Trust.

Historical summary

The *oppidum* at Bagendon is 5 kilometres north of the Roman town. This consists of a series of discontinuous dyke systems and areas of occupation on sloping ground close to a brook. Excavations have indicated occupation shortly before and during the Roman conquest of this area of southern Britain. Just east of Cirencester is a burial mound that may have formed a high-status burial site for a member of a dominant Late Iron Age family.

The site of a possible Roman fort was found during excavations beneath the centre of Cirencester and dated to the mid-50s or 60s CE. During this period, people started to move from the surrounding area to the low-lying riverside site where the town was to develop. Like many of the other *civitas* capitals in southern Britain, the street system and public buildings were constructed during the early to mid-second century, and a set of ramparts, later faced with a stone wall, was built during the latter part of the century. The mosaics and finds from the excavations indicate the wealth of some of the townspeople.

The rediscovery of ancient Cirencester

Knowledge of Cirencester's Roman past dates back to the later sixteenth century when the remains of the town wall were identified and an inscription recorded. Mosaics and other finds continued to be discovered during the seventeenth to nineteenth centuries. A growing appreciation of the scale of the Roman site led to the founding of an urban archaeological unit during the 1960s. Large-scale excavation work since the 1970s has created a detailed knowledge of the urban settlement, which has been well-served by recent publications. The Iron Age *oppidum* at Bagendon was recognized and first excavated during the 1960s. It has also been subject to recent excavations and surveys.

Iron Age Cirencester

The *oppidum* is marked by a series of earthwork dykes close to the village of Bagendon, which can be explored on foot. The dykes are broadly comparable to those at Verulamium and Colchester. Excavations have indicated that the main area of occupation within the dykes developed just a few decades before the Roman conquest. Iron Age coins were produced here, and imported pottery from the Continent has been found. The commonly used name of the Roman town today is *Corinium*, which may also have been the name of the *oppidum*. The meaning of this name is uncertain, but it could refer to 'the place of Carinos'.

The extent of the Late Iron Age activity in the landscape around Cirencester was much more extensive. To the north-east of the river crossing at which the Roman town was later to develop, and some distance south-east of Bagendon, are the earthwork remains of Tar Barrow (Figure 21, A). Interpreted as a high-status Late Iron Age burial site comparable to that at Folly Lane (Verulamium), this earthwork is on private land and cannot be visited. A geophysical survey indicates that it was the focus of an extensive area of burial activity, probably around the time of the conquest.

This *oppidum* probably played a significant role during the conquest of Britain since we hear that the Roman invasion force in the initial campaigns (in 43 CE) freed a people known as the 'Bodunni' from the overlordship of the Catuvellauni. 'Bodunni' may be a misspelling of Dobunni, and if our source is correct, a Roman military force was used to free this people from the control of the domination of the Catuvellauni. During the early period of conquest, the Iron Age ruling family at Bagendon may well have submitted to Rome and been adopted as a 'friendly' kingdom (as at Chichester, Silchester and Verulamium).

A Roman fort?

Excavations uncovered what may be part of the defences and several of the internal buildings of a Roman fort, although the identification of these remains is not certain. The dating of the finds from the site suggests occupation during the reign of Nero, probably *c.* 55–65 CE, sometime after the first arrival of Roman forces in the area. Two military tombstones from Cirencester, on display at the Corinium Museum, commemorate auxiliary cavalrymen. If this was a fort, the garrison might have played a role in the campaigns underway in Wales while providing security for the local ruling elite.

The *civitas* capital

During the later first century, the new town began to develop as a community settled here. Excavation indicates that the early settlement started to develop with the construction of roads and timber buildings. This low-lying riverine site required substantial work to channel the River Churn and raise the ground level to allow buildings to be constructed.

The grid of metalled roads and the masonry public buildings date to the early second century (Figure 20). As was the case at several other towns, the formal laying out of the urban centre may have marked the official foundation of the *civitas* capital as a central place for the Dobunni. As some early excavations showed, however, the forum was only constructed during the mid-second century. A gravelled marketplace or a timber forum may have preceded the grand masonry building. Although the forum is commemorated in the name of the Forum Car Park, the car park itself is located north of where the Roman building lies buried under the modern town. Fragments of impressive Corinthian capitals, some displayed in the Corinium Museum, probably formed part of the aisles of the basilica. A section of the apsidal western end of the basilica is marked out on the road surface at the north end of Admirals Walk with an information board offering a description (Figure 21, B). Cirencester may also have had a theatre, which would have accompanied a significant temple complex (Figure 20). The probable site of the public bathhouse has also been identified in the insula south-west of the forum.

The museum has an excellent display of objects and a well-informed interpretation of people, houses and urban infrastructure. This includes several stone sculptures of gods, although the remains of temple buildings have yet to be discovered. One significant discovery made during the nineteenth century is an inscription recording the restoration of a Jupiter Column (displayed in the museum). It was found close to the junction of Chester Street and Victoria Road, possibly marking the monument's original location (Figure 21, C). The inscription documents the restoration of the column by Lucius Septimius, the governor of *Britannia Prima*. This senior Roman administrator was probably based here during the early fourth century. There were many Jupiter Columns set up in the Rhineland, and fragments of a few others have been found in Britain. These columns, which could be up to 10 metres tall, were topped with a statue of Jupiter to celebrate his status as king of the gods.

Walking the walls

The defences of Roman Cirencester can be traced around most of their circuit. The earth rampart is prominent around part of its southern and eastern sections. North-east of the circuit, an excavated section of the foundations of the stone-facing wall is displayed in Abbey Grounds Park. Apart from that, most of the course of the ramparts is marked by modern streets. These defences are significant because, like those at Silchester and Caerwent, there was little rebuilding in medieval times.

The initial construction of the earthwork of the defences may date to the mid-second century, and the stone-facing wall to a century later than this. These defences surround an area of 96 hectares, making this the second most extensive walled town in Britain after London. A ditch will have lain in front of the earth rampart. The defences were punctuated by at least four stone gateways. In the past excavations uncovered the east (Verulamium) and west (Bath) gates, although no traces are visible today. These gates may have been built before the masonry wall was erected. The masonry wall was later widened and may have reached a height of *c.* 6 metres. Evidence of internal towers has been found, and several external bastions were added during the fourth century.

I began my walk at the location of the former north (Gloucester) gate (Figure 21, D). All four gates are named after the Roman towns reached by travelling from Cirencester along each road. The north gate was located close to the junction of Dollar Street and Thomas Street. Thomas Street then follows the line the defences once took (E–E). This street, which runs behind the course of the former rampart, features some of Cirencester's most impressive historical buildings. The course of these defences is then lost in the grounds of Bathurst Estate and Cirencester Park. Walking to the right down Park Street and then along Park Lane leads back to the original course of the defences located just west of the junction of Sheep Street with Tetbury Road (F), where there may have been a Roman gate.

The defences then ran on a line a little way to the west (right) of Sheep Street, now lost under the site of the former railway station and the building that houses Waitrose supermarket. The former site of the west (Bath) gate was where Querns Lane meets Sheep Street (G), although there is nothing to mark its location. Fragments of a statue of Mercury, found during the excavation of the residual remains of this gate, suggest that a figure of this god may once have adorned this entrance. Mercury was a god associated with commerce, travel and boundaries. Excavations indicate that this gateway had two carriageways and semicircular bastions projecting outwards.

To follow the line of the rampart from the west gate, turn left into Querns Lane for a short distance and immediately right across the traffic barrier into Querns Road (H–H). At the end of Querns Road, turn left into Trinity Road, which follows the outside line of the former defences (I–I). At the end of Trinity Road, a modern housing estate has been constructed over the line of the defences. To get back onto the course of the defences, follow School Lane (to the left), and then Six Gables. Turning right down Watermoor Road then takes you to a left turn into City Bank Road (J). A plaque at this location records the former location of the south (Silchester) gate.

Walking up City Bank Road leads to a footpath following the earthwork of the City Bank, the surviving remains of the Roman defences (K–K). Around the east of the town a lengthy section of the rampart survives, although very overgrown with trees and vegetation. This earthwork runs as far north as Beeches Road, beyond which most traces are lost. After crossing the line of the rampart, Beeches Road initially follows the course of the rampart's inner face and continues along the rampart's original course as far north as London Road (L–L). The point where Beeches Road meets London Road is the location of the east (Verulamium) gate (M). Excavations uncovered the poorly preserved foundations of this monumental gateway, and a plaque marks the location.

Crossing over the busy London Road, the line of the rampart lay just to the east (right) of the modern road named Corinium Gate, which runs into a housing development. One of two right turns off this road takes you into Abbey Grounds Park. In this park, you can appreciate the scale of the town defences because of the survival of the earthwork and the cutting of vegetation (N–N). This is the only place in Cirencester where traces of stone facing wall, uncovered by excavation, are displayed. This surviving section of the masonry wall includes an internal tower and the fragmentary remains of two of the late Roman bastions.

Further to the north in Abbey Grounds Park, additional sections of the banked rampart survive although covered with trees (O–O). Further to the north-west in the park the earthwork has been flattened, and its course is marked on the inner (left) side by the long duck pond. Walking northwards, with the pond to your left, you will reach the park's north end. The medieval gatehouse to St Mary's Abbey lies close to the Roman wall's course (P). The defences then turned to the south-west, and the line is lost in modern development. Walking down Spitalgate Lane takes you to Dollar Street, then turning left for a short distance, you arrive back at the site of the north gate (D).

The amphitheatre

This is the only significant public building visible in Cirencester, located 160 metres south-west of the closest section of the town defences (Q). Access to the amphitheatre would have been through the west (Bath) gate. The construction of the dual carriageway, Bristol Road, has divided the amphitheatre from the historic town.

The amphitheatre is displayed to the public by English Heritage, and there are several helpful information boards on site. It lies in an area known as the Querns which shows signs of extensive stone quarrying, some of Roman date. The surviving earthworks form a prominent grass-covered mound with entrances from the north-east and south-west. The banks rise to a maximum height of over 8 metres above the arena floor and enclose an elliptical area of *c.* 49 by 41 metres. As at Silchester, the arena was defined by a stone wall. Limited excavations in the 1960s indicated construction during the early second century when the earth excavated from the arena was used to create the seating bank. The bank held rows of seats formed by pressing flat stones into the underlying soil. The structure may have seated a maximum of *c.* 8,000 people. As the town's population may not have filled the seating, this would also allow space for visitors. The amphitheatre was rebuilt during the early to mid-second century, and later alterations suggest that it continued in use until the early fifth century.

Houses and mosaics

The museum displays several impressive mosaics from wealthy townhouses. Over ninety mosaics have been found at Cirencester, including some of the best-known examples from Britain. The Seasons Mosaic, for example, shows the four seasons of the year. Dating probably to the second century, this mosaic formed the floor of a wealthy townhouse uncovered below Dyer Street. Other mosaics from the town illustrate the rich lives of its late Roman elite (Figure 22).

The museum display also explains that not all the townspeople were wealthy and privileged. The partial reconstruction of a timber strip house is used to emphasize that such buildings were common in Roman towns. The presence of enslaved people and industrial workers is also addressed. This display emphasizes that many of the town's residents were relatively poor and worked for a living. Many museums document life in the Roman towns by displaying the lives of the elite, but the Corinium Museum provides a more balanced perspective. Despite this, visitors are likely to be impressed by the distinctive mosaics from the town and its surrounding region, which suggest that a school of mosaicists was based here. The sculptures, many of which are displayed in the museum, indicate a community of sculptors at Cirencester.

Figure 22 *Photograph of a detail from the Roman hunting dog mosaic found in a Roman townhouse in Cirencester. © https://www.gettyimages. co.uk/detail/news-photo/detail-from-the-hunting-dogs-mosaic-which-was-discovered-in-news-photo/117042040?adppopup=true.*

The urban hinterland

Unlike at many other urban centres, there is little evidence of extensive areas of extramural settlement outside the gates. The absence of extramural settlement may help explain why the walled area was so large. A few scattered farms and villas have been found some distance from the town, including a villa at The Barton (in Cirencester Park) and an aisled building just outside the south-east corner of the Roman town.

Recent excavations have explored the cemetery that lay outside the western gate, uncovering inhumation and cremation burials and the tombstone of a 27-year-old woman named Bodicacia. The seven tombstones displayed at the Corinium Museum attest the names of some of the men, women and children who lived here.

Later Roman Cirencester

Since the inscription on the Jupiter Column (above) describes its dedicator as the governor of *Britannia Prima*, it is possible that Cirencester may have become the capital of this province at the end of the third century (see introductory chapter). If so, the town would also have served as the base for a bishop mirroring the other three provincial capitals at London, Lincoln and York. Each of these towns sent bishops to the Council of Arles in 314, an important meeting of Christian clergy from the western areas of Rome's empire. Displayed in the museum is a palindrome (arrangement of 25 letters formed of 5 letters per line and row), found scratched on the wall of a Roman house in Victoria Road in 1868. This palindrome has long been supposed to contain a hidden reference to the worship of Christianity in Cirencester, although this is uncertain.

The town prospered during the late third and fourth centuries, and the defences were maintained into the late fourth century. Cirencester may have been abandoned during the early fifth century.

Further reading

For the status of the *oppidum* as a friendly kingdom of Rome, see Hingley (2022). For detailed information on the Late Iron Age in the Cirencester region, see Moore (2020). For Roman Cirencester, see Holbrook (2008a) and Holbrook (2008b). Detailed reports from decades of excavation are freely available online and offer more information about all significant discoveries in the town. For relevant web links, see the website connected with this book.

8

Colchester: Fortress of Camulos

Introduction

Colchester's ancient past has helped to build the identity of the urban community. The monumental town wall, much of which survives, has deeply influenced the development and layout of the medieval and modern town. Over the past hundred years, extensive excavations have produced information that has been used to lend a distinctively ancient flavour to Colchester. This includes using Iron Age and Roman names for streets, buildings and hotels (see Figure 2), and the displaying of Roman buildings and finds. Visitors can spot the use of ancient individuals associated with the town in street names such as Cunobelin Way and Boadicea Way.

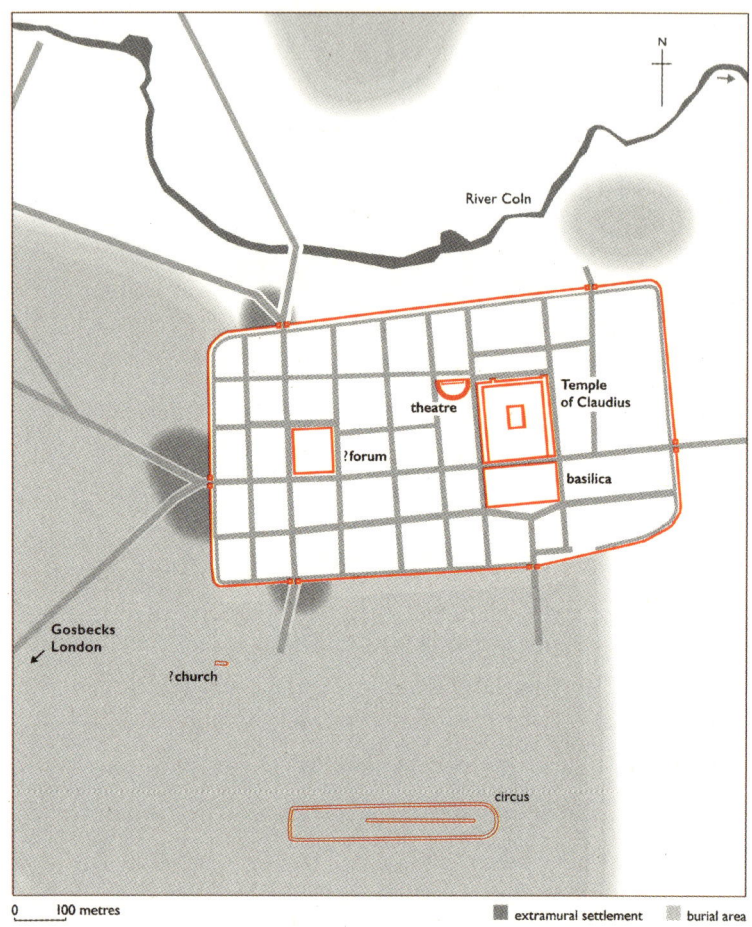

Figure 23 *Map of Roman Colchester (after Crummy 2008: Figure 2, and Gascoyne and Radford 2013: Figures 6.1, 7.1 and 7.9). Drawn by Christina Unwin.*

Colchester: Fortress of Camulos 119

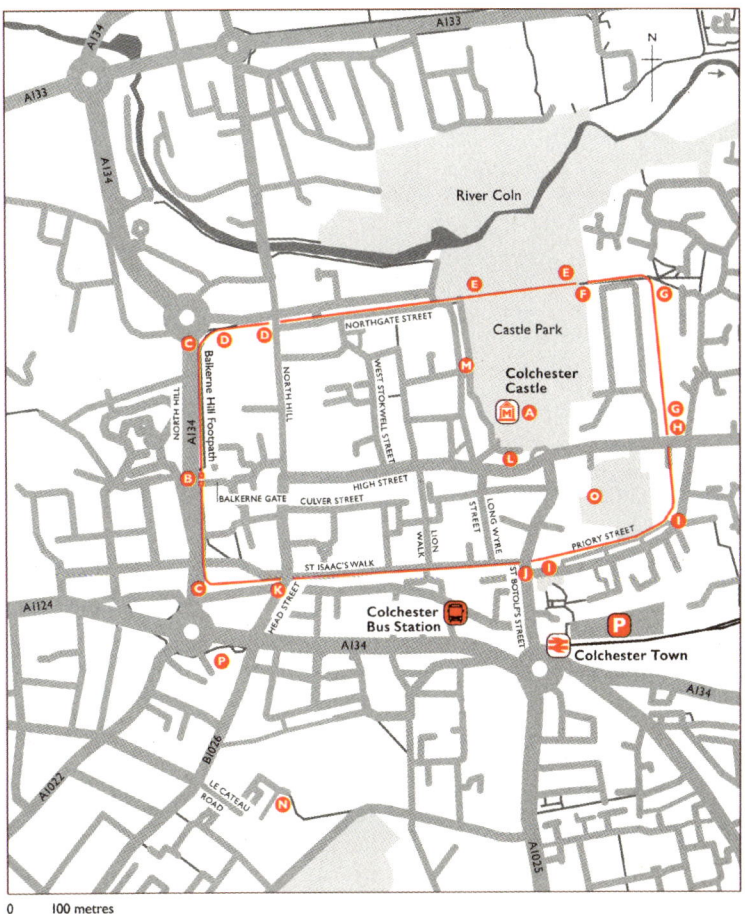

Figure 24 *Map of modern Colchester with locations mentioned in the text marked. Drawn by Christina Unwin using information from Google Maps.*

Main visible archaeological features with grading

	Star rating
Gosbecks Park	*
Temple of Claudius	***
Circus	**
Theatre	*
Church?	*
Town walls	***
Mosaic	*
Museum	***

Getting there

Colchester is well served by public transport and has two train stations. Colchester North is about a 20-minute walk from the town centre, and Colchester Town, which is on a branch line, is closer to the centre and the Roman remains. A wide range of places to eat, shop and stay overnight are available in the town.

Exploring ancient Colchester

It took me 2½ days to visit all the major archaeological sites, museums and heritage centres. The two maps provide information on the location of significant Roman sites, but it has not been possible to include the Iron Age sites west of Colchester on them. The town includes several important Roman monuments, an excellent museum set within the remains of the medieval castle, and a visitor centre for the circus. Most of the archaeological sites in and around Colchester are provided with up-to-date information panels, and there are helpful sources of information online. Highlights include the museum in the castle. This houses an extensive collection of Iron Age and Roman finds from Colchester and is built within the remains of the temple of Claudius. The Balkerne Gate is the most impressive of the surviving Roman buildings. These sites can be visited in 2–3 hours, although walking the circuit of the well-preserved town walls adds at least another hour to the tour.

There is much more to visit and see, including the interpretation centre for the Roman circus. The internationally important Iron Age and Roman site of Gosbecks is located south-west of the town centre. Sections of the Iron Age Colchester dykes can also be viewed, along with the surviving mound of the Lexden Tumulus. If you intend to visit Gosbecks Archaeological Park and the Colchester dykes, you are likely to require a bicycle, a car or to use public transport to avoid lengthy walks. The Ordnance Survey maps for exploring the archaeological sites outside the city centre are OS *Landranger* 168 and OS *Explorer* 184.

Historical summary

It is simplest to understand ancient Colchester by dividing the site into two phases: the Iron Age and the Roman period.

The main Iron Age focus was at the *oppidum* in and around Gosbecks, 3 kilometres to the south-west of where the colony later developed. Gosbecks was a significant meeting place during the final decades of the Iron Age. We know the name of a king called Cunobelin, who ruled from this royal centre during the early first century CE. The *oppidum* constituted an area of land defined to the west by the extensive Colchester dykes, including several dispersed clusters of settlements and high-status burials. The ditched enclosures at Gosbecks may have been the farm of Cunobelin, whose death *c.* 43 CE provoked the Romans to invade Britain. After the conquest Gosbecks developed into a cult centre, possibly associated with the cult of Cunobelin.

After the surrender of several British kings to Claudius at this *oppidum* in 43 CE, a legionary fortress for 5,000 soldiers was constructed within the dykes, a statement of Roman military victory. Six years later, the legion moved west to Gloucester, and the fortress was refounded as a colony. Many of the military buildings were repurposed as houses for veteran legionary settlers. The construction of the monumental temple of Claudius, the centre for emperor worship in Britain, was probably ordered by the deceased emperor's stepson, Nero, in the mid-50s CE.

Colchester was the first target of Boudica's uprising in 60 CE. The town was sacked and burned. After its refoundation, Colchester functioned as the primary urban centre of the province, with a grand rectangular masonry portico (covered walkway) constructed around the temple of Claudius. A circuit of stone walls surrounded the colony. Later, a monumental circus for games connected with the worship of Claudius was built to the south of the colony. Colchester was initially the provincial capital of Britain, although this role may have passed to London during the later first or second century.

Colchester included all the buildings expected in a Roman town, and the Castle Museum provides information about this urban infrastructure and the town's inhabitants. Occupation continued until the end of Roman rule, and a building displayed to the public outside the walls, set within one of the extensive burial grounds surrounding the colony, may have been a church.

The rediscovery of Iron Age and Roman Colchester

Although the Roman origin of Colchester was recognized during the sixteenth century, it took some time for antiquaries to realize that this was the site of *Camulodunum* referred to by ancient authors. Roman finds were recorded during the eighteenth- and nineteenth-century development of the town, and archaeological excavations commenced during the early twentieth century. In the 1920s Mortimer Wheeler recognized that the foundations of the medieval castle preserved the vaulted remains of the podium of the temple of Claudius.

In the 1970s, the creation of the Colchester Archaeological Trust under the inspirational direction of Philip Crummy focused new research directly on Late Iron Age and Roman Colchester. Important discoveries included the location of the circus and the recognition of the significance of the Iron Age structures around Gosbecks.

The *oppidum* of Cunobelin

Several lines of dykes (banks and ditches) defined the western limits of this *oppidum*. The extensive farmlands within the Colchester dykes were interspersed with settlements and high-status burials. *Camulodunum* was the royal centre of Britain's most powerful Iron Age ruler, Cunobelin (Shakespeare's Cymbeline). *Camulodunum* means 'fortress of [the war god] Camulos', a name which must have related to the dykes that defined the *oppidum*. The identity of the Late Iron Age people ruled over by Cunobelin is uncertain, although during the Roman period Colchester was in the territory of a people known as the Trinovantes. A visit to the Castle Museum provides insight into the extent and importance of the *oppidum*, and a range of artefacts is displayed.

The Colchester dykes

Pre-Roman Colchester was defended on the west by a series of earth banks and ditches, protecting lands defined on the east by the River Colne and its tributary, the Roman River. The most substantial of these discontinuous earthworks were originally *c.* 4 metres high and had ditches of a broadly comparable depth. Some sections are different in form and were probably not quite so substantial. The scale of these barriers emphasized the significance of the *oppidum*, constraining the movement of people and animals across the landscape, and may also have been designed to repel large-scale attacks, perhaps by warriors in chariots. The labour required to construct these extensive dykes shows the number of people who could be commanded to work at this *oppidum* by its rulers.

Many sections of the dykes have been flattened by agricultural operations and built over, although three can be visited and explored:

- The Triple Dyke (centred on TL 965 247) has multiple banks and ditches and may have been constructed on several occasions during the Late Iron Age and early Roman period.
- The Blue Bottle Grove Dyke (centred on TL 973 248) is an excavated section within a fenced enclosure close to a housing estate.
- Gryme's Dyke (between TL 961 246 and TL 964 232) was a further outlying section of the dykes, formed from a bank and ditch, and you can follow this earthwork for several hundred metres on foot.

Burials of the elite and settlements

There is no indication that Iron Age Colchester included a nucleated settlement. Several areas of high-status burials and settlements lay within the extensive Iron Age dykes. Much of this land was for farming. The *oppidum* was an important meeting place for the clients of the elite family that had its royal centre here. People probably gathered here at annual festivals to pay their respects to their rulers.

Several areas of high-status burial are known in and around the *oppidum*. Excavations at Stanway, located just west of Gosbecks and beyond the outermost of the Iron Age dykes, uncovered ditched enclosures containing several high-status burials. Displays in the museum feature these burials. One remarkable example has been interpreted as the remains of a doctor, since in addition to amphorae and feasting gear, it contained a gaming board and a set of surgical instruments. The community resident in this area of Colchester *c.* 50 CE had access to medical services, and the objects buried with this individual show he was of very high status.

The most important of all the burials around Colchester was interred within a tumulus at Lexden, close to one section of the dykes (TL 9753 2472). Lexden Tumulus, which survives as a mound on the edge of a housing estate in the western suburbs of Colchester, can be seen from the estate road. Excavation of this mound in 1924 indicated that it contained the burial of a Late Iron Age ruler. Since the offerings deposited in the grave included items dating to *c.* 16 BCE, the deceased individual cannot have been Cunobelin as this date is too early for the great king's death. They included lavish grave goods, such as a silver medallion of Augustus, and a considerable number of wine amphorae. Lexden Tumulus must have been the burial monument for one of the kings or queens who controlled *Camulodunum* over half a century before the Roman conquest.

The *oppidum* enclosed several areas of Iron Age settlement. The excavation at Sheepen (around TL 987 255) uncovered substantial occupation and industrial activity. There is nothing is to be seen at this site today. The most important site was at Gosbecks (centred at TL 965 227), a location constituting a focal point for several of the dykes. Aerial photography and geophysical surveys have located several ditched enclosures, including an impressively sizeable example that may have been the farmstead of Cunobelin. Perhaps Gosbecks was where Cunobelin's clients visited to help the great king celebrate festivals when he ruled from *Camulodunum*. These Iron Age enclosures are partly within Gosbecks Archaeological Park. A pleasant walk from the car park is supplemented with information boards offering interpretation of the buried remains.

Roman Gosbecks

This Iron Age site continued to develop during the first century of Roman rule. A few hundred metres north-west of the Iron Age enclosures noted above, aerial photography has located a Roman fort. It may have been the base of a unit of auxiliary soldiers sent to superintend this important Iron Age meeting place during the conquest in 43 CE, or it may date to the period of reprisals during the violent suppression of Boudica's uprising seventeen years later.

Small-scale excavations of the enclosure interpreted as Cunobelin's farmstead indicate that it developed into a sacred site during the decades after the conquest, with a small Romano-Celtic temple built in the south-east corner and a portico constructed around the four sides of the ditched enclosure. The Roman theatre built to one side of the temple enclosure is the largest known in Britain. It was of the standard D-shaped form, with a stage facing banks of seating. This timber-and-earth theatre was rebuilt with a stone retaining wall during the second century. Its substantial size, with enough seating for *c.* 5,000 people, may indicate the scale of the meetings held to celebrate Cunobelin's cult during the first two centuries of Roman rule.

The site of the temple and the theatre are displayed in Gosbecks Archaeological Park, marked out on the ground with white painted lines in the grass. Some slight earthworks are all that remain of the theatre, which was once a very substantial structure.

Roman fortress

The death of Cunobelin set off a chain of events that led Rome to invade Britain, and as the former capital of the great king, Colchester played a prominent role in the initial phase of the conquest. As Cunobelin's sons had fallen foul of Rome, Colchester was the main target of the invasion. The emperor Claudius instructed his military commander to sail across the ocean and conquer Britain. After several weeks of campaigning, Claudius travelled from Rome, joining his commander to superintend the surrender at Colchester of several kings, or Late Iron Age leaders, of the various British people. We do not know where Claudius received these kings, but Gosbecks may have been the place. This grand event will have involved all the high-ranking Roman officers, several of the legions involved in the conquest, and probably as many as ten British kings from across southern Britain. The role played by Claudius in securing control over much of south-eastern Britain explains the significance of Colchester during the first century of Roman rule.

A legion overwintered in tents in a temporary camp and quickly constructed a fortress as the base for the Twentieth Legion. This fortress, of timber and earth, was located to dominate the *oppidum*. Although no trace of the fortress is evident on the ground, the excavations have established its layout. The course of the fortress's western and southern defences was reused when the colony received its wall several decades later. Some artefacts displayed in the Castle Museum include the tombstones of a soldier of the Twentieth Legion, Marcus Favonius Facilis, and that of a centurion of the First Cavalry Regiment of Thracians called Longinus Sdapeze. These men served in the garrison during the first six years of the conquest.

Establishing the colony

In 49 CE the Twentieth Legion moved west, and a colony (a settlement of Roman citizens) was established at Colchester to replace the fortress. The author Tacitus remarked that this colony provided a home for retiring legionary soldiers while acting as a bastion against revolt. It had no defensive wall, which proved to be a disastrous mistake.

Tacitus suggests that the leading Iron Age families at Colchester were dispossessed of their land by the Roman settlers. High-status individuals nevertheless continued to be buried at Stanway (close to

Gosbecks) until 60 CE. These burials suggest that some families were allowed to retain their wealth. They may have been included as administrators in the colony. It is important to be aware of the biases in the writings of classical authors such as Tacitus.

Excavation has shown that the colony was established by reusing the remaining structures of the fortress, including the streets, many of its timber buildings, and the barrack blocks of the soldiers. The fortress defences were flattened. Since they could easily have adapted them to serve the new town, this indicates that the colonists felt confident about their security. The initial colony occupied the south-western area that was later enclosed within the town walls (Figure 23).

The temple of Claudius

The significant decision was taken to build a grand temple in memory of the deceased emperor Claudius, probably on the direct instructions of Nero when he succeeded his stepfather (in 54 CE). This temple was constructed just beyond the eastern boundary of the colony (Figure 24, A). This sizeable classical building was planned as the location at which the provincial council, the assembly of all the leaders of the *civitates* (peoples) of Britain, was to meet, probably on the anniversary of Claudius' birthday (1st August) each year. The construction work will have been in its early stages when the violent uprising led by Boudica broke out during the Spring/Summer of 60. The podium of the temple survives in the foundations of Colchester Castle, which now houses the museum. The temple, which was a massive structure, is explained and interpreted in the museum and discussed further below.

The Balkerne Gate

A second monumental masonry structure that dates to the colony's earliest years is the Balkerne Gate, located on the western boundary of Roman Colchester (B; Figure 25). The origin of the name is unknown.

Figure 25 *Photograph of the Balkerne Gate at Colchester from inside the town defences.* © *Richard Hingley.*

It is a massive and monumental triumphal gate with two portals, much of which survives. Constructed from masonry, with courses of stones and bricks, the Balkerne Gate was incorporated into the circuit of the colony's wall a few decades later. It is one of the best-preserved Roman structures visible in Britain. Anyone approaching the town from Gosbecks would have passed under this monumental statement of victory. This triumphal gate and the temple of Claudius flanked the colony to its west and east.

Boudica and the destruction of Colchester

As the most important town in the province of *Britannia*, Colchester was the first target for the Britons who rose under Boudica in 60 CE. Boudica was the wife of the deceased king of the Iceni. She led her people and the Trinovantes in a campaign to drive the Romans out of Britain. The destruction of *Camulodunum* is described in detail by Tacitus. The final scene in this drama was the burning of the temple of

Claudius and the killing of all who had taken shelter inside. Excavations have also demonstrated that the colony was destroyed by burning. One fascinating recent find from these excavations is the so-called Fenwick Hoard, displayed in the Castle Museum. A highly significant collection of coins and gold and silver jewellery, the items contained in this hoard must have belonged to one of the retired legionaries and his partner.

The colony re-established

Order was restored and the colony was refounded. The killing of its occupants means that decades passed before Colchester fully recovered. The colony was rebuilt on a substantial scale to reflect its role as the primary town in the province (Figure 23). An impressive circuit of stone walls, enclosing a larger area than the early town, were the first Roman urban defences in Britain to be constructed. The roads and property boundaries of the earlier town were retained, and the destruction debris cleared.

New timber houses were constructed, and the urban facilities re-established. No trace of these is visible today, although the Castle Museum includes some interpretation of the early town. The forum was probably centrally sited, but little trace has been found during excavation. There were other public buildings, including temples and bathhouses.

Walking the walls

The substantial stone wall enclosed an urban area of 40 hectares. These walls provided a sense of security for the new generation of urban settlers and symbolized Colchester's elevated status as the only colony in the new province. The Roman colonies on the Continent also had circuits of stone walls to indicate a status higher than that of ordinary towns. Colchester's walls originally stood at a height of 6 metres. A substantial external ditch encircled the wall, and an earthen rampart was added inside the wall. Towers were built against the inside of the wall, a few of which have been uncovered by excavation. Unlike many other Roman towns, Colchester's walls appear not to have been strengthened by the addition of bastions during the fourth century. The bastions on the south-eastern circuit are known to be medieval. When planning the stone walls, a larger area than the original extent of the early colony was enclosed, including the surviving remains of the temple of Claudius. As the population continued to expand, the street system was extended and houses built across much of the enclosed area.

The Roman wall was later reused to form the medieval defences. Substantial remains survive, including two out of the six gates. Information boards on the course of this wall provide additional detail. Two narrow pedestrian walkways and external guardrooms were added to the Balkerne Gate, which was included in the circuit of town walls (Figure 24, B). The entire structure of this gate is well-preserved. When walking the walls, take a moment to examine the inner view of this gateway. This was the main gate of the colony, and gave access to Gosbecks and London.

Well-preserved sections of original stonework of the Roman wall, with brick coursing, survive, especially along most of the west of its circuit where it has not been so thoroughly rebuilt (C–C). You can view this section of the wall from the Balkerne Hill Footpath. At the north-west corner of the defences, this footpath turns a corner at the roundabout, following the wall, and runs east as far as the site of the former north gate (D). To follow the course of the wall, walk down Northgate Street. Where Northgate Street meets Maidenburgh Street (on your right), turn left down a path with a metal fence on your left and a brick house on your right. This takes you into the parkland of Castle Park. After 50 metres, you will find traces of the rebuilt town wall on your right (E–E). Approximately 100 metres from the north-east corner of the defences is the second surviving Roman gate, Duncan's Gate (F). Named after the man who led the Victorian excavations here, this gate was a single-arched entrance with a guard chamber above. It is visible today as a gap in the wall.

Turning right at the north-east corner of the defences, you can walk along the grassed area to follow the outside of the wall around most of the eastern limits of the colony. Much of the wall's fabric was rebuilt, however, in later centuries (G–G). The east gate, uncovered by excavation, was a single carriageway flanked by foot passageways (H). This gate gave access to the colony's port on the River Colne. Turning left down East Hill and then right down Priory Street brings you to an impressive section of the town wall, heavily reconstructed during the medieval period. This wall section, with its massive medieval bastions, forms the boundary of the Priory Street Car Park to the south-east of the colony (I–I). Turning right onto St Botolph's Street for a short distance brings you to the site of the south gate (or St Botolph's Gate), which has not been excavated (J). This gate gave visitors to Colchester access to the temple of Claudius.

Turn left onto Short Wyre Street and follow straight on to Eld Lane and Sir Isaac's Walk to follow the course of the wall (immediately to the right) to the site of the Headgate (K). This gateway was double-arched. Walking up Crouch Street allows you to follow the original course of the outer face of the wall to the south-west corner of the defences. Here you can turn right onto the A134 and join the Balkerne Hill Footpath to return to the Balkerne Gate.

The temple of Claudius and its portico

The other major monumental building project undertaken during the late first century was completing the temple of Claudius (A). This building spanning two insulae formed a grand imperial complex dedicated to worshipping Claudius the God. Parallels include the grand forum-basilica complexes at Tarragona (Spain) and Augst (Switzerland). Like these imperial complexes in their respective provinces, the temple of Claudius was probably where the provincial council of Britain met. This assembly included the leading individuals from the *civitates* of the province.

The classical temple was 32 metres north–south by 23 metres east–west and set on a substantial podium to emphasize its scale. It is the largest classical temple known in Britain. The only surviving traces are the vaults of the foundations, preserved below the surviving Norman Castle (in the basement of Colchester Castle). It is possible to visit these vaults by arrangement (see the museum website). Nothing of the temple superstructure survives, but this would have been a colonnaded building, probably *c.* 20 metres tall. It included marble imported from the Mediterranean. Unfortunately, no traces of the building's dedicatory inscription survive.

The temple building was enclosed within a massive masonry courtyard *c.* 150 metres north–south by 164 metres east–west (see Figure 23). The ranges that formed the courtyard's east, north and west sides may have consisted of rooms. Excavations have uncovered the base of a massive altar in the courtyard in front of the temple, the focus of the festivals associated with the cult of Claudius. The southern range of the courtyard was a monumental arcade with a substantial arch in the centre. A visitor approaching from the road to the south would have walked through this arch and faced the altar, with the south facade of the temple behind it. Although few traces of the masonry courtyard are visible today, recent excavations uncovered part of the monumental arcade. It is sometimes possible to see these remains beneath the glass floor of the aptly named Claudius Gateway Cafe Museum in Castle Bay (Figure 24, L). On display are the bases of three piers which supported four of the twenty-six arches forming the arcade, and the remains of walls and foundations. Unfortunately, the cafe itself is currently closed.

Traces of another monumental building, found during excavations in the insula of the Roman town to the south of the temple portico, have been interpreted as a substantial courtyard building incorporating a basilica. This hall may have been for the location of meetings of the provincial council.

The theatre

A theatre lay just west of the temple (M). Constructed in masonry during the second century, it was built into the slope of the hill and replaced the earlier timber-and-earth theatre mentioned by Tacitus in his account of the events of Boudica's uprising. Used for religious gatherings, it was of the standard D-shaped form with a stage in front of banks of seating. The displayed remains, uncovered in 1981–2, can be viewed through a glass window in Maidenborough Street. The course of part of the buried stone structure is marked by dark-coloured bricks crossing the modern street surface. Its proximity to the temple of Claudius suggests that the theatre played a role in the rituals of the imperial cult. A relatively small structure with a capacity of *c.* 3,000 people, it was smaller than the theatre at Gosbecks. The imperial sanctuary, however, was also provided with a circus.

The circus

This monumental masonry structure, built during the second century, was positioned south of the colony (N). The circus was unknown until the excavations located its remains in 2004. All traces of this substantial structure were destroyed by centuries of urban development, but its plan was established by targeted excavation. At *c.* 460 metres long by 73 metres wide, the seating of the circus was carried on an earth bank revetted by two stone and brick walls. This monumental structure may once have seated *c.* 8,000 spectators. As some of its circuit is marked out, visitors can gain an idea of the extent of the circus. The reconstructed foundations of the starter gates, built of stone and brick, are displayed close to the visitor centre.

That this is the only circus in Britain is another clear indicator of the importance of Colchester during the second century. Important Roman towns across the empire, including Merida (Spain) and Milan (Italy), often possessed a circus, and the most famous example, of course, was the Circus Maximus in Rome. The games held in circuses were expensive to stage, and the stone structure at Colchester would have been very costly to construct and maintain. The games probably formed part of the celebrations of the cult of Claudius. The urban community must have met the costs of maintaining the circus and holding the games, including the priests of the imperial cult.

Houses, mosaics and industry

The Castle Museum contains displays of information and artefacts collected during the excavations of houses, industrial buildings and cemeteries across the town. Some large and elaborate masonry houses were constructed during the second to fourth centuries, decorated with mosaics and painted plaster. There were also small areas of housing and industry outside at least three of the gateways. One of Colchester's mosaics is displayed under a glass panel at the Firstsite Art Museum, close to where it was uncovered during the early twentieth century (O). This mosaic has a central design of a rose motif surrounded by four panels depicting sea monsters chasing dolphins. Other mosaics are displayed in the Castle Museum.

The Butt Road building: A late Roman church?

During the fourth century, Christian worship gradually replaced the previous religions as the state cult of the empire. This change in religion will have influenced urban communities. Some of the temples excavated in Colchester appear, however, to have continued to be used during the fourth century.

Just off Maldon Road, close to the Police Station, the foundations of a small masonry building are on public display (P). At *c.* 25 metres long and 7 metres wide, this building is orientated east–west with a small apse at its east end. Located in an extramural area of the town within an extensive cemetery, the building, constructed during the fourth century, had aisles formed by wooden screens. There was no entirely definitive indication from the excavations undertaken during the 1970s and 1980s that it served as a church. It could also have been a banqueting hall for funerary feasts or a temple of the god Mithras.

The late Roman occupation of Colchester is explored in the displays at the Castle Museum. By the early fifth century, the monumental buildings were in decline, and the urban community would not have continued long beyond this time.

Further reading

Gascogne and Radford (2013) is the most up-to-date detailed archaeological account of Iron Age and Roman Colchester. The Late Iron Age and early Roman history of Colchester, including the roles of Cunobelin and Claudius in the history of the *oppidum* and the colony, is addressed in Hingley (2022). For the town walls, see Crummy (2003). For relevant web links, see the website connected with this book.

9

Corbridge: Hosting Place on the Frontier

Introduction

The town at Corbridge developed during the second century CE on a site the Roman military had first occupied a century earlier. This may already have been a significant meeting place during the Iron Age, however. From the late 80s to the mid-second century, a sequence of auxiliary forts was constructed at this strategic location. Although the final fort was demolished *c.* 160 CE, the site's military function continued. Inscriptions indicate the presence in the developing town of legionary detachments associated with the Hadrian's Wall frontier. Corbridge retained its military functions in the later Roman period and was abandoned during the early fifth century.

The English Heritage site at Corbridge includes extensive and well-preserved archaeological remains and a museum with an impressive collection of artefacts. Although there is no evidence that the town became a *civitas* capital, the scale of the buildings and the quality of some of the sculptures indicate its importance. The visible archaeological remains are displayed within a fenced area, part of the centre of an extensive urban settlement lying mainly beneath the surface of the surrounding fields.

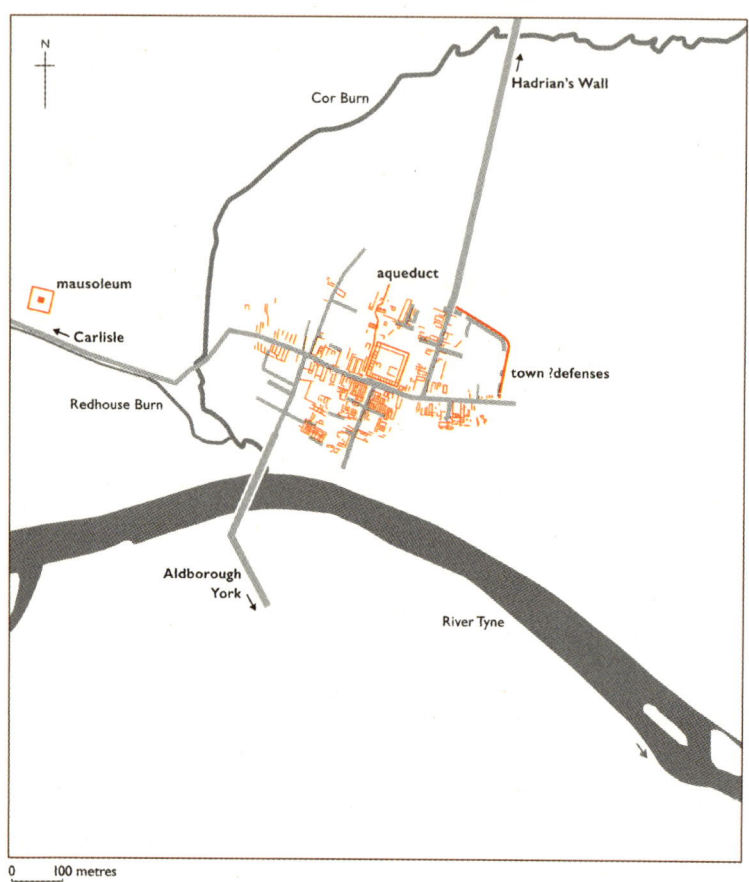

Figure 26 *Map of Roman Corbridge (after the English Heritage map included in Hodgson 2015: 3).*

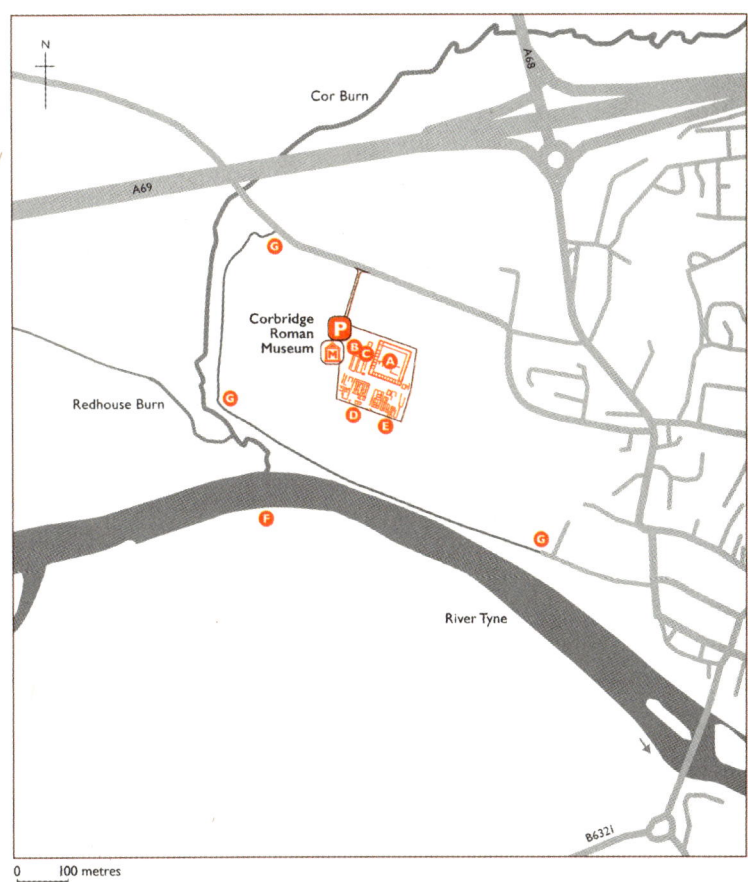

Figure 27 *Map of modern Corbridge with locations mentioned in the text marked. Drawn by Christina Unwin using information from Google Maps.*

Main archaeological features with grading

	Star rating
Granaries	***
Houses/shops/storehouse	***
Aqueduct and fountain house	***
Museum	***
Bridge	*

Getting there

The archaeological remains are on display a few hundred metres west of Corbridge village. There is a car park, and it is also possible to find alternative parking in and around the attractive village. The site is on cycle route 72 (the Hadrian's Wall Cycleway), and the surrounding roads are usually not too busy. Alternatively, you can reach Corbridge by rail from Newcastle or Carlisle and walk through the village to the Roman site. A bus service taking passengers to the site entrance is also available.

Exploring Roman Corbridge

The site is open to the public every day in the summer months, and during weekends in winter. Make sure to check the English Heritage website for opening times before visiting. A visit to the museum and archaeological remains may take *c.* 2 hours. Toilets and light snacks are available onsite. If you have time, however, there is more to explore. A visit to the attractive village of Corbridge, with its shops and eateries, is highly recommended. Many of the buildings are built from stones derived from the Roman site. St Andrew's Church is especially of interest. You can also visit the site of the Roman bridge across the River Tyne to the south of Corbridge. The Ordnance Survey map of Hadrian's Wall (OL 43) will help you explore the surrounding landscape. It is easy to spend an entire day in the summer wandering around the Roman remains, the village and the surrounding area.

Historical summary

The earliest fort close to Corbridge may have dated to the initial Roman push into the region in the late 70s CE. After the communication system in the area had been established, Corbridge lay at a key point at the intersection of two Roman roads: the Stanegate, which ran from Carlisle to just east of Corbridge, and Dere Street, which ran north from York, through the frontier lands at Corbridge and then into unconquered territory beyond. During the mid-80s, a new fort was constructed to serve as one of the garrisons on the Stanegate. During the 120s, this fort was modified and held a garrison in the hinterland of the new monumental frontier of Hadrian's Wall. After the final fort was decommissioned in *c.* 160, Corbridge became the base for legionary detachments. The town began to develop as a supply base for military activities further north, and as a marketing and supply centre for soldiers living along the Wall. Corbridge served as a trading centre into the early fifth century. It was one of two towns on the northern Roman frontier of *Britannia*. The other frontier town, at Carlisle, does not feature in this book.

The rediscovery of Roman Corbridge

After the Roman buildings fell into ruins, this site became the source of the stone used to construct buildings in Corbridge and Hexham. There is a record of an attempt to dig for treasure here under King John in 1201, and during the sixteenth century antiquaries began to record the surviving remains. From 1906 to 1914 excavations were undertaken across a very extensive area. The excavations from the 1940s to the 1970s uncovered the central part of the site, which is now within the area managed by English Heritage. More recently, large-scale geophysical survey has added information about the layout of the settlement, and excavation has revealed several buildings to the north of the Roman town.

The Roman forts

The place name of the fort and town, *Coria*, is thought to mean 'hosting place' in the Celtic language. One later Roman source gives the name *Corie Lopocarium*, possibly including the name of the people who had their meeting place before the arrival of the Roman military. An Iron Age settlement found during early excavations beneath the fort also indicates that this may have been a site of significance before the Romans invaded. These deposits lie deeply buried beneath the remains of the fort and town, however, and the extent of the Iron Age occupation is unknown.

The first Roman fort in the area was at Corbridge Red House, 800 metres to the west of the site of the town (nothing is visible). Although a sequence of at least four successive auxiliary forts was later constructed at the main Roman site at Corbridge, the early date and character of the excavations have limited our knowledge. The first fort to occupy the gently sloping site 200 metres north of a ford over the River Tyne was constructed of timber *c.* 86 CE. It may have been the base for a unit of cavalrymen. Several of the wooden writing tablets from Vindolanda mention soldiers stationed at *Coria*, and during the 90s there was a close connection between these two Stanegate forts. One of the tablets includes a request from an auxiliary soldier called Messicus to spend his leave at Corbridge. This suggests that a civil settlement connected to the auxiliary fort at Corbridge may have played a significant cultural and economic role on the Roman frontier. Why else would a soldier want to spend his leave there?

There is very little information on the extent and character of the early fort. A second timber fort was constructed during the early second century, and a third dated to the 120s. A fourth fort, which may date to the 140s, included several stone-built buildings. Traces of the foundations of two of these buildings can be seen, including part of the north range of the headquarters building and the fragmentary remains of the commanding officer's house (Figure 27, A). You can walk on the remaining metalling of the east–west road of the fort, onto which these two centrally positioned buildings faced.

If you wish to visit a better-preserved Roman fort, travel to Housesteads, 20 kilometres west of Corbridge. The more impressive structures at Corbridge date from the civil phases.

The town

In c. 160, the final fort was demolished and the town started to develop. The new town was probably undefended, and the ramparts of the earlier forts were demolished and infilled. The central area included two monumental granaries, a substantial courtyard building and two military compounds. Surrounding these structures were many houses and shops, which now lie under the surrounding fields. Aerial photographs, geophysical survey and limited excavations indicate that this town covered an area of c. 20 hectares, probably surrounded by a circuit of later defences. The onsite museum has an impressive and extensive series of finds from the site, including a significant collection of sculptures and inscriptions.

The Stanegate road, granaries, fountain and courtyard building

The archaeological remains within the English Heritage site are confusing since they date to several periods from the first to fourth centuries. Most easily recognizable is the uneven paving of the Stanegate Roman road. To the north of this are the foundations of a monumental fountain, two very substantial granaries and a large courtyard building. To the south of the Stanegate are the remains of parts of two military compounds and several shops.

The first structures you reach along the Stanegate after leaving the museum are two immense granaries (B). These buildings, which are well-preserved, may have been constructed to support the military campaigns undertaken north of the Wall under the emperor Septimius Severus (during the early third century). Roman forts across the empire contained granaries to store the grain and dried food stuffs their garrisons required. The Corbridge granaries are particularly substantial, however, and may have been used to store grain for the military forces on campaign. Characteristic features of granaries, well-displayed by these Corbridge examples, are the buttresses supporting the thick outer walls and the raised floors that helped to keep the grain dry. In front of the doors to each granary, along the northern edge of the Stanegate, are the fragmentary remains of loading platforms that were once covered by porticos.

Just east of the granaries is an elaborate fountain built during the late second or third century to provide water to the people of the town and the soldiers in the compounds (C). An aqueduct, visible beyond the substantial stone remains of the fountain, supplied water from a spring north of the town. The small fountain structure, initially with a pedimented roof, contained the spout from which water poured into the first of two stone basins. The sides of the second basin, visible by the side of the Stanegate, were worn down by people drawing water in buckets and sharpening their metal tools (Figure 28). Flanked by statue bases, the fountain formed a sacred focus within the town – springs and fountains were considered sacred in the Roman world.

Further east are the remains of a very extensive courtyard building constructed on the site of the earlier fort buildings already discussed

Figure 28 *Photograph of the stone basin supplied with water by an aqueduct at Corbridge, showing the wearing of the sides of the basin caused by sharpening tools and weapons.* © Richard Hingley.

(A). Known as Site XI since its discovery in the early twentieth century, this large building is square in plan and surrounded by four ranges of rooms. The masonry foundations are particularly substantial and indicate that this building, dating to the late second century, was an important project. Probably serving a market and storage function, it was never completed. The entrance to this building was on the Stanegate, from the south. Its southern wing was probably completed and used for storage during the third century.

One possible explanation is that this building project was interrupted by a serious conflict on the frontier. Leaving such a significant structure incomplete seems very surprising, especially since it lay at the centre of a thriving town. Like all the buildings at Corbridge, the stone from the walls of this building has been very heavily robbed in post-Roman times.

The military compounds

To the south of the Stanegate are two enclosures interpreted since the excavations as military compounds (D, E). These compounds, which probably date to the late second or early third century, lie partly within the area open to the public but extended into the fields to the south (outside the area displayed by English Heritage). The simplest way to appreciate these confusing remains is to identify the wide retaining walls of each compound. Although over 1 metre in width, these walls were not defensive, but separated the military from the civil areas of the town. The compounds may have housed legionary detachments of c. 100–200 men. Each compound included a headquarters building, meeting rooms, barracks, a shrine, a strongroom and granaries. Each compound housed soldiers from different legions. At one time these were the Twentieth Legion Valeria Victrix and the Sixth Legion Victrix, who made joint dedications at Corbridge. These legionaries may have managed and overseen the town's supply depot and market, reflecting the key role of Corbridge as a strategic frontier location on one of the roads leading north out of the province.

To both the east and west of these military compounds, the fragmentary remains of shops fronting onto the south side of the Stanegate are displayed. It is unclear why the construction of the retaining walls of the legionary compounds avoided these civilian buildings. There are many unanswered questions about this site.

Other areas of the town

To both west and east the Stanegate continued beyond the boundaries of the area displayed today, lined on both sides by strip buildings that served as shops and houses for trading families (Figure 26). By the early third century, an extensive town had developed around the supply depot. The buildings and streets outside the English Heritage site have been studied through aerial photography and geophysical surveys, but lie on private land with no public access. Several of the sculptures in the museum originate from temples which were outside the area displayed by English Heritage. Inscriptions on display include dedications naming divinities such as Sol Invictus (the Unconquered Sun) and Jupiter Dolichenus. These sculptures were used to surface the Stanegate when the temples were demolished. The Corbridge Lion, which may have formed a fountain head, is displayed in the museum.

Finds from excavations indicate industrial activities, including metalworking, pottery production and leatherworking. Recent excavations in Corchester Playing Fields, north of the Roman town, uncovered a section of Dere Street and buildings lying alongside this road dating from the mid-second to mid-third century. At this period the town was probably defended by a circuit of banks and ditches and, possibly, by a wall. An account of 1725 described a circuit of walls. These earthworks may have been flattened during agricultural operations, and the circuit has yet to be fully identified.

We know little about the townspeople, although several military gravestones have been found. Two gravestones with the names of young girls, Vellibia Ertola and Ahtehe, represent the civil population. Relatively little is known about the cemeteries at Corbridge, although in the 1950s a monumental tower tomb within a walled enclosure was located and excavated at Shorden Brae, to the west of the town (Figure 26). The site of this tomb is on private ground and not accessible. The substantial tomb is unique in Britain. The best parallels are on the Continent, including one well-preserved tomb at *Glanum* (Provence, France). Although the identity of the deceased is unknown, he or she was evidently a very important individual. One of the town's cemeteries lay close to this monumental tomb. Alongside the other roads outside the town boundaries, especially to the north, there were additional burial grounds.

A bridge over the River Tyne

Around 200 metres south of the town is the site of the Roman bridge that carried Dere Street across the River Tyne. To reach the site, walk across the seventeenth-century bridge south of Corbridge village and turn right to follow the footpath along the river's south bank. The bridge was a substantial masonry structure with as many as eleven arches. The massive stone blocks displayed on the river's south bank once formed part of the ramp that led up the bridge (Figure 27, F). To view some of the sculpted stonework from this bridge, visit Hexham Abbey, where the seventh-century crypt includes reused Roman masonry from Corbridge. This crypt also reused stone from the tower tomb and other Roman buildings at Corbridge.

Another option for visitors is to walk along the footpaths to the west and south of the Roman town (G–G). This attractive walk provides a view of the sloping ground across which Roman Corbridge was constructed.

Further reading

The English Heritage guidebook (Hodgson 2015) provides an up-to-date summary of the archaeological information and a more detailed guide to the visible archaeological remains than is possible here. Rivet and Smith (1979: 317–18, 322–4) discuss the potential meaning of the name *Coria*. For *Coria* and the Vindolanda Tablets, see Bowman (1994). Bishop and Dore (1988) describe some of the early excavations. For more detailed information on the tombstones, that of Ahtehe is RIB 1180, and of Vellibia Ertola RIB 1181. For Messicus and Corbridge, see Vindolanda Tablet 175. For the reuse of stones from Corbridge in the Anglo-Saxon crypt at Hexham Abbey and information on the tower tomb, see Bidwell (2010). For relevant web links, see the website connected with this book.

10

Dorchester: A Town with Henges

Introduction

Dorchester is an attractive country town and most significant for the insight its archaeological remains provide into the transition from the Iron Age to Roman rule in this part of Britain. On a spur of chalk downland just outside the boundaries of the modern town lies Maiden Castle, one of Britain's most impressive Iron Age hillforts. The Roman military may have had to fight to gain access to the territory of the local Iron Age people, the Durotriges. The *civitas* capital at Dorchester developed as the capital of the Durotriges during the first century CE.

The most impressive visible remains of the Roman town are the very substantial earthworks of its amphitheatre. Intriguingly, the excavations indicated that this structure was created early in the Roman period from the ancient earthwork remains of a Neolithic and Early Bronze Age henge. Other Neolithic and Bronze Age monuments nearby suggest that the new urban centre, close to a ford over the River Frome, developed at a location that had long been a significant meeting place. The Roman Town House is a notable feature, and although the remains are highly fragmentary, the course of the defences forms an attractive walk.

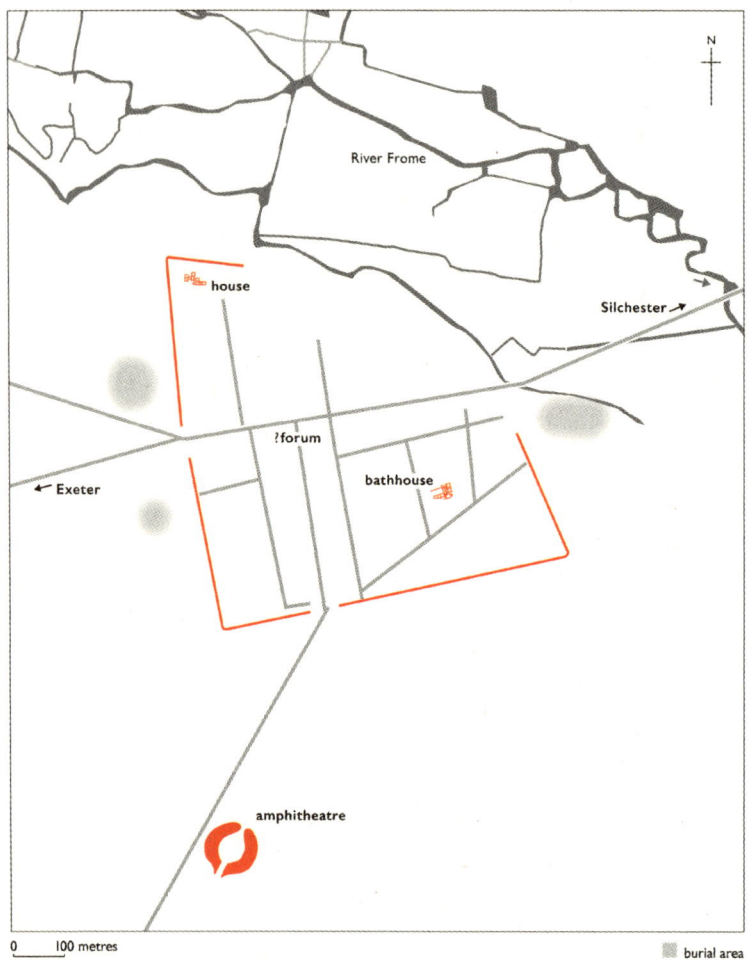

Figure 29 *Map of Roman Dorchester (after Wacher 1995: Figure 145). Drawn by Christina Unwin.*

Dorchester: A Town with Henges 151

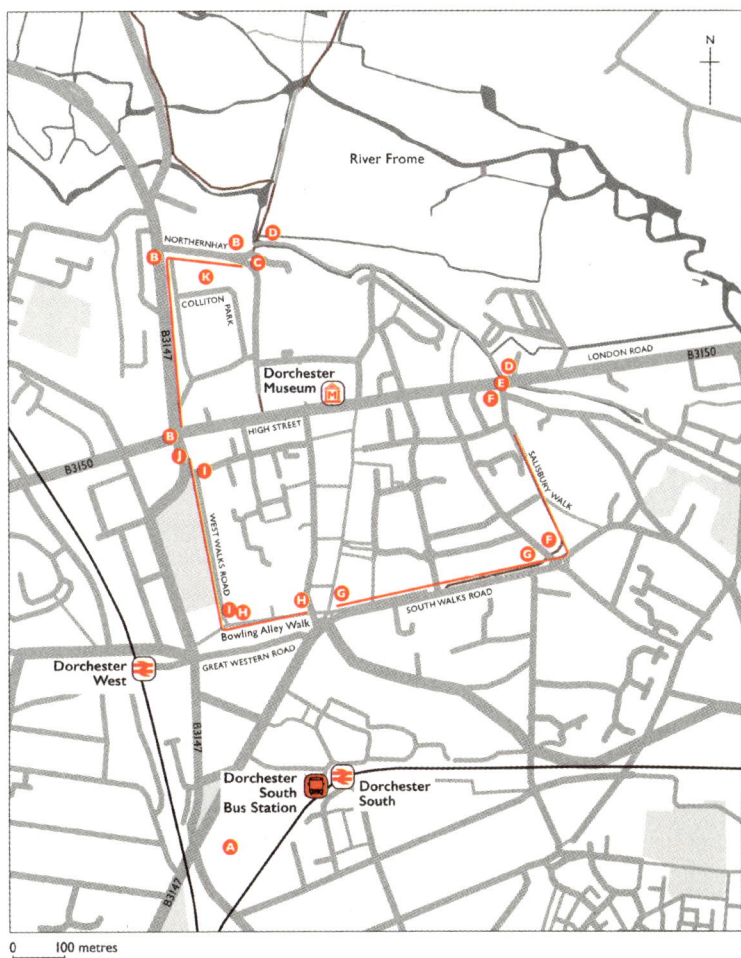

Figure 30 *Map of modern Dorchester with locations mentioned in the text marked. Drawn by Christina Unwin using information from Google Maps.*

Main visible archaeological features with grading

	Star rating
Maiden Castle hillfort	***
Poundbury hillfort	*
Amphitheatre	***
Townhouse	**
Town walls	*
Museum	**

Getting there

The Roman urban centre lies buried underneath the modern town. Two train stations and a public bus service provide access to central Dorchester. There is also plentiful public car parking and a good range of places to eat, shop and stay overnight.

Exploring ancient Dorchester

The key sites in the Roman town are the substantial remains of the amphitheatre, traces of the town wall, and the Roman Town House. Archaeological finds from Dorchester and its surrounding area are displayed and interpreted at the Dorset Museum in the town centre.

Although some distance from the town centre, nearby there are two significant Iron Age hillforts which can be visited. Both can easily be reached by car or bicycle. The locations of Maiden Castle and Poundbury hillforts are marked on the Ordnance Survey maps covering the area around Dorchester, *Landranger 194* and *Explorer OL 15*. You can park on public roads close to Poundbury Fort, and there is ample public parking at Maiden Castle.

It took me 4 hours to explore the main sites in Dorchester during my visit, but you could easily spend a day looking at all the historic sites interspersed with visits to cafes and shops. A visit to the Iron Age fort and Roman aqueduct at Poundbury will take no more than half an hour. Maiden Castle hillfort is a highly significant site that warrants at least 2 hours to explore fully.

Historical summary

Unlike many Roman towns in southern Britain, Dorchester appears not to have been preceded by an Iron Age *oppidum*. Despite this, the area was obviously important during the Iron Age. Three kilometres south-west of Dorchester lies the highly impressive Maiden Castle hillfort, one of southern Britain's most spectacular Iron Age sites. Less than 1 kilometre west of Dorchester is a second significant Iron Age fort known as Poundbury. The proximity of these two sites indicates that this area of Dorset provided a focus for local populations in the centuries before the Roman military arrived.

The history of this region goes back far further, however, as the area around Dorchester was a focal point for people during the Neolithic and the Bronze Age. Several significant henges underlie the town, and there was a causewayed enclosure at Maiden Castle hillfort. Many of these early earthworks survived into the Iron Age and Roman periods. At Maumbury Rings, very early in the Roman period, the earthwork of the henge was remodelled to form an amphitheatre. One wonders what ancient people thought of these already ancient monuments that were so common across this area. Dorchester's significance in the Iron Age appears to have built on a lengthy history of its use as a gathering place.

During the Roman period, this area was in the territory of a people known as the Durotriges. It has been suggested that the Roman military conquered this people by attacking their hillforts one by one. A Roman fort may lie underneath the modern town. Dorchester became the capital of the Durotriges during the first century CE, and it is probably significant that the Roman town developed close to the major hillfort at Maiden Castle.

The rediscovery of Iron Age and Roman Dorchester

Interest in Roman Dorchester commenced early, and the archaeological investigation of the amphitheatre took place from 1908 to 1913. This excavation provided detailed information on the structure and its adaptation from the preceding henge. The 1930s excavations at Maiden Castle by Mortimer and Tessa Wheeler have long been famous for their discovery of the so-called war cemetery. The Roman Town House was also located and excavated during the 1930s. Although the scale of development in Dorchester during the later twentieth century led to other important discoveries, no additional Roman buildings are currently displayed.

Iron Age forts at Maiden Castle and Poundbury

Maiden Castle (NGR SY 668884) is one of the best-known hillforts in southern Britain. The imposing ramparts and ditches are curated for public display by English Heritage. This hill was occupied in several periods, starting during the Neolithic when a discontinuous series of short ditches formed a monument known as a causewayed enclosure. During the Early Iron Age, the site of the Neolithic enclosure was reused as a hillfort. During the Middle Iron Age, perhaps c. 300 BCE, this was extended to the west with the strengthening of the banks and ditches to enclose an area of c. 19 hectares. The eastern gate, on the side of the hillfort with the weakest natural defences, has a series of complex outworks. Much of the interior of the hillfort was taken up by timber roundhouses.

Although the hillfort appears not to have been intensively settled during the half-century before the invasion, it is clear that people were still living here when the Roman military forces first moved into the area (43–4 CE). During the 1930s excavations, human burials were uncovered in and around the eastern entrance. Some of the deceased had been injured by offensive weaponry and finds included a ballista bolt and iron arrowheads. One possibility is that a battle may have pitched the resident community of the hillfort against a Roman military unit. Alternatively, the injured individuals may have died in a conflict between local Iron Age peoples who possessed Roman weaponry.

It seems likely from discoveries made during the excavations that a temporary Roman military base was established within the hillfort. After this, the hillfort was abandoned, although its earthworks remained, and local people will have kept knowledge of this site alive. During the late third century, a small Romano-Celtic temple was constructed inside the eastern part of the hillfort, probably on a site of ancient sacred significance. You can inspect this temple and a small two-roomed building with masonry foundations, interpreted as a priest's house. A bronze plaque found at the site suggests that Minerva was worshipped here.

The Iron Age hillfort at Poundbury (NGR SY 682911) is less well known and has been far less thoroughly excavated. Sited on publicly accessible open land, the surviving ramparts of the hillfort are well-defined. They indicate that this was once a very substantial earthwork with two circuits of ramparts defining an enclosed area of just over 5 hectares. Occupation of the area in and around the hillfort offers evidence of Neolithic, Bronze Age, Roman and post-Roman activity. We know relatively little of the chronology and character of the Iron Age occupation of this hillfort. It is possible that the wide separation between the two series of ramparts to the south, where the approach is least steep, indicates a later Iron Age construction, not long before the Roman occupation.

The early town

Dorchester's Roman name was *Durnovaria*, which probably refers to the town's location close to the River Frome. Its exact meaning remains obscure. It has long been thought that Dorchester developed on the site of a Roman fort, as is the case at several other urban centres in southern Britain. The excavations uncovering the earlier phases of the town's development have yet to produce convincing indications of a fort. The earliest Roman military finds could derive from soldiers visiting the urban site in its early phases. An important recent discovery from Dorchester is the tombstone of a veteran of the Second Legion, Lucius Didius Bassus, from Macedonia. While this has reignited an old discussion of whether there might have been a legionary fortress here, only excavated traces of a Roman fort or fortress would settle the debate.

It seems likely that the urban settlement at Dorchester started to develop *c.* the mid-60s CE at a river crossing close to the Iron Age hillforts of Maiden Castle and Poundbury. The houses were initially made of timber and earth. All the public buildings are later in date, apart from the amphitheatre.

The amphitheatre

The vast earthworks of the amphitheatre of Maumbury Rings, to the south of the urban settlement, are a particularly remarkable aspect of the early town (Figure 30, A; Figure 31). Archaeological excavation in the first decade of the twentieth century indicated that it was

Figure 31 *Photograph of the Roman amphitheatre at Dorchester from the south. © Richard Hingley.*

constructed in the 50s or 60s. This structure modified the earthwork remains of a Neolithic henge several millennia old.

The henge was formed of a circle of pits surrounded by a bank. The amphitheatre was constructed by excavating soil from the central area of the henge and building up the surrounding bank. The massive grass-covered remains of the amphitheatre's banks are still over 9 metres high. They form a roughly circular earthwork *c.* 100 metres in external diameter enclosing an elliptical arena with entrances to north and south. The earth bank supported timber seating for the audience in the arena. Only the northern entrance is original. The southern entrance was a secondary feature dating from a later phase of the construction of the amphitheatre. The arena had a gravel surface, and timber walls formed a gangway around the circumference. Small rooms which probably served as shrines, or sheltered people waiting to perform, lay to the south, east and west of the arena.

The building of this amphitheatre predated the establishment of the Roman town, at a date comparable to the early amphitheatre at Silchester. Why was such a substantial amphitheatre required at Dorchester by what must have been a small-scale community? The reuse of this ancient monument, one of many henges in the area, raises the possibility that the structure was a meeting place during the Iron Age. The local community may have monumentalized this ancient structure, adapting it for an amphitheatre. It may have been used in Roman times for games or gladiatorial combat on festive occasions. Amphitheatres were also places for holding public meetings and performances. Maumbury Rings has continued to function as a meeting place in recent times.

The *civitas* capital

Little has been discovered about the public buildings of the Roman town, although excavations have uncovered parts of several townhouses and the layout of the street system (Figure 29). There was a large public bathhouse in the south-eastern area of the town, but little is known about this building and even less about the forum.

The aqueduct

In many Roman towns an aqueduct was built to bring in water. The example at Dorchester is well-preserved in parts. In Britain, aqueducts were usually open channels making use of the natural contours of the landscape, to provide water to the urban community from a spring or stream source. The Dorchester aqueduct was an earth-cut channel supplying the town with water from springs 20 kilometres to the north-west. One recently excavated section suggests that a rectangular conduit was created with wooden planks to keep the water fresh. This aqueduct provided water to both public buildings and private houses. The course of the aqueduct survives as an earthwork cut into the north-west defences of Poundbury Iron Age hillfort. It is visible at this location as a slight earthwork marked by a track. The Ordnance Survey maps show the course of the aqueduct here, and sections further from the town can also be explored.

Walking the walls

Another significant feature of the town is the circuit of ramparts which you can trace at several locations along their course. Initially, the defences consisted of an earthen bank and ditch built in the late second or early third century. During the early fourth century, a stone wall was added to the outer face of the earth rampart. The approximate locations of several Roman gates are known. The walls enclosed an area of $c.$ 32 hectares, although there were also areas of housing and industrial activity outside the four gates. The physical remains of the defences were removed and flattened during the eighteenth century. Walks constructed at this time commemorate the course of the walls to the west, south and south-east of the town. The development of the medieval and modern town obscured the course of the walls to the north-east.

The west gate was located close to the Top of the Town roundabout. A substantial earthwork scarp, the best-preserved section of the rampart, marks the location of the northern part of these western defences alongside (to the east of) the B3147 (Figure 30, B–B). This earthwork increases in size as it runs north, and its rounded corner remains visible on the right at the junction of the B3147 with Northernhey (road), from which it runs almost as far east as the probable original site of the north gate (C). This is immediately to the east of the road junction where Northernhey runs downhill to the left and Glyde Park Road curves to the south. The defences then ran along the southern bank of the south stream of the River Frome, under the site of Dorchester Prison.

To get back to the course of the defences from the site of the north gate, turn down Carters Place and cross the footbridge over the River Frome. Turning right takes you onto a footpath along the river's north bank until you reach London Road (D–D). Turn right onto London Road, and the site of the Roman east gate is straight in front of you, where London Road meets the High Street (E). Turn left into High Street, Fordington, with the Terracotta Warrior Museum to your right, then fork right down the narrow Salisbury Street, forking left to continue following Salisbury Street (marked as a dead end), which leads to the Salisbury Walk footpath (F–F). Salisbury Walk follows the line of the rampart around the south-eastern corner of the defences.

Crossing over Icen Way, follow South Walks Road to the west along the original course of the Roman wall (G–G). The path running alongside the road follows the course of the outer face of the rampart, and the point at which you cross Trinity Street is the probable location of the original south gate. From here, go straight on and follow the path along the tree-lined Bowling Alley Walk that runs along the line of the rampart (H–H). At the end of this path, walk right onto West Walks Road, which follows the line of the southern section of the western rampart (Borough Gardens is to your left; I–I). On reaching Prince's Street, turn left for a short distance and right onto the B3147. A short section of the town wall survives in the roadside boundary wall (J). A stone plaque records that it was donated to the town (by Lucia Catherine Stone) in 1886. From here, it is a short walk back to the site of the west gate (B).

The Roman Town House

The other site on public display is the Roman Town House in Colliton Park – the best place in Britain to explore the remains of an urban

Figure 32 *Photograph of the Roman townhouse at Dorchester from the east.* © Richard Hingley.

dwelling (K). Although the main living area is covered with a modern building, the large windows help visitors view the remains (Figure 32). It is possible to pre-arrange a tour of the internal structures by payment of a small fee.

The house was first uncovered during the 1930s when excavations in advance of new development at Dorchester located eight buildings in the north-western area of the town. The remains of the masonry walls survive to a height of almost 2 metres. This building, which dates to the third and fourth centuries, has a slightly unusual plan, including two ranges of rooms. The north-west range (under the modern roofed structure) consisted of residential rooms. Several rooms had mosaics, one of which survives almost complete. The south-eastern range of rooms, not covered by a modern roof, may have originated as a bathhouse. Two rooms in this house had hypocausts (underfloor heating systems).

Timber buildings lay alongside this late Roman house. Additional excavations have uncovered timber-framed and masonry houses in

Dorchester. Significant finds, including several mosaics, are displayed in the museum.

Cemeteries and religion

Like all the Roman towns, Dorchester had extensive cemeteries. The well-excavated example at Poundbury to the west of the town included many late Roman burials. Little evidence of the religion of the urban population survives, but the potential Christian significance of the Poundbury cemetery has been widely debated. This cemetery has been extensively excavated and lay to the east of the Poundbury hillfort, almost entirely under the buildings of a modern industrial estate. The foundations of a Romano-Celtic temple can be seen at Maiden Castle (above).

Further reading

An account of Roman Dorchester is included in Putnam (2007). Wacher (1995: 323–35) remains a relevant account but is dated. Manley et al. (2024) updates the information on the Dorchester aqueduct. See also Fulford and Holbrook (2015). For the potential Christian associations of burials at Poundbury, see Sparey-Green (2002). For relevant web links, see the website connected with this book.

11

Exeter: Riverine Place

Introduction

Exeter is a pleasant city to visit, but more could be made of its significant Roman past. A legionary fortress was first constructed *c.* the mid-50s CE, at the lowest crossing point of the River Exe, during the conquest of south-western Britain. When the fortress was decommissioned, the legion moved to a new base. A civil settlement developed alongside the fortress and continued when the legion moved on. The community moved within the fortress defences, and the construction of public buildings started during the late first century. At this time, Exeter became the *civitas* capital of the Dumnonii. Excavations have revealed important information about the basilica, which formed part of the forum. The only structure visible today is the circuit of the walls, much of which survives. The Royal Albert Memorial Museum displays some Roman finds from Exeter.

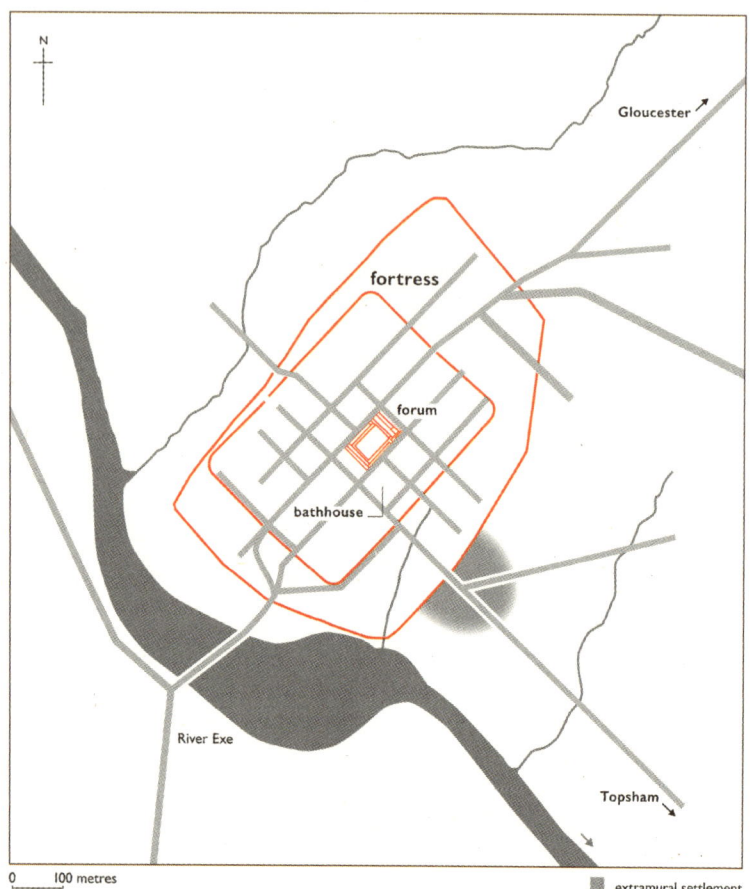

Figure 33 *Map of Roman Exeter (after Rippon and Holbrook 2021: Figures 6.1 and 6.6). The course of both the first-century defences and later walls are marked. Drawn by Christina Unwin.*

Main visible archaeological features with grading

	Star rating
Town walls	**
Museum	**

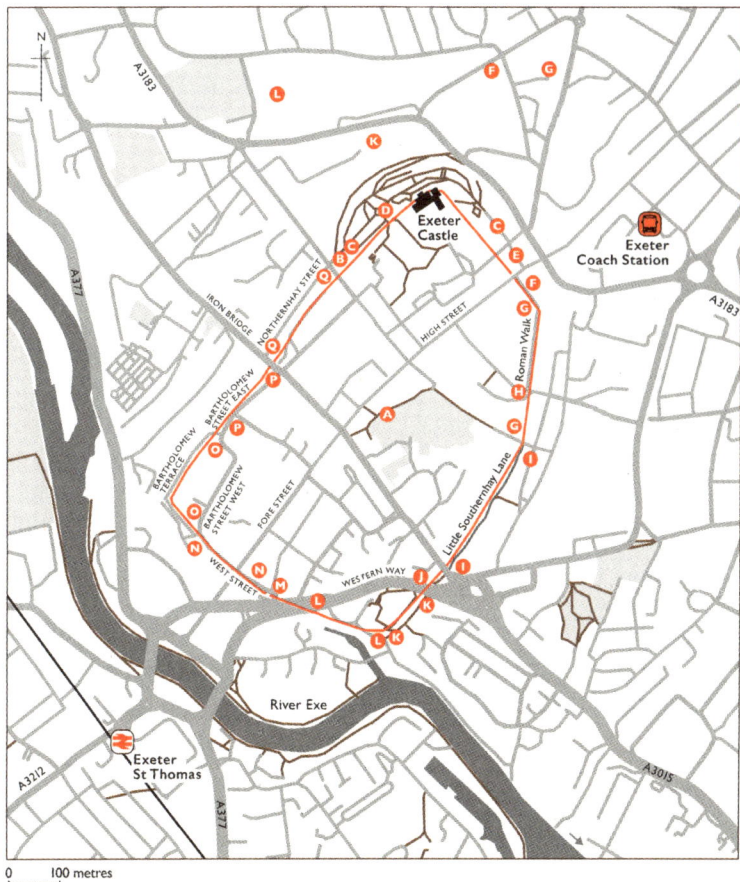

Figure 34 *Map of modern Exeter with locations mentioned in the text marked. Drawn by Christina Unwin using information from Google Maps.*

Getting there

Exeter is well-connected by both trains and buses. Central Station, located just south-west of the city walls, gives easy access to the Roman remains and the museum. Exeter can be a busy place for drivers, and there are several car parks and Park and Ride services on the outskirts. There are many places to eat and stay in the city.

Exploring Roman Exeter

The simplest way to explore the Roman sites is on foot. Cycling around the city centre is also possible, although less good for exploring the walls which involves crossing several busy roads. It took me 3½ hours to walk around the city walls and visit the Royal Albert Memorial Museum, with its collection of Roman finds. There are other historic buildings and museums to explore if you have more time to spend.

Historical summary

Exeter was a significant location in the Roman conquest of south-western Britain and was established as a legionary base early in the conquest period, *c.* 55 CE. This fortress was strategically positioned to defend a port at the head of the River Exe at Topsham, 6½ kilometres to the south-east. Excavations have uncovered a series of military fortifications connected with the Second Augusta Legion in and around Exeter. An extensive civil settlement developed outside the east gate of the fortress.

By *c.* 75, when the south-west had been conquered and settled, the Second Legion moved to a new base at Caerleon. A decision was made at this time to found a town within the ramparts of the decommissioned fortress. By *c.* 90, construction work was underway on the forum, and other public buildings may also have been constructed at this time. The urban street system reused some of the roads of the fortress. The enclosed area was increased in the second half of the second century by a new circuit of ramparts, indicating a thriving and expanding urban community. A stone wall was added to the face of the rampart during the early third century. Although the density of settlement declined, occupation of the city continued into the late fourth and early fifth centuries.

The rediscovery of Roman Exeter

From the sixteenth century onwards, the discovery of Roman finds drew the attention of Exeter's population to the early phase of their city's history. Archaeological excavations commenced in the 1930s. In 1971, the scale of new building in Exeter led to the establishment of an archaeological field unit to undertake rescue excavation work. Excavations uncovered the substantial remains of a Roman legionary bathhouse. Substantial excavations have continued around the city, revealing additional information about Exeter's Roman past.

The fortress

The Roman name for Exeter was *Isca*, which as it seems to have meant 'watery place' probably referred to the River Exe and its floodplain. Excavations have uncovered much of the plan of the fortress, located on a raised but sloping site close to the River Exe. A bridge was built, possibly soon after the conquest, to cross the river just south of the fortress. Archaeological work has established the approximate location of the river banks, which formed a lake just to the south-east of the fortress (Figure 33). The legionary defences comprised an earth bank with timber revetment and four timber gates, with an external ditch occupying the smaller enclosed area marked on Figure 33.

The only trace of the layout of the fortress visible today is the line of High Street and Fore Street, which follow the approximate route of the north–south road of the fortress (and that of the town that succeeded it). The excavations uncovered the substantial remains of the military bathhouse, the only masonry building in the fortress. This monumental building dated to the late 50s or early 60s. Stretching south-east from the fortress, alongside the road running towards the Roman port at Topsham, was the extensive civil settlement which remained after the Second Legion left Exeter in *c.* 75.

The *civitas* capital

Exeter was the *civitas* capital of the Dumnonii, a people that occupied a substantial area of south-western Britain. The foundation of *Isca* enabled the local elite families to take over control of the governing and taxing of their people. As at Wroxeter, military veterans will have settled at Exeter and encouraged the development of the early town. Unlike many towns developing from a Roman fortress, however, Exeter has produced no stone inscriptions, and we know very little about its occupants.

The circuit of legionary ramparts was retained and refortified with the addition of a more substantial external ditch. Some of the fortress's streets were reused, although the timber military buildings were demolished and levelled, apart from the masonry legionary bathhouse.

Public buildings

The forum was constructed in the centre of the town, perhaps as early as 90 CE. The legionary bathhouse was rebuilt to form the basilica within the forum complex, and the excavations also uncovered a small part of the forum south of the basilica (Figure 34, A). The excavations were located just south of Cathedral Yard, in front of Exeter's medieval cathedral. The remains were then backfilled to protect the archaeological deposits. A public bathhouse, supplied by an aqueduct, was constructed south-east of the forum. Occupation within the early town seems not to have been dense.

Walking the walls

In *c.* 160–80 CE, it was decided to extend the defended area. At Lincoln, a comparable decision resulted in adding a new walled area (the Lower City) to the original defended area. At Exeter, the defended town was extended by levelling the earlier ramparts and constructing an entirely new circuit. This enclosed area of 37 hectares is around twice the extent of the original circuit. The earthen rampart and external ditch now enclosed an area of sloping ground, including both low-lying land alongside the River Exe and higher ground to the north. This new defended area included extensive areas not subsequently developed for housing, and it is unclear why the new ramparts were required.

At the start of the third century, a stone wall was added to the front of the rampart. Four stone gateways probably replaced the earlier timber gates, although there has been little excavation to test this assumption. Exeter does not appear to have had external stone towers (bastions). Much of the course of the circuit of the walls survived because Exeter was refortified in the ninth or tenth century, and the city walls maintained throughout the medieval period. Little of what is visible today is Roman, although the medieval wall was built on Roman foundations.

I started my exploration of the walls in Northernhay Gardens (Figure 34, B). Substantial remains are visible in the park, but the Roman masonry has been altered substantially by medieval and modern rebuilding (C–C), including a lengthy section in which the wall forms the base for the north-western fortifications of eleventh-century Rougemont Castle. Just to the north-east of Athelstan's Tower (part of the medieval castle), a section of the facing of the Roman wall survived the later rebuilding (D). Follow the path skirting the exterior of the wall as far as the gates, and into Northernhay Place (E). The line of the wall is lost in the houses to your right. Cross over Bailey Street, then follow a lane called Roman Gate to the High Street.

Turn right for a short distance along High Street, then left again along the pedestrianized Eastgate (F). At this point, you are close to the Roman and medieval east gate, of which there is no longer any trace. This gate gave access to the north-east, towards Gloucester and eventually London. Walking down Eastgate takes you to a short section of the surviving wall (with a plaque dated 1977) where Eastgate meets Princesshay. At this point, proceed down Roman Walk to follow the rear of the heavily restored stone wall that continues much of the way to Bedford Street (G–G). A preserved length of wall can be viewed in a car park behind the shop fronts facing you on the south side of Bedford Street (H). To continue following the wall, turn east onto Bedford Street for a short distance and then turn right and follow Southernhay West.

When you reach the Cathedral Close, turn right and follow Little Southernhay Lane. This lane leads along the outer face of a well-preserved section of wall until you reach South Street (I–I). At this point you are at the location where the south gate once stood. Just after crossing South Street, the location of the south-western tower of the south gate is marked out on the pavement in pink tiles, adjoining a surviving section of the town wall to the south (J). This gate, which gave access to the road to the port at Topsham, survived until the nineteenth century, as an engraving depicts a single Roman archway.

Beyond this gate another short section of the wall is visible. To follow the defences further you then need to cross a footbridge across the busy Western Way. From here a stretch of wall runs down a steep hill to the Custom House Visitor Centre, a pedestrian walkway (K–K) following just above the bank of the River Exe. Turning right at the Custom House takes you up Quay Hill, and when you reach Lower Combe Street on the left, you have crossed the line of the urban defences and are back on top of the wall, now visible to your left (L–L). Where Lower Combe Street meets Western Way, you can turn left into an area of managed ground that contains a well-preserved section of the wall's outer face.

To continue following the wall line, you must cross Western Way again. A short section of the town wall is visible in a car park just west of where West Street meets Western Way (M). A sign on the wall commemorates the location of the west gate, although no traces of it survive. This gate gave access to a bridge crossing the River Exe to the south. Continue up West Street and straight down Bartholomew Street West. This route runs on top of where the defences once stood (N–N). All signs of the rampart are lost, although the ground level falls to your left at the point where Bartholomew Street West curves to your right. Now, continue straight ahead along Bartholomew Terrace and follow the top of the defences (O–O). The Catacomb built into the outer face of this section of the city wall provides a fascinating glimpse of life in nineteenth-century Exeter. Catacombs were a popular way to bury the dead in ancient Rome. This substantial structure, built into the outer face of Exeter's city wall in 1835–7, drew on the Roman practice.

Walking past the Catacomb leads you onto Bartholomew Street East, where the fall of the ground outside the town walls is still visible, although the road gradually leaves the course of the defences (P–P). On North Street, with Iron Bridge Street on your left, you have reached the location of the north gate, all traces of which are lost. Now cross the road and turn left onto Iron Bridge Street for a short while, then down the steps into Lower North Street. Turn right down Northernhay Street (Q–Q). This follows the exterior line of the defences, with the occasional traces of the wall visible between the houses to the right of the road, and takes you back to our starting point in Northernhay Gardens (B).

Housing, extramural occupation and burial

Little is known about the early housing, although as with other towns, Exeter had many masonry houses in the later Roman period. Some of the wealthier houses had mosaics, including two displayed in the Museum.

People may also have lived in extramural settlements such as outside the south-eastern gate, where excavations have uncovered some traces. There is no clear indication of the location of Exeter's cemeteries, although some burials have been found outside the south and north gates. Exeter has produced no Roman tombstones, and as a result we know little about the identities of the townspeople.

Further reading

A recent volume by Rippon and Holbrook (2021) provides a thorough summary of the Roman archaeology of Exeter. Salvatore (2024) includes a less detailed but helpful summary of the evidence for the fortress, and more limited information about the town. For relevant web links, see the website connected with this book.

12

Gloucester: The Bright Place

Introduction

Gloucester was the third in the sequence of colonies established in Britain. Although relatively little trace of the Roman colony is visible today, this was an important place. Gloucester originated as a legionary fortress established in the 60s CE during the Roman military campaign to conquer southern Britain. The colony succeeded the fortress, reusing its defences and some of its internal buildings. The Museum of Gloucester features artefacts from the Roman settlement, including some impressive tombstones and also the foundation of the town wall. Walking the line of the wall and the axial streets of the colony, reflected in the arrangement of the modern roads, gives an impression of the layout of the Roman town.

Main visible archaeological features with grading

	Star rating
Town walls	*
Museum	**

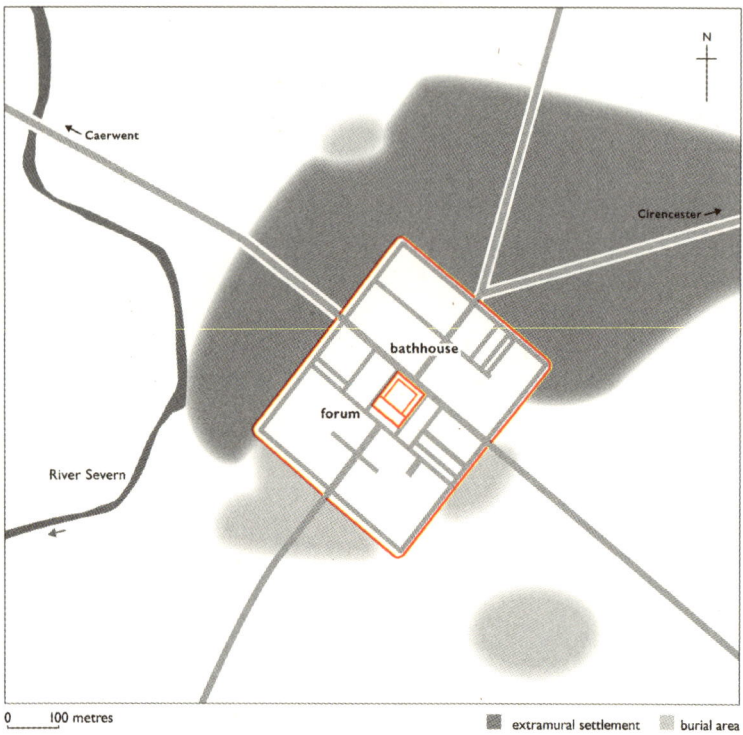

Figure 35 *Map of Roman Gloucester (after Wacher 1995: Figure 66). Drawn by Christina Unwin.*

Getting there

Roman Gloucester lies beneath the centre of the modern city. This busy city is well-served by trains and buses, and there are also several multistorey car parks if you want to drive into the city centre. It is best to explore the Roman town on foot. There are numerous places to eat and drink.

Exploring Roman Gloucester

I explored the sites described below in 3 hours. There is little to see apart from the collection at the Museum of Gloucester. Traces of the

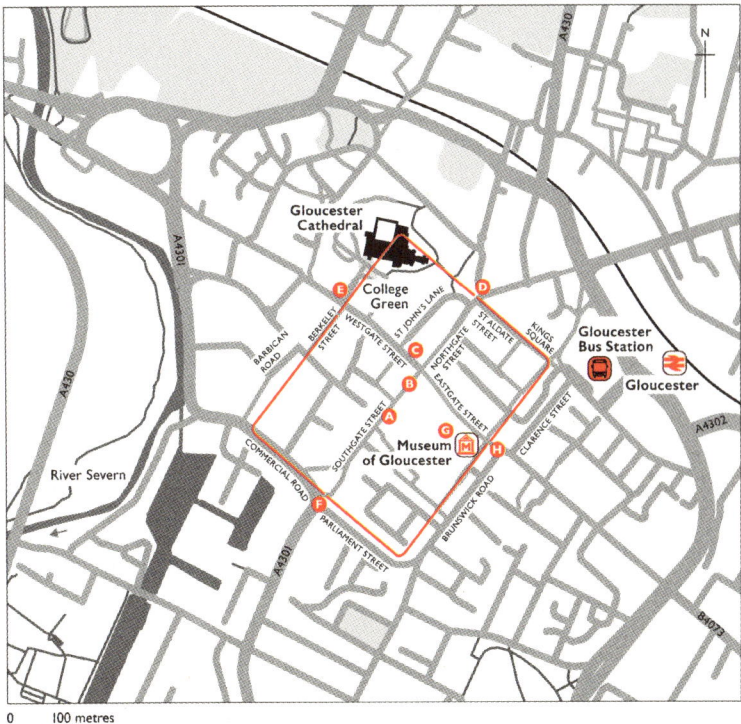

Figure 36 *Map of modern Gloucester with locations mentioned in the text marked. Drawn by Christina Unwin using information from Google Maps.*

urban defences are visible in two locations in the city centre, along with a fragment of the base of a massive Roman column and a modern statue of the emperor Nerva, marking the foundation of the colony during his reign. It is worth spending more time in Gloucester to examine the grand cathedral and other historic buildings.

Historical summary

Gloucester served as a legionary base, probably from the late 40s CE. Although recent excavations have produced indications of Iron Age settlement pre-dating Roman activity here, there is nothing to suggest that this was a place of significance. The first fortress was at Kingsholm, north of the city centre (further north than the area shown on the maps). Two decades later, during the late 60s, the decision was made to replace the earlier fortress with a second legionary fortress. The decommissioning of this second fortress resulted in the colony's foundation during the 80s or 90s. The townspeople reused the fortress rampart as their town defences and rebuilt some barrack blocks for houses. Although no traces of either legionary fortress can be seen at Gloucester today, the museum provides some interpretation of this period of the city's past.

The rediscovery of Roman Gloucester

Early discoveries of Roman tombstones in Gloucester created local interest in this period in the city's history. As with many Roman towns beneath modern urban centres, archaeological research during the 1970s revealed information about the history of the fortress and colony, as well as the buildings and walls. Archaeological excavations undertaken before recent redevelopment have uncovered an extensive cemetery and two military gravestones. The number of recent excavations has been limited, however.

The fortress

The timber and earth defences of the second fortress at Gloucester, built during the late 60s, enclosed an area of 17 hectares. These ramparts lay along the same course later used for the colony's defences (Figure 35). The name of Gloucester in Roman times was *Glevum*, probably meaning 'the bright place', which may have referred to the appearance of the ground before the fortresses was built. The excavations in the city centre have uncovered some military buildings.

Although the second fortress was probably decommissioned during the late 70s, there may have been a military garrison here into the early 80s.

The museum displays information and finds from the legionary fortresses. Two of the military tombstones found in Gloucester are on display. The memorial to Rufus Sita, a trooper of the Sixth Cohort of Thracians, depicts him riding down a naked barbarian, a stock image used on many Roman cavalry soldiers' tombstones. Another fragmentary tombstone commemorates Lucius Octavius Martialis, a soldier of the Twentieth Legion.

The colony

There was probably a break in time between the decommissioning of the fortress and the formal establishment of the colony. The people resident in the civil settlement outside the fortress's gates presumably remained to form part of the colony's population. Retiring legionaries also settled here. The townspeople reused parts of the fortress, including the earth ramparts and some barracks that became houses.

A tombstone from Rome provides information about the foundation of the colony. This inscription names Marcus Ulpius Quintus of the Sixth Legion, and the formula on the words suggests that he was from the *Colonia Nervia* (or *Nerviana*) *Glevensium*. It therefore appears that the colony was founded during the reign of the emperor Nerva (96–8 CE). It is also possible, however, that the act of foundation occurred at least a decade earlier. The preceding emperor, Domitian, had been condemned by the Senate in Rome after he died, and as a result the colony may have adopted the name of the new emperor, Nerva. Marcus Ulpius Quintus gave Gloucester as his home colony. He was a Roman citizen who had joined the Sixth Legion and helped manage the corn supply to Rome. He may have been the son of one of the legionary veterans who settled here.

In 2002, the Gloucester Civic Trust erected a bronze statue of Nerva on horseback in Southgate Street (Figure 36, A). A stainless-steel time capsule housed in the hollow plinth on which the statue rests includes items relating to the Roman foundation and life in the present city.

Gloucester is remarkable as one of only two Roman towns in Britain where the course of the main east–west and north–south streets is reflected in the modern layout. The forum, which has been partly excavated, lay south of the intersection of these roads, replacing the headquarters building of the fortress on the same site (B). Probably constructed in stone during the early second century, the forum is likely to have replaced an earlier building.

The only other trace of the buildings of Roman Gloucester is a fragment of masonry redisplayed behind a glass window at the branch of HSBC in Westgate (C). This fragment of column base is displayed close to where it was found during an excavation in 1971. Further traces found in the course of excavation along Westgate Street indicate that the column formed part of the colonnade in front of a public bathhouse sited on the north front of Westgate Street. The scale of this column and other monumental masonry found in Gloucester indicates the importance of the colony. The museum displays another impressive column and some other masonry from urban buildings.

Walking the walls

The population of the colony reused the timber-and-earth defences of the legionary fortress and a stone wall was soon added to the outer face of the earth rampart during the early second century. There was a substantial ditch outside the walls. Recent excavations to the south-east of the walled circuit uncovered traces of an internal stone tower, comparable to towers on the walled circuits of other towns. In later centuries the wall was rebuilt as a substantial structure as much as 2 metres wide. The date of the masonry gates is unknown, and they were probably contemporary with the masonry wall. The medieval walls reused the Roman defences, although the medieval city spread further to the west and north.

The walls have been traced around the full extent of the colony and enclose a relatively small area of 17 hectares. The walled area at Lincoln was insufficient for the developing town, and the creation of the defences of the Lower City extended the urban area. Extensive extramural settlements lay to the north and west of Gloucester, although there is no indication that these were defended.

The town walls can be followed around the circuit, except to the north-west, where the cathedral was built across their line. I started at the site of the north gate on Northgate Street (D), where a blue plaque and information board mark the former site of the gate, just north of where Northgate Street joins St John's Lane. Turning west up St John's Lane for a short while before taking the path through St Lucy's Garden leads to the east end of Gloucester Cathedral. This massive building was constructed in the north-west corner of the town defences and has obscured the line.

Walking past the south side of the cathedral leads you to College Green. Outside the main entrance to the cathedral, turn left into College Street, which follows the outside line of the west defences to the west gate. The west gate was to the south of the junction of College Street and Westgate Street, (E). Walking down Berkeley Street allows you to follow the outer line of the defences. Barbican Road diverges slightly from the line of the defences. In the medieval period a castle was built over the south-western section of the defences. Although no trace is visible today, the name 'Barbican Road' serves as a reminder of the castle's existence.

Turn left down Commercial Road and walk to the site of the south gate, marked by the junction with Southgate Street (F). Go straight down Parliament Street, which follows a short distance outside the former defensive line and curves into Brunswick Road. This takes you past the Museum of Gloucester on your left (G). You can view the remains of the surviving basal courses of the town wall inside the museum, where the excavated foundations have been displayed and interpreted in an underfloor alcove. The Roman remains in Gloucester, including this section of the wall, lie buried 2 metres below modern ground level.

Walk from here for a short distance to Eastgate Street (H). Just to your left, outside a branch of Boots, is the site of the east gate. The scant remains are displayed in an underground alcove covered in glass, accompanied by an information board. Excavation has demonstrated that the Roman east gate was more substantial than the north gate and had a twin carriageway with square towers to each side, flush with the face of the town wall.

Follow Eastgate Street to the south-east for a short distance before turning left into Clarence Street, which runs parallel to the town wall but just beyond the line where the Roman and medieval ditches were located. Turn left down Station Road and continue onto Market Parade, past the entrance of King's Walk Car Park, then straight on into King's Square. Walk straight onto St Aldate Street, leading you back to the site of the north gate (D).

The people of Gloucester

Several houses have been uncovered by excavation, although nothing can be seen today. Areas of extramural occupation lay outside the four gateways, with the main settlement to the north approximately equivalent to the extent of the walled town. Recent excavations just outside the west gate have uncovered traces of an inlet of the river and late-first-century timber wharves connected with trade. Later in the Roman period, this land was reclaimed and built over for housing.

Cemeteries lay outside each of these gateways. The excavation of burials at 120–121 London Road uncovered many inhumations of late-second-century date, dumped in a pit for reasons unknown (further to the east than the area shown on the maps). It was highly unusual for people to have been buried in this manner, and one theory suggests that they may have been victims of a plague.

The late Roman colony

During the fourth century the walled circuit was reconstructed and strengthened, and the forum appears to have been abandoned. There are indications that some of the houses continued to be maintained and occupied, but little of the later history of the colony is known.

Further reading

Wacher's account of Gloucester (1995: 150–67) is still important and less dated than his account of many other Roman towns because of the lack of more recent excavation. Fulford and Holbrook (2015) provides additional information. Hurst (2020) contains some relevant details. Other excavations are summarized in Hart (2021), Hart (2022) and Symmonds, Márquez-Grant and Loe (2008). For the memorial to Rufus Sita, see RIB 121; for the fragmentary tombstone of Lucius Octavius Martialis, see RIB 3073. For relevant web links, see the website connected with this book.

13

Leicester: The Earthen Fort

Introduction

Leicester was a significant Iron Age settlement which became the *civitas* capital of the Corieltauvi. As at many Roman towns, the ramparts and walls were reused and modified in the medieval period. Despite the scale of modern urban development, it remains possible to follow the course of the defences, though only one small length of the medieval wall survives. Excavations since the 1980s have revolutionized our knowledge of Iron Age and Roman Leicester.

The remains include one of the most substantial sections of standing masonry from Roman Britain, the Jewry Wall. Little else of Roman Leicester survives above ground. Our knowledge of this *civitas* capital derives from extensive archaeological excavations, which have provided some informed insights into the population. Most remarkably, a lead curse from one large townhouse includes the name of a god previously unattested in Britain. It also names twenty enslaved people who may have been part of this household.

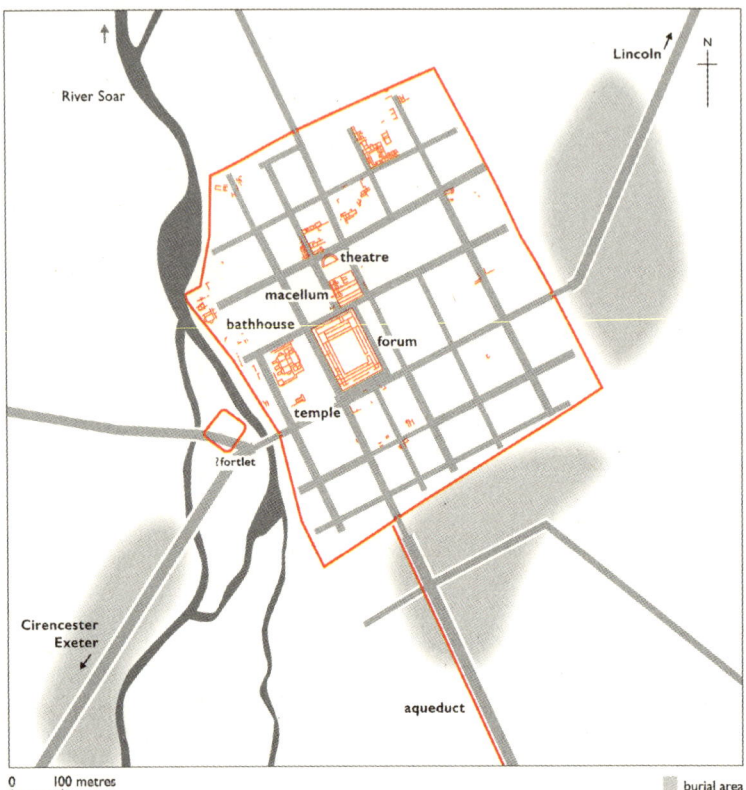

Figure 37 *Map of Roman Leicester (after Buckley, Cooper and Morris 2021: Figure 4.6). Drawn by Christina Unwin.*

Main visible archaeological features with grading

	Star rating
Bathhouse	***
Town walls	*
Museum	***

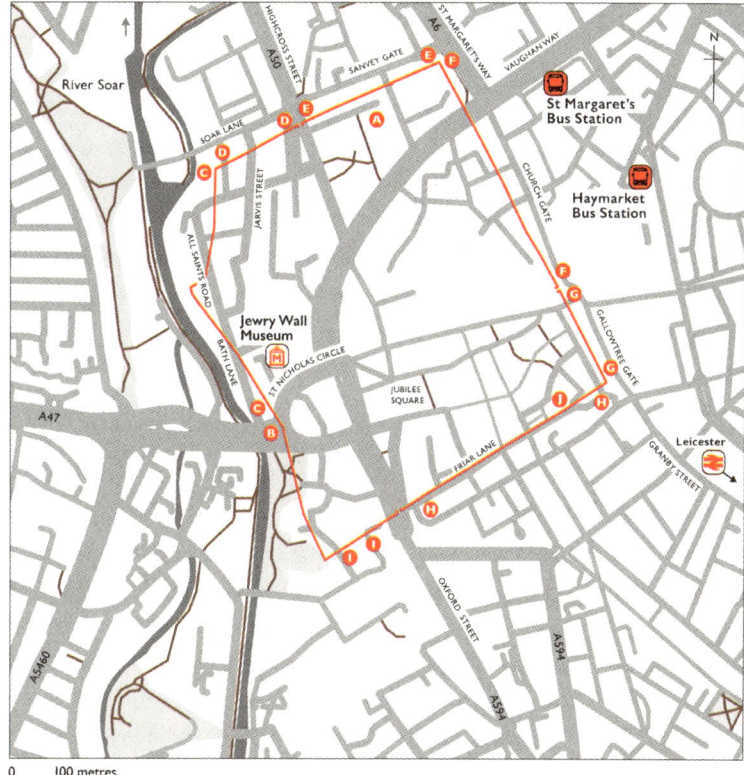

Figure 38 *Map of modern Leicester with locations mentioned in the text marked. Drawn by Christina Unwin using information from Google Maps.*

Getting there

The remains of the Roman town lie beneath the medieval and modern city. The train station is south-east of the city centre on London Road, and the main bus station is at St Margaret's (in the city centre but outside the former line of the walls). Leicester has plentiful parking and many places to eat, shop and stay overnight. The best way to explore Roman Leicester is on foot.

Exploring ancient Leicester

The main Roman attraction for visitors is the Jewry Wall Museum which, during my visit, was closed for major refurbishment, but reopened in 2025. A visit will give access to the impressive remains of the bathhouse and the highly important archaeological collections. It is intended to use the Roman collection in the museum to tell stories of the everyday life of Leicester and its people. This will draw upon some of the recent discoveries from excavations in the city, including the lead curses from Vine Street (below).

Today, visible traces of the Roman town are few. They are limited to the impressive remains of the bathhouse at Jewry Wall and a few fragments of monumental masonry in the graveyard of St Nicholas Church. Exploring the city centre gives access to areas where archaeological excavations have uncovered important information about the Iron Age and Roman past.

Historical summary

During the early decades of the first century CE, a significant Iron Age settlement flourished close to a ford over the River Soar. Leicester may have been an *oppidum*, and there appears to have been a concentration of population here. These people had access to a range of pottery imports comparable to those at other high-status Late Iron Age *oppida* across southern Britain. It is possible, although uncertain, that the leader of the local people, the Corieltauvi, became a pro-Roman ruler at the time of the emperor Claudius' invasion of Britain in 43 CE. A Roman fortlet may have been established close to the river crossing.

From the 60s the town developed across an extensive area. Replanned as a more formal urban settlement during the early second century, at this point Leicester took on the role of *civitas* capital for the

Corieltauvi. The extensive excavations undertaken in advance of development in the city centre have provided significant insights into the community living here. During the late second to third centuries a circuit of defences was constructed, defining the town. Much of its course has been located during excavation. Occupation probably continued into the early fifth century.

The rediscovery of Leicester's ancient past

Roman finds began to be recorded in the eighteenth century. Although in the early to mid-twentieth century attention focused mainly on the public and high-status buildings in the western half of the Roman town, over the past twenty-five years numerous excavations over a wider area have been undertaken in advance of urban development. These have provided knowledge of the Iron Age occupation underlying Leicester and an increasingly detailed understanding of many aspects of the Roman town.

Iron Age Leicester

In the Late Iron Age, Leicester was probably a significant *oppidum*. Intriguingly, the Roman-period place name, *Ratae*, is thought to mean 'rampart'. Since the Roman defences were not constructed until the late second century, the name must have derived from the Iron Age settlement. To date, however, excavations have uncovered only limited traces of Iron Age dykes.

At least 10 hectares in extent, this settlement was on the east bank of the river. The recent discovery of another area of Iron Age settlement located 400 metres further to the north-east shows that there is far more to be discovered. One indication of the significance of pre-Roman Leicester is the quantity of imported ceramics from the Continent.

This suggests that the elite families of this community, in common with their neighbours at other *oppida* in southern Britain, shared the international connections enabling them to obtain these materials. Excavated finds also indicate that coins were produced at Leicester, as at several other *oppida*. No traces of Iron Age Leicester can be seen today, but the Jewry Wall Museum displays examples of the finds.

The early town

As with several other *civitas* capitals addressed in this book, the early history of Leicester is challenging to characterize. Excavation has located a possible Roman fort on an island in the river which may have served to control the crossing point of the Fosse Way road over the River Soar (Figure 37). This military occupation is far from clearly established, however, and the Roman town may initially have developed as incomers joined the local population of the *oppidum* and established a civil settlement east of the river. The early settlement consisted of timber buildings, some with painted plaster walls. Trackways and roundhouses were constructed on higher ground to the east. The low-lying land alongside the river must have been a regularly flooded wetland. This low-lying situation resembles other Roman towns with Iron Age predecessors (Canterbury, Verulamium and Winchester). Substantial groundworks helped to level the site in preparation for development.

The *civitas* capital

The laying out of the street system probably began in the early second century. There also appears to have been an increase in the density of settlement at this time. As at many other *civitas* capitals, recent work has suggested that the street system was not quite as regular as was once believed. The area covered by streets expanded during the second and third centuries. Exploring the city on foot, it is possible to locate several significant features of the Roman town (Figure 37).

Several public buildings have been discovered during excavations, including a theatre to the north of the market hall and a temple, possibly dedicated to Mithras. One of two lead curses found during recent excavations at Vine Street provides fascinating information about a ritual structure (Figure 38, A). Dedicated by a man named Sabinianus, this curse referred to the theft of silver coins from a building titled the *septizonium*, naming three potential culprits. The most famous example of a *septizonium* was on the Palatine Hill in Rome, and there were comparable structures in Sicily and North Africa. The *septizonium* in Rome was a monumental fountain. There must have been a *septizonium* in Leicester, perhaps close to the findspot of the curse.

The forum

The construction of the forum, which has only been selectively excavated, was probably undertaken during the mid-second century, which is decades later than at several other *civitas* capitals. An extensive gravelled area that pre-dated this building had probably served as a market place. The masonry forum was an elaborate structure now buried under Jubilee Square. If you stand in this square looking north, you are facing the main entrance to the forum. The view from St Nicholas Circle bridge over the Southgate underpass gives a striking impression of how 1960s urban development ripped the heart out of historic Leicester.

No traces of the forum are visible onsite today, although some fragments of monumental masonry (including columns) lie in the graveyard of St Nicholas Church. A restored section of the row of columns (stylobate) forming part of the facade of the forum used to be displayed at the Jewry Wall Museum. St Nicholas Church has Saxon origins and much of the building contains stone and tile taken from the ruins of the bathhouse and possibly also the forum.

A market hall

The market hall (*macellum*) occupied a position north of the forum. Constructed during the late second or early third century, this substantial courtyard building demonstrates the importance of Leicester as a market for the surrounding area, not least because the courtyard of the forum would also have served as the location for market activity. The massive scale of the market hall is indicated by a 16-metre-high section of the eastern gable wall of the basilica (hall) which collapsed outward during the early medieval period. Recent excavations uncovered this section of wall. Details of the arcade separating the nave and the basilica's south aisle survived. Although there is nothing to be seen on the ground today, it is an interesting coincidence that the well-appointed Highcross Shopping Centre is built partly over the remains of this *macellum*.

The public bathhouse

Just to the west of the forum are the remains of a substantial public bathhouse, constructed around the same time as the forum (Figure 37). The remains of the Jewry Wall, which formed part of the east wall of the baths, include the twin entrance to the building (Figure 39). One of the most sizeable sections of a Roman masonry building to survive in Britain, the Jewry Wall still stands since it was reused as the west wall of St Nicholas Church during the early medieval period.

The surviving section is 33 metres long, 9 metres high, and 2½ metres wide. It features six types of masonry, including granites and substantial quantities of tile. The small 'putlog' holes on the

Figure 39 *Photograph of the Jewry Wall in Leicester from the south. By permission of University of Leicester Archaeological Services.*

surface of the wall mark the position of scaffolding used during the construction of the building. When built, the walls of the bathhouse were plastered, and the interior was painted. The base of the twin arched entrances represents the Roman floor level. The ground level of the area to the east of the museum building was lowered as a result of the excavations.

Excavations directed by Dame Kathleen Kenyon during the late 1930s led to a fuller understanding of the purpose of the Jewry Wall and the building of which it formed part. The excavated foundations of the rest of the bathhouse lie to the west between the Jewry Wall and the museum. On the eastern side of the Jewry Wall, partly within the graveyard of St Nicholas Church, there was an exercise hall (*palaestra*). Niches to either side of the doorways through the Jewry Wall formed part of the original decorative scheme and may have held statues. After exercising, the bather walked through one of the entrances into the cold room, which may have been open-air. There were changing rooms and toilets on either side. Beyond were the three warm rooms heated by pillared hypocausts, allowing hot air to circulate under the floors. The bases of these tiled pillars are displayed. Closest to the furnace, the hot rooms acted like saunas and included heated plunge pools. The furnace and pools are buried (but preserved) under the Jewry Wall Museum.

An aqueduct

Several Roman towns in Britain, including Leicester, had aqueducts. An earthwork known as the Raw Dykes is thought to have brought water from a brook *c.* 2 kilometres to the south of the town to the area of the south gate. Most of the course of the Raw Dykes is now lost. Close to the stadium of Leicester City Football Club, however, the earthwork of a channel with banks to either side survives for a length of *c.* 100 metres. This lies just west of the junction of Aylestone Road and Saffron Lane, well to the south of the area shown on Figures 37 and 38.

Walking the walls

Recent excavations indicate that the defences were constructed during the late second century. Initially consisting of an earth bank and two, or possibly three, massive external ditches, a stone wall was added to the front of the rampart during the third century. The medieval walls reused these fortifications, and their course is known as a result of excavations in several locations. As they ceased to play a defensive role, from the fifteenth century, Leicester's walls were gradually demolished. In several places, the former gateways are marked by blue plaques to help the visitor locate them.

The west gate was on the riverside, close to the current West Bridge (Figure 38, B). Presumably there was also a Roman bridge over the

River Soar at this location, replacing the earlier ford. From this point, Bath Lane and All Saints Road roughly follow the line of the defences traced during excavations (C–C). Following Jarvis Street to the left leads into Soar Lane. This follows the outside line of the north defences to the original location of the north gate at the top of Highcross (D–D). From here, Sanvey Gate follows the outside of the defences as far as the north-east corner (E–E).

St Margaret's Way more or less follows the exterior line of the northerly section of the eastern defences. Their line is then picked up to the south of the busy crossing of Vaughan Way, by Church Gate (F–F). This takes you to a street called East Gates, where the Roman and medieval east gate once stood. Keeping straight on from East Gates along Gallowtree Gate leads you to the south-east corner of the former defences (G–G).

Turning right into the market area, past the display of the Cherry Orchard Mosaic (below), your route along Friar Lane follows the inside line of the defences (H–H). When you reach Vaughan Way/Oxford Street, you are close to the site of the Roman south gate. The only surviving trace of the medieval defences, built on the Roman line, is preserved in the wall that divides the Newarke House Museum from the churchyard of St Mary de Castro Church (I–I). This wall is visible through a gateway in Castle View (right turn just past the museum). The medieval castle obliterated any further traces of the town walls. The south-eastern corner of the defences was presumably around the site of the Castle Motte, and the walls would then have run north along the river to the west gate (B).

Before the construction of the walls the town extended slightly further south. There were also some later Roman houses lining the road outside the south gate. As elsewhere, substantial cemeteries developed in the urban periphery.

Urban housing

The scale of recent redevelopment means that Leicester is one of the most impressive sources of information for Roman urban housing in Britain. Besides producing traces of houses and industrial activity, investigations also suggest that quite substantial areas of the town remained undeveloped, serving as storage spaces and market gardens. Excavations have uncovered several mosaics, including the fragment known as the Cherry Orchard Mosaic displayed on the wall of a modern building in Leicester's market area (J).

The most recently published excavation has produced a unique insight into the life of a household in the north-east quarter of Leicester. At Vine Street, the initial phase of Roman occupation dated to the early second century (A). Several timber strip houses built on stone foundations were found. During the early third century a substantial masonry courtyard house was constructed featuring hypocausts, floors decorated with mosaics, and painted walls adorning the range of principal rooms. The significant finds from the excavation include two lead curse tablets, including the one mentioned above. Such curses have been found in large numbers at two temple sites in Britain, including at the Sacred Spring in Bath. In towns, however, they are rare.

Servandus, the dedicator of one curse from Vine Street, called on the god Maglus to take revenge on whichever of sixteen men or three women (named individually on the curse) had stolen his cloak. The god Maglus was previously unattested in Britain, although there is another dedication to this deity in France. This curse included a word (*paedagogium*) which seems to mean 'slave-quarters', probably indicating that the household of this substantial property included at least twenty slaves (the dedicator of the curse among them). This lavishly decorated courtyard house will have been home to a wealthy family. It was occupied for decades and reconstructed on several occasions. It is a revelation, however, that such a household included as many as twenty slaves. Another find from the house was a small relief panel from an Egyptian ivory box, a highly unusual and valuable item in Roman Britain. This imported object may suggest that one of the occupants of this house was Egyptian or Middle Eastern in origin.

Before this excavation, only a handful of Roman Leicester's residents were known by name, including a gladiator (Lucius) and an actress (Verecunda). The two curse tablets added another twenty-four names. Clearly, enslaved individuals will have formed a significant proportion of the town's population. Equally unusual finds from Vine Street were lead sealings (originally from bags containing documents or goods) bearing the insignia of three legions: the Twentieth, the Sixth and the Third Cyrenaica. The lead sealings from Leicester indicate that, for reasons unknown, the Roman military played a significant role in the economy during the second and third centuries. Perhaps Leicester, at the centre of the road network in Britain, served as a transport hub.

The density of settlement declined in the late Roman period. Although occupation continued, the town was probably sparsely populated after the beginning of the fifth century. Finds of fifth- and sixth-century occupation within the walls, and early medieval burials in the suburban cemeteries, show that Leicester was not entirely abandoned.

Further reading

The recent volume by Buckley, Cooper and Morris (2021) contains a detailed and thoughtful analysis of excavations in the north-eastern quarter of Roman Leicester, including the Vine Street excavations, and an assessment of the Iron Age and Roman history of Leicester. For the bathhouse and aqueduct, see Speed (2023). For connections between the Roman town and North Africa, see Morris (2022). For relevant web links, see the website connected with this book.

14

Lincoln: Place by the Pool

Introduction

As one of three colonies founded during the first fifty years of the Roman conquest of Britain, Lincoln was a highly significant town. Initially the site of a legionary base, the colony developed after the decommissioning of the fortress. The town was built on steeply sloping ground north of an important crossing point over the River Witham. Extensive wetlands lay alongside the river, and archaeological finds indicate that this river crossing was important before the military arrived.

The colonists reused the ramparts of the legionary fortress, and the community rapidly expanded, requiring a downhill extension to the defensive circuit during the later second century. The area originally within the walls is known today as the Upper City, and the expanded area as the Lower City. All the urban centres considered in this book are termed towns, although the accepted terminology for the two walled areas is adopted below.

Lincoln retains some impressive archaeological remains, including much of the town wall's north gate, fragmentary remains of two other gateways, and additional sections of its walls. Traces of the forum are also accessible, and the city has an informative museum.

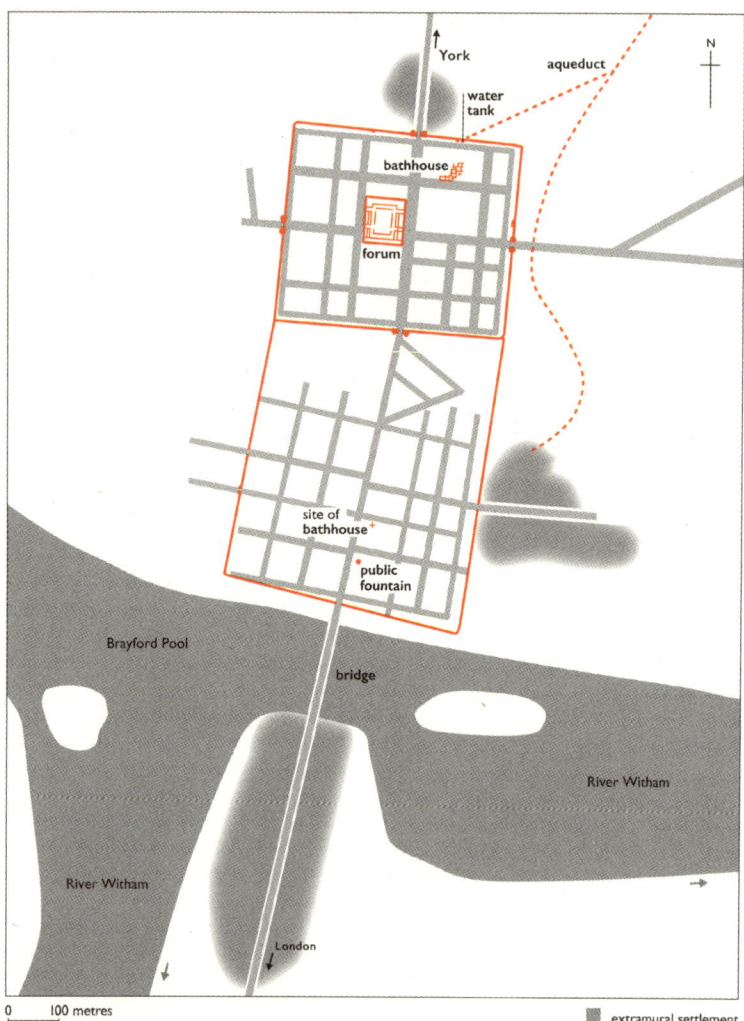

Figure 40 *Map of Roman Lincoln (from Jones, Stocker and Vince 2003: Figure 7.38). Drawn by Christina Unwin.*

Lincoln: Place by the Pool 199

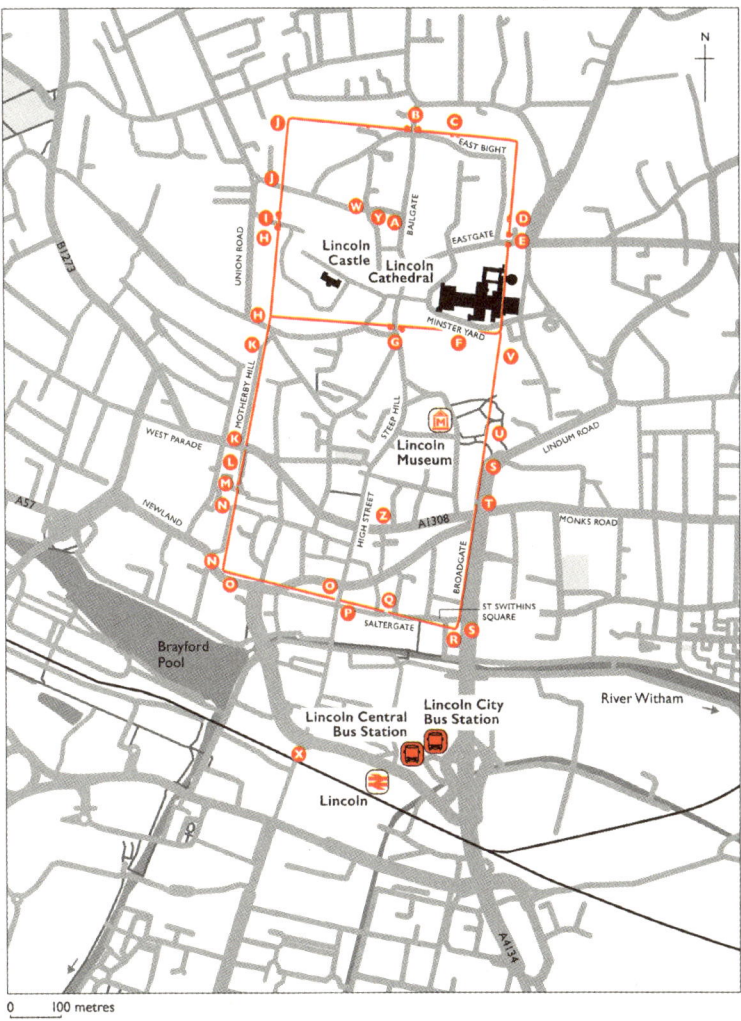

Figure 41 *Map of modern Lincoln with locations mentioned in the text marked. Drawn by Christina Unwin using information from Google Maps.*

Main visible archaeological features with grading

	Star rating
Town walls	***
Museum	***
Forum	**
Inscription	**

Getting there

Lincoln is well-served by public transport. There are railway and bus stations close to the Roman remains and a Park and Ride service north of the city. The Roman sites can be explored on foot, and there are plentiful places to eat and stay. Many other historic buildings and attractions exist within and around the city.

Exploring Roman Lincoln

I visited Lincoln for a day. Exploring the Roman remains involves a lengthy walk and climbing a steep hill. It is advisable to plan a route around the dispersed remains mentioned below if you wish to visit them all. I began by walking from the station up the eastern defences of the colony as far as the Usher Gallery. I then visited the Iron Age and Roman collections at Lincoln Museum before walking the length of the town walls of the Upper City. After this, I explored the remains close to the cathedral. On the way back to the station I visited the Lower City walls and St Mary le Wigford. A 2-day stay would allow a more leisurely exploration of the city and its impressive medieval buildings.

The most significant places to visit if time is short are the museum and the Newport Arch. Walking the course of the walls provides an insight into the topography and layout of Roman Lincoln, and traces of three gates can be explored. Fragmentary traces of the forum and the site of an early church are also worth visiting. Information boards are provided at many sites, although some, being old and weathered, are difficult to read.

Historical summary

Lincoln served as a legionary base from the late 50s CE and was already a strategic location before the Roman military built the fortress. The Lincoln Gap formed a communication route through the high grounds to the west and east. During the Iron Age, a significant crossing over the River Witham existed at Lincoln. Artefacts found in the river were deposited as offerings to the gods.

The construction of the Roman fortress controlled this river crossing. In the 80s CE, an urban settlement developed on the site of the decommissioned legionary fortress. Lincoln was designated Britain's second colony in *c.* 96, late in the reign of the emperor Domitian. This probably predated the colony at Gloucester by a few years. These two urban centres were required to house soldiers who retired from the legions based in Britain, there being no space at Colchester. The colonists reused the fortress's ramparts, and excavations have revealed a forum, two public bathhouses, a fountain, a temple and houses. The town declined in the later fourth century. A building in the central courtyard of the forum, which may date to the late fourth or early fifth century, was possibly a church.

The rediscovery of Roman Lincoln

Lincoln's Roman past was recognized by antiquaries from the late sixteenth century, with the discovery of substantial remains recorded during urban development in the eighteenth and nineteenth centuries. Excavations after the Second World War began to untangle the sequence of occupation, as evidence for a legionary fortress emerged to supplement the information provided by several tombstones of soldiers from Lincoln. In the 1970s, more extensive excavation work developed under the auspices of the Lincoln Archaeological Trust, leading to a fuller understanding of the archaeology of Iron Age and Roman Lincoln. In contrast to other towns in this book, recent discoveries have been relatively rare, although new information is available from the cemeteries.

Iron Age Lincoln

Lincoln was known as *Lindum* in Roman times, meaning 'Place by the pool'. This suggests that at the time of the invasion in the 50s CE the extensive wetland on either side of the River Witham formed a significant feature. Although there is no indication of an *oppidum*, Lincoln was a key location as it offered a transport corridor (the Lincoln Gap) of lower ground through higher ground to its east and west. People living to the north and south of Lincoln exploited this transport corridor.

The Brayford Pool forms a substantial lake where the River Till flows into the Witham. One of the main attractions of modern Lincoln, it is a much-reduced remnant of this extensive former wetland (compare Figures 40 and 41). A causeway may have been constructed during the Iron Age to cross these wet grounds. The significance of Lincoln at this time is evident from the artefacts deposited in the river and wetlands. A reproduction of the most famous of these objects, the Witham Shield (found east of Lincoln), is displayed alongside other artefacts in the museum. Although there is little to indicate substantial occupation of the area beneath the modern city, excavation has produced traces of occupation on an island in the Witham.

As at Colchester, the Roman fortress dominated a significant Iron Age location. The situation at Lincoln is also broadly comparable to pre-Roman London and Verulamium, where strategic riverside locations developed into towns. The difference at Lincoln is that a fortress, rather than a town, was constructed to control the river crossing.

The fortress

On the evidence of three tombstones commemorating soldiers of the Ninth Legion, the Roman military occupation of Lincoln may have begun *c.* 50 CE, just seven years after the invasion of the south-east. During the late 50s or early 60s, a new timber-and-earth fortress was constructed on higher ground north of the ford. These remains lie buried deep beneath the modern city, and excavation of part of the headquarters building has provided knowledge of this fortress. Its defences defined an area of *c.* 16 hectares, comparable (at 20 hectares) to the fortress at Colchester.

In *c.* 71 CE, or slightly earlier, the Ninth Legion moved north to a new base at York. The Second Legion Adiutrix took over the fortress at Lincoln. This legion had only recently been recruited and sent to Britain, suggesting it may have been intended to reinforce the Ninth. A civil settlement developed alongside the road to the south of the fortress in the area later occupied by the Lower City. Although the fortress was probably abandoned during the later 70s when the Second Legion Adiutrix moved to Chester, a smaller garrison may have remained at the urban site which developed in the vicinity of the disused fortress.

Little archaeological trace of the Roman military occupation is visible in Lincoln. The headquarters building lay close to the centre of the walled circuit, and its entrance was probably on its eastern side, accessed from the east gate of the fortress. At St Paul in the Bail, it is possible for visitors inspect the remains of a deep well that lay in the courtyard of the headquarters building (Figure 41, A). This well is located under a cover (designed to be see-through) and surrounded by a metal barrier in a public area. An information board provides some background, but the cover is currently impossible to see through and needs replacing. This well was reused when the colony was established (below).

The museum includes a display that addresses the military phase of Lincoln's development. Several military tombstones found at Lincoln are also on display in the British Museum, including stones dedicated to soldiers of the Ninth and Second Legion Adiutrix. The fragmentary tombstone of Gaius Valerius, standard bearer of the Ninth Legion, is displayed in Lincoln Museum.

The colony

The people of the civil settlement connected to the fortress remained after the legion had left. The next step was the granting of colonial status, which required the authority of the provincial governor and possibly the emperor himself. The colony is believed to have been founded during the reign of the emperor Domitian (81–96 CE). This is known as a result of the information recorded on an inscription found at a Roman fort in Mainz (Germany), a dedication to the goddess Fortuna made by a citizen of the colony named Marcus Minicius Marcellinus. A senior centurion of the Twenty-Second Legion Primigenia, he had been serving in Germany but was previously resident at Lincoln.

The Roman colony reused the earthen ramparts and street system of the fortress, still reflected in places in the course of the city streets of modern Lincoln. Most notable is Bailgate, which follows the approximate route of the Roman road from the northern to the southern gates of the Upper City. During the later second century, as the walled area of the colony was no longer sufficient for the population, a new walled circuit enclosed the extramural settlement on the hill slope to the south (the Lower City). Excavation has found some evidence that the hillslope was terraced to provide level ground for building, as also seen at Aldborough.

The Brayford Pool still formed a significant landscape feature at this time (Figure 40). A bridge carried Ermine Street across the course of the River Witham. Extensive wetlands followed the course of the rivers, particularly on the southern banks.

Walking the walls of the Upper City

During the early second century, the earthen rampart of the legionary fortress was faced with a substantial masonry wall. This stone defence, which reached a height of at least 4 metres, was a symbol of the status of the colony. The construction of the stone wall required the abandonment of the fortress ditch and the new ditch lay further out. During the second or third century, the height of the wall was increased to 6 metres and interval towers were added to the inner face of the wall.

Several sections of the walled circuit survive. The best-known element of Lincoln's walls is the north gate, known today as the Newport Arch (Figure 41, B; Figure 42). One of Britain's two best-preserved Roman urban gateways, its rear arch still stands while the foundation of the front of its west tower is also displayed. Constructed in the early second century as a simple stone gate, it was rebuilt in monumental form during the third century. In plan, this monumental gateway consisted of a single carriageway through the town wall for traffic with pedestrian arches to either side. The main arch is still used by traffic today. To either side of

Figure 42 *Photograph of the Newport Arch in Lincoln from the south.* © Richard Hingley.

the gateway were massive flanking towers with curved fronts, projecting slightly beyond the line of the town wall.

Two parts of the gateway structure are displayed. The southern wall includes the arch for traffic, originally *c.* 5 metres wide and 7 metres high, and the eastern pedestrian arch. These elements of the Roman structure remain because of their reuse in the medieval arch of the northern gateway of Lincoln. The walls projecting to the north from the southern face of the Newport Arch are post-Roman. If you consider that the Roman ground level was *c.* 3 metres lower than the modern roads and pavement, you can appreciate the substantial scale of the Newport Arch. This also explains why it appears rather squat.

The second part of the Roman gateway still visible is the excavated base of the western tower. The curved face of this tower projected beyond the town wall. You can view the foundations by walking north through the Newport Arch and looking left into a fenced enclosure beyond the Chinese restaurant. Looking back from this location helps you to understand the layout of the gateway and the extent of the surviving Roman masonry. The back and front faces of the town wall, where it crossed the Newport Arch, are marked out in the modern road surface with red and grey cobbles.

From the Newport Arch, turn right into East Bight, a lane which runs slightly to the south inside the line of the Roman defences. A short section of the town wall, rebuilt in the fourth century, can be viewed in a fenced enclosure (with information board) just to the north of this road, beyond the brick house (Figure 41, C). Marked out on the grass in front is the footprint of a substantial water tank found during excavation (see the description of the aqueduct below). The colony's public baths were just behind you to the south of the lane. East Bight runs further east and then turns a right angle, roughly following the inside line of the defences, although all traces have been lost in the gardens to the east. A well-preserved section of the town wall can be viewed in the car park just north of the Lincoln Hotel (D). If you want to look at this section of the defences, ask at the hotel reception.

Just south of the hotel, the remains of the east gate are displayed in a sunken area defined by a low wall (E). This was the principal gateway into the colony, built at the same location as the main gate of the (preceding) fortress. Unlike the north gate, the eastern gate had twin carriageways. Like the Newport Arch, it had projecting semicircular towers, probably constructed during the third century. Although only the north tower of this gate is displayed, the south tower, which lay on the other side of the road on the edge of the cathedral's lawn, was also excavated. The distance below the current street level occupied by this structure indicates how far the ground level has been built up since the Roman period. South of Eastgate, the course of the town wall of the Upper City lies under Lincoln Cathedral, which was constructed partly over its line.

The south-east corner of the town wall, which was located within the ground of the medieval Bishop's Palace, is lost. A section of the southern wall survives in the grounds of the palace, accessible from the south side of Minster Yard (F). You can find this by walking through the main vehicle entrance to the Bishop's Palace from Minster Yard. A heavily rebuilt section of the town wall is visible on the right (north) at the top of a bank.

The only other remaining sign of the course of the wall on the southern side of the Upper City is on Lincoln's famous Steep Hill. On the left (west) of the road going uphill, there is a section of stone wall between two properties. This marks the former location of the wall at the south gate (G). On the opposite (eastern) side of Steep Hill, a plaque outside House 44 records that the remains of the eastern carriageway of the Roman south gate are within. This house is currently a shop which was closed when I visited. Excavations near this point demonstrate that the south gate had a twin portal passageway comparable to the east gate. Wordsworth Street and Drury Lane then follow the outer line of the western section of the southern defences. These are lost beneath the houses and the castle defences.

The south-west corner of the walled circuit lay just to the east of the junction of Drury Lane and Union Road, and Lincoln Castle's western curtain wall was constructed along the line of the Roman town wall, which may survive buried in the massive medieval earthworks (H–H). The entire west gate is buried within the defences of the medieval castle, as discovered in 1836 by a disreputable innkeeper, trying to expand his premises by digging into the castle mound (I). This single portal gateway, which was located immediately in front of the Norman gate, was reburied after discovery. From here, Reservoir Street follows the original course of the wall (J–J). After this point, the wall line lies buried beneath the gardens and school grounds to the north of the rather grand (neoclassical) Westgate Water Tower (which is also well worth visiting).

Walking the walls of the Lower City

A later addition to the circuit of the Upper City, these walls probably date to the late second century. The defences, which appear to have had an earthen rampart as well as the stone-facing wall, may have taken some time to complete. At least one ditch encircled the wall and, as with the wall of the Upper City, towers were added to the rear. These defences enclosed an area of settlement previously lying outside the Upper City's south gate.

From Reservoir Street, you can walk back down Union Road, Drury Lane and Spring Hill to trace the line of the western defences of the Lower City. After an initial dog-leg, this follows the steep cobbled footpath and cycleway called Motherby Hill (K–K). The footpath lies directly on top of the course of the wall. The external ditch used to be visible (to our right) but has more recently been obscured by housing development.

At the bottom of Motherby Hill, cross West Parade, where an information board marks the location of a secondary west gate. The road called The Park follows the course of the town wall and takes you into a car park at the City of Lincoln Council Offices (L). You can view the remains of Lincoln's lower west gate to the right of the car park in front of you. The City Council offices were constructed in part over the defences. The excavated and displayed remains, which include an impressive section of the masonry wall and the foundation of the west gate, are in an awkward location partly under the Council offices (M). Excavations in 1968 indicated that this gate was a simple gap cut through the pre-existing wall and was a fourth-century addition to the circuit.

It incorporated earlier masonry into its structure, including some monumental fragments that hint at the magnificence of the public buildings of the colony. The substantial foundations of the two small rectangular towers flanking the outside of the entrance are displayed. Sections of the town wall survive on both sides of this gateway.

Walking further along the line of the wall leads to a public car park under the Council offices (N–N). The dimensions of the bank to the left (east) of this indicates that the Roman defences are well-preserved along this length.

Fun Farm Day Nursery, where you should turn left, is more or less the original location of the south-western corner of the defences. Newland follows the outside line of the southern defences (O–O). The Roman south gate lay where High Street meets Guildhall Street at the remarkable Stonebow Gateway (P). Excavations on the waterfront near here produced some organic objects that survived in the waterlogged conditions, including shoes and wooden tools. Saltergate follows the route of the eastern section of the southern defences to Bank Street, and in this section of the ramparts a postern gate gave access to the river (Q). It is sometimes possible to join a tour to see the remains of this gate in a basement under the Stonebow Centre shopping arcade (information is available at Lincoln's Visitor Centre). St Swithin's Square follows the remainder of the southern defences to their south-east corner (R).

The line of the eastern defences is picked up by the course of Broadgate and then Lindum Road, which runs alongside the former outer line of the wall (S–S). The east gate of the Lower City was just north of the junction of Monk's Road with Broadgate (T). This gate has not yet been located through excavation. Where Lindum Road swings to the right, the defences originally ran straight onward into Temple Gardens, which is the park surrounding the Usher Gallery. The southern part of the Temple Gardens includes traces of an earthwork section of the massive ditch that lay in front of the defences. This is just in front as you enter the park (U). A surviving section of the masonry town wall is also visible in the northern part of Temple Gardens (V). The south-east corner of the defences surrounding the Upper City was just north of this point.

The forum

The forum was located in the approximate centre of the Upper City, approached from the east through the main gate. It replaced the headquarters building of the fortress on the same site. The first masonry forum was constructed during the early second century and completely rebuilt during the late second century. The limited excavation which has been possible has produced a confusing picture of this significant building. Fragments of a bronze statue found in the remains of the building may perhaps have depicted the emperor Domitian.

Bailgate follows the course of the colonnade that formed the eastern front of the forum. On the west side of the road, granite roundels set in the paving of the road mark the locations of the nineteen stone columns of the colonnade. Since the building was almost square, this eastern frontage conveys an impression of the scale of the forum. The only other trace of the building is a remarkable survival. Part of the structure of the north wall of the basilica survives today in a section of Roman masonry known as the Mint Wall (W). This is located behind the Castle Hotel, accompanied by an information board (which is rather tricky to spot). This massive section of wall, *c.* 7 metres high and 23 metres long, lies in line with the most northerly columns of the Bailgate colonnade. The tile courses visible in the masonry helped strengthen the wall.

The well originally within the fortress's headquarters building was reused as a source of water within the courtyard of the forum (A). At this stage, a vaulted stone-and-tile well-head was constructed, but nothing of this is visible through the cover over the well. Traces of the foundations of the walls forming part of the forum's east range have also been marked out in this public area. There may have been a temple to the south of the forum, and an inscription records that an imperial freedman donated money to restore a temple to the imperial cult at Lincoln. Nothing survives to be seen of what may have been a major temple complex.

The supply and use of water

Lincoln was supplied with water by an aqueduct, part of the most sophisticated water supply system in Roman Britain. Wells also provided water to the townspeople, including the substantial example in the forum (above). The scale of the investment required to construct the bathhouses and the fountain (below) and to supply the water for these facilities indicates centralized control and planning. The urban council of the colony may have met the cost of building the aqueduct. The townsfolk will have been charged for the use of bathhouses and for supplying water to their houses, which will have recompensed the urban elite for their investment.

The aqueduct may have originated at a spring called Roaring Meg, 2 kilometres north-east of the colony. The site of this spring, which has been lost in the development of the outskirts of Lincoln, was north of the St Giles area, just south of the junction of Nettleham Road and Searby Road. The aqueduct ran from this spring on a course west of and roughly parallel to the Nettleham Road, leading to the north-east corner of the colony. The water ran through a terracotta pipe encased in concrete and buried in the ground. Excavations have uncovered the aqueduct at several points along its course, and the remains of the various engineering works required to pipe water to the town.

Excavations to the north-east of the Upper City uncovered a structure *c*. 17 metres long built into the back of the city wall at East Bight (C). The site of this substantial tank, supplied from the aqueduct, which probably held *c*. 12,000 litres of water, is marked out just inside the town wall. To the south of the tank, excavations uncovered a public bathhouse, well-positioned to exploit this water source. During excavations in the Lower City a second bathhouse was located. The foundations of a masonry structure, probably an octagonal fountain, were found just downhill from this bathhouse.

Housing and people

Although little is known about housing in Roman Lincoln, as is common in most towns it is clear that from the mid-second century early timber dwellings were replaced by stone-constructed houses. Some of these houses had hypocausts and mosaics. Excavations at the museum and the castle uncovered the remains of substantial townhouses which had mosaic floors. In addition to the finds displayed in Lincoln Museum, the castle also has a small collection of finds from excavations. Mosaics are displayed at the museum and at the Wren Library in the cathedral. Traces of less substantial strip houses have also been found during the excavations. As usual, settlement developed outside several of the gates, and cemeteries ringed the city.

Several tombstones name deceased residents of the colony. The west front of the church of St Mary le Wigford incorporates a remarkable Roman inscription (X; Figure 43). This commemorates Sacer, son of Brusus, a citizen of the Senones, his wife Carssouna, and son Quintus. The Senones were a Gallic people from the Seine Basin, a reminder that many of the townspeople were settlers from other parts of the empire. Intriguingly, an additional inscription was added, probably in the eleventh century, to Sacer's memorial to record that Eirtig commissioned and endowed the building of this church. Other

Figure 43 *Photograph of the inscription to Sacer, son of Brusus, at St Mary le Wigford, Lincoln. © Richard Hingley.*

notable residents included Volusia Faustina, wife of one of the town's *decurions* (elected officials), and Claudia Crysis, who died at the age of 90, the oldest known woman from Roman Britain.

Late Roman Lincoln

During the early fourth century, when Britain was divided into four provinces, Lincoln became the capital of *Britannia Secunda*. Around this time, the defences were strengthened by increasing the thickness of the town wall and recutting of the ditch. Unlike many other towns, there is no indication of the addition of towers (bastions) to the outer face of Lincoln's wall. By the mid-fourth century, the forum and public bathhouses probably became disused. At Flaxengate a huge basilican hall of later Roman date has been identified. This must have dominated the Lower City, but its complete form and function are unclear. Although occupation continued into the later fourth century and possibly beyond, substantial signs of early medieval settlement within the walled area, indicating longer-term occupation, are lacking. There is, however, one site that may indicate continuity beyond the end of the Roman period.

Excavations at St Paul in the Bail have revealed traces of two successive timber buildings constructed in the courtyard of the forum (Figure 41, Y). Although few archaeological finds were made, these buildings may have been constructed during the late fourth or early fifth century and were possibly early churches. The outline of the second building, which had an eastern apse, is marked in the paving of the public square. If the identification of these buildings as churches is correct, this area of the colony may have seen a continuity of Christian worship into the medieval period. This area of Lincoln is known by the name of the medieval church of St Paul, demolished in the eighteenth century, which lay close to the site of these two timber buildings. Perhaps a memory of the sanctity of the site of the early churches survived the ending of life in the Roman colony.

Further reading

Jones (2002) provides a helpful summary of the archaeology of Iron Age and Roman Lincoln. A fuller and more detailed study of Lincoln's history and archaeology is provided by Jones, Stocker and Vince (2003). Green (2012) discusses early medieval Lincoln. For relevant web links, see the website connected with this book.

15

London: A Place Frequented by Traders

Introduction

London was the most substantial and populous town in Roman Britain. It is also the place that has seen the most extensive excavation. With informal origins as a settlement of traders in a Thames-side location, London developed as a port soon after the Roman conquest of southern Britain. With a population estimated to have been as many as 35,000 people during the later second century, this was the largest town in Britain before the medieval period.

Despite relatively humble origin, Roman London probably became the provincial capital in succession to Colchester, possibly during the early second century. The urban community also had close connections with the Roman military. London played a prominent role in several historical events during the third and fourth centuries. As I write this book, London Museum (formerly the Museum of London) is temporarily closed and moving to a new location at West Smithfield. The new museum, reopening in 2026, will contain a groundbreaking display of London's Roman past.

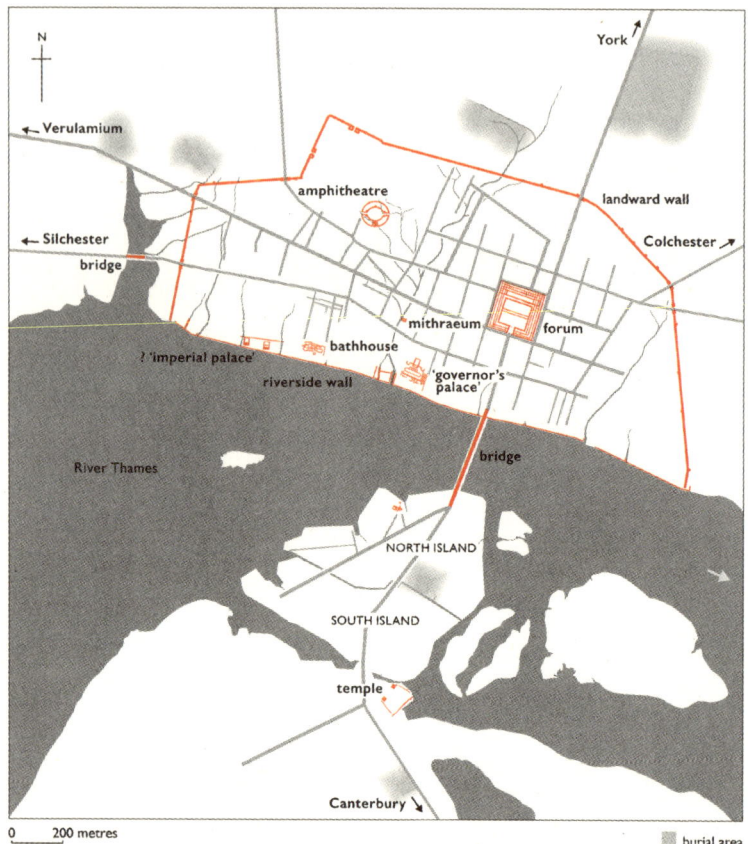

Figure 44 *Map of Roman London (from Hingley 2018: Figure 8.1). Drawn by Christina Unwin.*

There are many archaeological sites to explore. These include the remains of the town walls, and several Roman buildings. This chapter focuses on the archaeological remains that can be visited. Many other significant archaeological sites across the city have left no physical traces, although several of these are discussed because they have a particular significance.

London: A Place Frequented by Traders

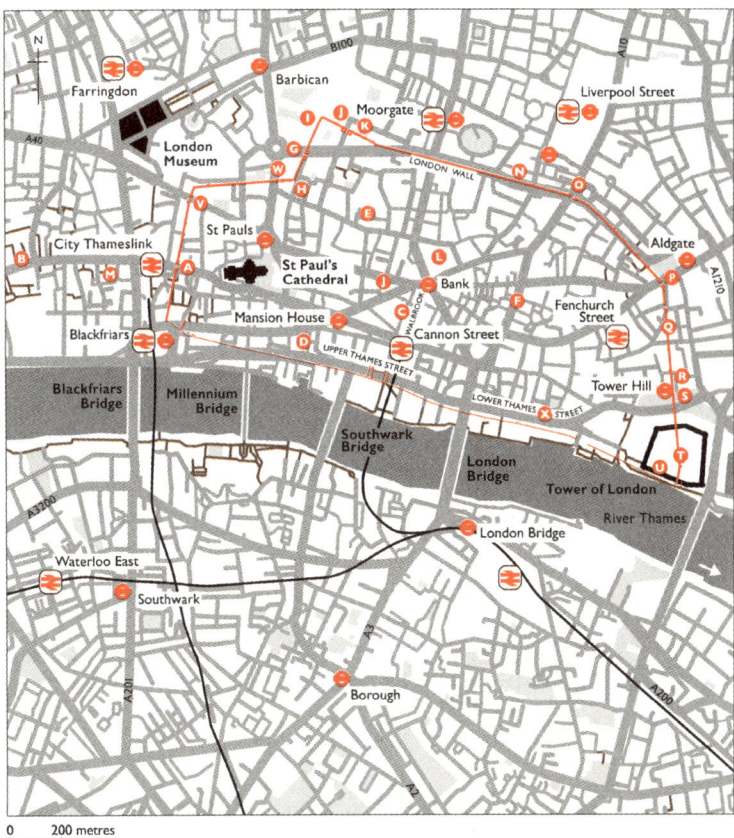

Figure 45 *Map of modern London with locations mentioned in the text marked. Drawn by Christina Unwin using information from Google Maps.*

Main visible archaeological features with grading

	Star rating
Amphitheatre	**
Second forum	*
Cripplegate fort walls	**
St Bride's Church mausoleum?	**
Town walls, including the city walls at Vine Street centre	**
Billingsgate bathhouse	**
Mithraeum	***
Museum	***

Getting there

The City of London is well-served by public transport, with many train and underground stations and regular bus services. There is very little public parking in central London, and an ultra-low emission charge is usually payable for private vehicles entering the city. The town spanned both banks of the River Thames. The archaeological sites that can be visited are all on the north bank. Several underground stations provide access, including Barbican, Moorgate, Liverpool Street, Aldgate, Tower Hill, London Bridge, and Bank. There are several mainline stations located close to this area of the Roman town. To the south of the river, Borough underground station is within the area once occupied by the town. Numerous restaurants and cafes are available for food and drink. Accommodation can be expensive, but a range of more economical hotels and bed and breakfasts are available on the outskirts of London.

Exploring Roman London

The sites discussed below are best visited on foot as this central area of London is very busy. People also cycle in the busy streets, although finding a safe place to leave a bicycle is problematic, and urban cycling requires patience and skill. As the archaeological sites are spread across central London, you will need adequate time to visit all of them. I have developed my knowledge by visiting these sites during several trips.

Some explanation is required of the two maps as they differ in detail from the maps for other chapters. These maps are printed at half the scale of those for other towns to fit all the archaeological information onto a single page. Figure 44 shows the main Roman buildings with an approximation of the extent of the Thames's waters at high tide during the third century. The Roman occupation resulted in the gradual containment of the river through the creation of waterfronts and the building up of land. The pushing back of the riverbanks exploited two islands in the Thames at Southwark, which became part of the Roman town's built-up area. Despite the land reclamation, an extensive watery area bisected the town from east to west. Comparing Figures 44 and 45 shows the substantial areas reclaimed since the third century to provide land for buildings across London.

London Museum reopens at the Smithfield General Market building in 2026. Other highly recommended locations include the Mithraeum and the amphitheatre. These are both free to visit, although booking is required to visit the Mithraeum. The British Museum's Roman Britain gallery also includes artefacts from London.

Historical summary

London had informal origins as a focus for traders settling here to exploit the port on the riverbank during the decade after the conquest of south-eastern Britain (43 CE). It was probably already a significant location during the Iron Age, however, since the islands in the Thames at Southwark provided the fording point closest to the mouth of the Thames. The Roman-period name *Londinium* is of uncertain origin but probably refers to a characteristic of the river. Early in the Roman period, a bridge was built over the Thames, replacing an earlier ford. From the earliest phase of the conquest, the riverbank also provided a convenient site for unloading ships. In 60 CE, this fledgling settlement of traders was sacked and burnt by the followers of Boudica.

Refounded swiftly after this uprising, the port was used as a base to disembark soldiers brought in to punish the peoples from north of the Thames who had rebelled against Roman rule. The first forum and the amphitheatre were built during the 70s or 80s. Substantial groundworks during the centuries of occupation created waterfronts to restrain the flow of the multiple courses of the Thames and to form dry areas for buildings. During the early second century an imposing new forum replaced the earlier forum. London had become the largest and most important town in Britain by this time. A circuit of walls constructed in the third century enclosed an area larger than at any other town in Britain.

The port's significance declined during the third century. In the final decade of the third century, however, London served as the political centre for the usurper emperors Carausius and Allectus when they broke away from the Roman empire. During the 360s CE, the town featured prominently in the campaigns of the Roman general Theodosius to restore order, retaining significance until the early fifth century, after which the walled town was abandoned.

The rediscovery of Roman London

Interest in the city's Roman past increased during the early seventeenth century when medieval stories about its origin first came to be questioned.

These tales suggested a grand ancient origin for London, founded many centuries before the Romans came to Britain by a group of Trojans fleeing from the sacking of their city by the Greeks. London's famous city walls were supposedly constructed slightly later by the mythical King Lud: 'Lud's City' later became known as London. Lud's Gate was one of the medieval gateways through the city wall, commemorated by the modern street name Ludgate (Figure 45, A). This medieval gateway replaced one of the Roman gates of *Londinium*. During the sixteenth century, an ornamental sculpture of Lud and his two sons adorned the gate. Moved at the time of the demolition of the gate, it is displayed in the west porch of St Dunstan in the West on Fleet Street (B).

From the early seventeenth century, however, historians paid increasing attention to the classical texts mentioning London, and the medieval myth about Lud was dismissed. Roman finds uncovered during building work gradually resulted in an increased appreciation of the town's extent and character. During the nineteenth century, there was a growth in excavation and recording, and the rebuilding of London after the Second World War led to some remarkable discoveries. There have been far more excavations here than at any other Roman town in Britain, particularly during the past twenty-five years. Owing to the very deeply stratified character of much of London's Roman archaeology, many of these sites consist of keyhole excavations in complex sequences of buildings.

Origins

Iron Age finds from the islands in the Thames at Southwark indicate their use for settlement, which was probably seasonal. At this time the main route from north to south was across a ford that exploited these islands, and the Thames was also a significant communication and trade route. The place where London was to develop was at the edges of the territories of several Late Iron Age people. The rise to power of the great King Cunobelin, whose political base was at Colchester, suggests that in the decades before the Roman invasion this river crossing would have been under the control of his people. This is likely to have been where the invading military forces crossed the Thames in the summer of 43, on the march from Kent to Colchester.

London before Boudica

Before the uprising of 60 CE, there is no clear indication of the presence of the Roman military at London. The Roman author Tacitus tells us that London, unlike Colchester, was not a colony, although traders frequented it. Archaeological research indicates that the laying out of the town involved the construction of metalled roads, property boundaries and timber houses. There may have been several thousand people settled here by 60 CE. At this early date, the settlement lay mainly north of the river crossing, extending to the north island of Southwark. The first in a series of Roman bridges may have already spanned the Thames. Many timber strip houses lay alongside the streets. Although excavations have uncovered only small parts of this settlement, the early town to the north of the river probably had a regular layout of streets and properties.

One highly significant recent find is the 400 writing tablets unearthed during excavations in advance of the construction of the Bloomberg SPACE Building (Figure 45, C). These owe their preservation to the waterlogged conditions regularly encountered by archaeologists in the early Roman layers of the stratigraphy. One of the early tablets names two freedmen, ex-slaves who had been set up in business by their former masters and were residents of London.

The regular plan of the early town indicates a considerable investment in the urban facilities by wealthy settlers from overseas, aiming to exploit new trading opportunities. During this time the first waterfront was constructed on the north bank of the Thames. A gravelled marketplace was also established close to the junctions of Cornhill and Gracechurch Street, in the area later occupied by the forum. Building materials from sites to the north and south of the Thames suggest the presence of one or more bathhouses at this early date.

Boudica's uprising led to the sacking and burning of Colchester, London and Verulamium. Tacitus explains that everyone who could fled London before its destruction, but others did not escape the violence. Thick layers of burning have been found right across the area of the town.

Re-establishing London

London was swiftly refounded as the Romans re-established control of *Britannia*. The initial reconstruction focused on the infrastructure, including a fort, a more substantial timber waterfront, and an urban water supply. One of the Bloomberg letters records the ordering of twenty loads of provisions by a trader in London from another trader at Verulamium. This indicates that the market in both towns had been re-established by October 62. The port on the north bank of the Thames played a vital role in re-establishing the security of the province. The Bloomberg letters indicate that London acted as a trans-shipment centre for the troops used to quell the rebellious peoples north of the Thames, where the Boudican uprising was focused. The other significant activity at this time involved clearing the debris from the sacked town. The lines of the roads were re-established, and the residents who returned were housed in temporary insubstantial homes.

The provincial procurator Gaius Julius Alpinus Classicianus was based in London immediately after the uprising. Classicianus' grand burial monument, originally located in a cemetery east of the town, is displayed in the Roman Britain gallery at the British Museum. Of equestrian rank, Classicianus was one of many Gauls resident in London. Equestrians were the second rank of the Roman elite, below the senators. Following the uprising, London probably became the base of the provincial procurators.

Early Roman London

During the 70s and 80s CE, a significant phase in the construction of monumental buildings, including a forum, temples and amphitheatre, began. Since London was not a *civitas* capital, a council of wealthy traders may have taken control of urban administration and arranged for the construction of these buildings. There is no indication that the Roman military maintained a permanent fort here, although London's military connections were maintained throughout its history.

The first forum

The high ground of Cornhill in the centre of the town was the site of the first masonry forum, replacing the gravelled market area. Just west of the forum was a small classical temple. The remains of the forum have been uncovered on several occasions. Recent excavations have located the eastern end of the basilica at 85 Gracechurch Street (there are plans to display these remains for visitors). These two buildings were relatively small-scale compared to the temple of Claudius at Colchester. Few towns in Britain had a forum at this early date, however, and this building shows the ambitions of the urban council. The forum faced the recently constructed bridge that crossed the Thames.

A public bathhouse and a possible palace

Several other masonry buildings were constructed at this time, including the Huggin Hill bathhouse and a grand building identified by the excavators as the 'governor's palace'. The slight traces of the terrace that supported the bathhouse are visible at the southern end of Cleary Garden (Figure 45, D). Nothing is to be seen at the second of these sites, a substantial and ornate courtyard house that may have been the provincial governor's home. The idea that London may have been the centre of operations for both the provincial procurator and the governor suggests that the town had already become the prime urban centre in Britain.

The amphitheatre

Unknown until its discovery during excavations in 1988, the remains of London's amphitheatre are displayed at the Guildhall Art Gallery (E). Initially constructed in timber and earth on the north-western periphery of the early town, during the early second century the amphitheatre was reconstructed with stone retaining walls. The timber amphitheatre probably accommodated an audience of c. 7,000 people. The black line in the paving of the Guildhall Yard marks the original location of its outer wall. The archaeological remains of the excavated section of the amphitheatre are accessible in the Undercroft of the Guildhall Art Gallery. Visitors can view the foundations of the eastern area of the seating bank and the entrance. An audiovisual display provides information about the site.

Houses and people

During the late first and early second centuries, an extensive town developed north of the Thames and on the islands in the river at Southwark. Many of the houses were of timber and earth, but there is also evidence of substantial masonry buildings across much of the settled area. The masonry houses indicate the higher status of some of the occupants. At the other end of the scale were the enslaved people and low-status industrial workers and traders ubiquitous across London. A writing tablet found in the Walbrook Valley provides a fascinating insight into urban life. This deed of sale names an enslaved woman called Fortunata, bought by a man named Vegetus, who was himself enslaved. Since he paid 600 denarii to acquire Fortunata, a sum equivalent to two years' pay for a legionary soldier, Vegetus was clearly a wealthy man.

The largest town in Roman Britain

Because of its role in the provincial administration London may have been elevated to the status of colony during the second century. The reconstruction of the amphitheatre at this time included a masonry arena wall and stone-walled entrance passage, increasing the seating capacity to *c.* 10,000 people. The waterfront along the north bank of the Thames was also extended and supplemented to improve the port facilities. In addition, several substantial masonry buildings were constructed, including one on the north island in Southwark.

A new forum

The new forum was one of the largest such buildings in the north-western provinces, symbolizing the ambitions of this urban community. The basilica was so substantial that it took around two decades to complete. A single fragment of the foundations, located in the basement of Nicholson & Griffin hair salon, on the corner of Gracechurch Street and Leadenhall Market (Figure 45, F), is the only trace to be seen today. When I visited, the staff were happy to take me downstairs to explore these fragmentary remains. This masonry foundation supported the base of one of the arches in the basilica's arcade.

The fort on Cripplegate

London is unusual since, in addition to the early fort mentioned above, a second fort was constructed on the north-western periphery of the town in c. 120 CE. About 5 hectares in extent, this fort probably accommodated c. 1,000 soldiers and may only have been in use for one or two decades. The four gates had flanking towers, while excavation has uncovered several towers attached to the back of the defences. The remains of the masonry wall of the fort can be viewed at several locations along its western and northern defences. These sections of the fort walls were later incorporated into the Roman town wall, explaining their survival (below). The eastern and southern defences were demolished and levelled after the abandonment of the fort.

Locating these sections of the walls of the fort presents difficulties since it involves crossing several busy roads. The foundations of the western gate of the fort are preserved and displayed in an underground car park below London Wall (G). Formed from a double portal flanked by towers, the foundations of the north tower and the guard chamber of the gate are well-preserved. To visit these remains, you can join a guided walk around London which must be pre-booked with London Museum. All the other sections of the fort walls are accessible without prior arrangement.

The foundations of the fort's south-western corner and part of the southern part of the western defences can be viewed on the west side of Noble Street (H). This section includes one of the corner towers and an internal turret. Just to the north of the location of the (now disused) Museum of London, in a small area of parkland, is another section of the wall (I). This section of wall with its substantial bastions was thoroughly rebuilt in medieval times.

To the south of St Giles Cripplegate, a section of the wall overlooking a pond on the site of the former town ditch is visible (J). This section includes another medieval bastion. Although nothing is visible today, the north gate of the fort was close to this location. Just to the east, in St Alphage Gardens (K), is another section of the Roman wall heavily rebuilt in the medieval period. The foundations show that the fort wall was thickened when incorporated into the town wall.

Temples, houses and cemeteries

London grew to its maximum extent during the second century CE. Little is to be seen of the private houses. The fragmentary remains of two mosaics of probable second-century date are displayed at the Bank of England (L). Discovered during construction work in 1933 and 1934, these were lifted and redisplayed. One is at the foot of a staircase in the basement, while the other is on display at the Bank's museum. Other mosaics from across London can be viewed at the British Museum.

One sacred site has been excavated at Tabard Square on the south bank of the Thames (Figure 44). This consisted of two small Romano-Celtic temples in a *temenos* (sacred enclosure) just east of the Roman road that ran to Canterbury. An inscription found during the excavation mentions the dedicator of the temple, Tiberinius Celerianus, a Gallic trader resident in London.

The urban cemeteries developed on all sides of London, north and south of the Thames. Considerable research has been undertaken on the human remains recovered during excavations, which indicate the multicultural character of a population drawn from across the Roman empire. There is growing evidence for masonry mausolea, particularly on the roads running to the south, including the recent discovery of a remarkably well-preserved building in Southwark.

At St Bride's Church, in a burial site on the western edge of the Roman town, two fragments of tessellated floors are displayed in the crypt along with some artefacts discovered during the excavations here (Figure 45, M). Painted plaster indicates that the building had decorated walls. The proximity of burials to this building may suggest that this was a mausoleum. The display in St Bride's Church suggests that this was a place of worship.

The later town

London continued to prosper during the third century CE, although the population may have reduced. The falling water level in the Thames gradually required an extension of the waterfront wharves further into the river. The quantity of inter-regional trade declined, possibly undermining the economic role of the town. London nevertheless remained a highly significant political centre.

Walking the town walls

The landward section of the defences was constructed during the early third century, incorporating the west and north walls of the Cripplegate fort, which had been decommissioned by this time. As the riverside wall was only added in the late third century, this means that the north bank of the Thames was undefended for half a century. This reflected the continuing importance of the waterfront during these years, and implies that by the time the riverside wall was constructed, trade had declined.

The walls enclosed 133 hectares, the largest defended area for a Roman town in Britain. The building of the wall involved substantial engineering operations and must have disrupted town life for years. The masonry wall was backed by an earth rampart. At *c.* 2 metres wide at the base, the wall may have been up to 6 metres in elevation. Small turrets were built into the rear of the wall. Fronted with one or more ditches, the wall had at least six gateways.

Several fragmentary sections of this wall survive, and walking the entire length is a challenging but worthwhile experience that took me most of a day. You can follow the course of the town wall from the last surviving eastern section of the Cripplegate fort's wall (Figure 45, K), by walking east along London Wall, then Wormwood Street. A section of modern wall, possibly containing the heavily rebuilt remains of the town wall, forms the northern boundary of the churchyard of All Hallows on the Wall (N). The location of the former gateway at Bishopsgate is at the busy junction of Wormwood Street and Bishopsgate (O). Follow Camomile Street to the east to continue walking along the course of the inner side of the wall. The site of Roman and medieval Aldgate is marked by an information board describing its history (P).

The next surviving section of the wall is at a new development called The City Wall at Vine Street (Q). This new venture includes a gallery, museum and cafe. This centre offers an interpretation of the entire walled circuit of Roman London, featuring artefacts from the excavation at Vine Street. Walking south, the next surviving section of the wall is in the courtyard at 8–10 Cooper's Row, squashed between modern buildings (R). It is simplest to find this by visiting the section of the wall at Tower Hill Underground Station and tracing your way back north. This next and best-preserved surviving section to the south is in a public garden directly south of Tower Hill Underground Station (S). The Roman wall survives to a height of over 4 metres, to the level of the sentry walk (Figure 46). The wall was faced with coarse sandstone blocks with regular courses of tile at intervals to provide stability.

Two sections of the wall can be visited in the grounds of the Tower of London, although this requires the payment of an entry fee to this

Figure 46 *Photograph of the London city wall just south of Tower Hill Underground Station.* © *Richard Hingley.*

popular and busy tourist attraction. A short section of the surviving foundations of the town wall is displayed in the outer bailey just east of the main tower (Figure 45, T). A short distance to the south, again within the medieval bailey, a section of the riverside wall is displayed (U). This is the only fragment of the riverside wall visible today.

This riverside wall, which followed the north bank of the Thames, ran from the south-eastern corner of the defences almost as far east as Blackfriars Station before it joined the south-western corner of the landward wall. Its buried remains have been excavated and protected on three sites in Upper and Lower Thames Street, which once formed the foreshore of the Thames. Bridgegate was a medieval gate on the site of a Roman gate, located on the north–south road that crossed the Thames over the Roman bridge before climbing the hill towards the forum. The gate was close to the church of St Magnus the Martyr on Lower Thames Street.

Black Friars Lane follows the southern section of the western boundary formed by the landward wall quite closely as far north as

Ludgate Hill. This marks the approximate location of Ludgate, a Roman and medieval gate (A). From here, the original course of the outer face of the town defences can be followed by walking along Old Bailey as far as Newgate Street, the location of another of the Roman and medieval gates, Newgate (V).

Giltspur Street initially follows the line of the defences. The northwest corner once lay close to this point, but its course has been lost under modern development. To return to the course of the defences, find your way to the London City Presbyterian Church on Aldersgate Street, just north of the site of the final Roman gate at Aldersgate (W). Excavations at this site suggest that this gateway was a late Roman addition to the circuit.

Turn back down St Martin's Le Grand, and Gresham Street (to your left) takes you back to the area of the south-western corner of the Cripplegate fort (H). At this location, discussed above, the relationship between the corner of the fort wall and the town wall was revealed through excavation and is visible. The ruined foundations of the wall clearly abut the corner of the fort, indicating that the fort wall is the earlier. The fort's western and eastern defences were reused and widened to form the next section of the town wall.

The Billingsgate bathhouse

Excavations have revealed several bathhouses on both sides of the River Thames. The well-preserved remains of the Billingsgate bathhouse, located in the basement of 101 Lower Thames Street, can be visited (X). Advanced booking is required. Discovered in 1848, additional excavations from 1967 to 1970 provided information on the building's chronology. The displayed remains include three connected rooms: a cold room entered from the north, leading to warm and hot rooms to either side of the entrance passageway. Hypocausts heated the warm and hot rooms. Since this building was attached to a house, it would probably have been a private bathing facility for a wealthy family and their clients. Traces of earlier timber-and-earth buildings were found at this site.

The Mithraeum

The temple of Mithras, located in the Walbrook Valley and displayed in the basement of the Bloomberg SPACE Building, was one of many small temples and shrines constructed by the occupants of London (C). The Walbrook was one of several rivers that bisected Roman London, running from the north into the Thames. The city's development from medieval times has gradually built over and obscured its course. Today, the Walbrook flows underground. Part of its former course is commemorated by the street named Walbrook, running just east of Bloomberg SPACE. A modern sculpture called 'Forgotten Streams' to the south of Bloomberg Arcade draws upon the idea of the former location of the Walbrook, a sacred river. Several temples, including the Mithraeum, lay along its banks.

The discovery of the Mithraeum in 1952 had an immense impact on the population of London and helped promote public interest in the Roman past. Its surviving foundations have been moved twice since it was excavated. In 2010, Bloomberg embarked on developing a new site for its European headquarters, including an ambitious redisplay of the remains of the Mithraeum. Finds from the recent excavation and artworks inspired by the history of this part of London are displayed at Bloomberg SPACE. The venue is free to visit, although advance booking is required.

The foundations of the Mithraeum are displayed accompanied by an audiovisual presentation, which gives the visitor a sense of the original structure and the worship of Mithras (Figure 47). The Mithraeum has the standard form of a small rectangular aisled

Figure 47 *Photograph of the London Mithraeum. Photo by Sam Mellish. © https://www.gettyimages.co.uk/detail/news-photo/atmospheric-lighting-helps-display-the-reconstructed-mid-news-photo/887666158?adppopup=true.*

building, orientated approximately east–west with an apse at the western end. The temple's entrance was to the east, close to where the visitor enters an underground room where the remains are displayed. The interior was divided into three sections by low sleeper walls supporting seven pairs of columns. The floor of the aisles was raised to a higher level than that of the nave. Only a small group of worshippers would have been able to gather in this temple at one time. An inscription from the temple records a man called Ulpius Silvanus, a veteran of the Second Augustan Legion, who probably paid for it to be built.

An imperial palace of the riverfront

A more substantial sacred site was constructed on the north bank of the Thames close to the Millennium Bridge, just north of the City of London School (Figure 44). It consisted of two very substantial classical masonry temple buildings, but no traces of these buildings are visible today. The temples are of particular significance because of the dates obtained from tree ring analysis of timbers included in the foundations – these dates suggest that the temples were constructed during the reigns of Carausius and Allectus (286–96 CE).

The emperor Maximian made Carausius a naval commander to rid the Channel of pirates, but Carausius later rebelled by seizing power over Roman territories of Britain and the near Continent. Allectus succeeded him. Although we know little about these twin temples, they may have formed part of an imperial palace constructed by the two usurpers. London formed the prime target for the emperor Constantius I's military action when he defeated Allectus and returned Britain to the rule of Rome. The role of London in the activities of Carausius, Allectus and Constantius indicates the town's continued significance during the late third century.

The decline of London

Although it retained its political significance, London, like many towns, gradually declined during the fourth century. It served as a base for Theodosius, a senior Roman general who later became emperor, in his military campaigns to restore order in Britain during 367–8 CE. We also know that in the early fourth century London had a bishop.

While the scale of trade and industry continued to decline, within the walled town and on the islands in Southwark occupation continued. Although many public buildings, including the forum, ceased to be used, the bridge over the Thames was maintained. The amphitheatre probably continued in use into the middle of the fourth century.

To strengthen the defences, bastions were added to the outer face of the town wall to the east and north-west of its circuit. The foundations of one of the eastern bastions are visible at the Vine Street interpretation centre (Figure 45, Q). Some of the finds from burials and areas where people lived and worked indicate that on the periphery of London occupation continued during the fifth century. The walled town was abandoned as the increasingly unstable condition of the masonry buildings made it dangerous to visit.

When the cathedral of St Paul's was established, probably in 604, it was deliberately sited in the western part of the walled circuit, drawing on the history and status of the Roman town. Although the town walls were reused after 886, when a burgh was founded in London under King Alfred, by this stage the lines of many of the Roman streets had been lost. Few buildings will have remained as more than grass-covered ruins.

Further reading

A vital source of information is the Museum of London Archaeology Roman Map (2011). This well-designed map features most of the sites mentioned below and several archaeological sites not included in this chapter. As two additional archaeological sites have been made available since the map was published, however, it is not entirely up to date. Two recent books including detailed information are Hingley (2018) and Perring (2022). These accounts take different approaches to the archaeology and history of Roman London. Tibbs (2024) gives an accessible account of the Roman town. For relevant web links, see the website connected with this book.

16

Silchester: Place in the Woods

Introduction

This Roman town is significant both because of the series of excavations undertaken since the Victorian period and the excellent preservation of the town walls and amphitheatre. As the remains are situated mainly in open agricultural land, aerial photography, excavation and geophysical survey have revealed much of the urban plan (Figure 48). Since the 1970s a fresh programme of excavation has revealed considerable information about ancient Silchester. In the decades before the Roman invasion this was an *oppidum* of some consequence, and probably became the capital of a pro-Roman king after the conquest in 43 CE. After the death of its ruler, Silchester became the *civitas* capital of a people known as the Atrebates. The modern excavations provide considerable insight into the early phases of this urban settlement, while the walls and amphitheatre are impressive features to explore.

Figure 48 *Map of ancient Silchester. The Iron Age earthworks that underlie the town are shown in grey (after Creighton and Fry 2016: Figure 13.8, and Fulford 2021: Figure 1.24). Drawn by Christina Unwin.*

Main visible archaeological features with grading

	Star rating
Amphitheatre	***
Town walls	***

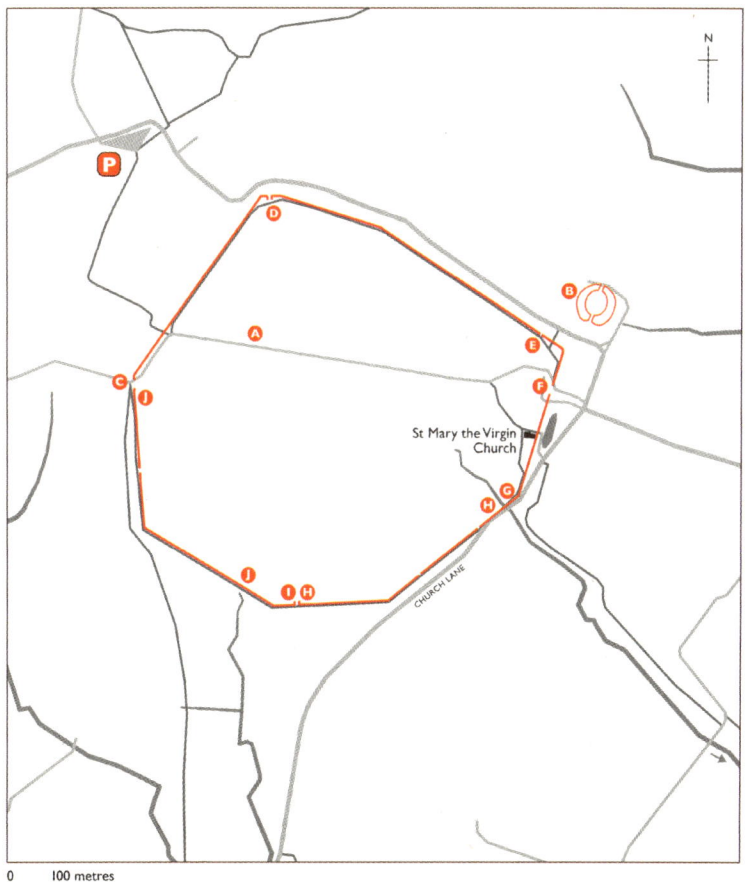

Figure 49 *Map of modern Silchester with locations mentioned in the text marked. Drawn by Christina Unwin using information from Google Maps.*

Getting there

As Silchester is a rural site, it is best to visit by car or bicycle. The surrounding roads are not usually busy, and this is a popular cycling area. The site can be reached by National Cycling Route 23 from Reading to Basingstoke, known as the Calleva Way. The public car park for the site is on Wall Lane, a short distance to the north-west (Figure 49).

Information boards at the car park provide the background to the *oppidum* and Roman town. From here, the town walls are a short walk. No shops or services are available onsite, so take any food and drink.

Exploring ancient Silchester

Since there are no places to refuel, walking around Silchester requires some stamina. The information boards to guide your visit are up to date and it took me 4 hours to explore the entire site. Having walked from the car park to the site, you can walk around the defensive circuit, visit the amphitheatre on the way, and make your way back to the car park. If you have less time available, the southern section of the defences is the best preserved, and the amphitheatre is also well-displayed. You could then walk back along the public right of way that crosses the walled area from east to west. English Heritage provides an audio tour of Silchester, which is also a helpful source of information. The Silchester Gallery at Reading Museum includes the finds from the excavations.

Historical summary

The *oppidum* and succeeding Roman town are in an unusual location. While most of the towns in this book were close to rivers, Silchester is on a raised plain some way from one. There were several springs, however, including one that supplied the early Roman bathhouse. The first significant occupation here dates to the later first century BCE, although Silchester may have been a meeting place before this. Some decades before the Roman invasion, a settlement started developing as people moved here. This *oppidum* differed from others addressed in this book (e.g. Colchester and Verulamium) since it was a significant centre of occupation, not just a meeting place, before the invasion.

During the invasion, the ruler of Silchester probably submitted to Rome and was allowed to continue as king. We do not know the name of this individual, but Silchester may have been in one of the territories given to Togidubnus, who probably ruled from Chichester. Togidubnus may, therefore, have had at least two capitals and perhaps a relative ruled at Silchester on his behalf. During the 50s CE, a significant programme of building works started with the construction of a bathhouse, and the emperor Nero played a significant role in the history of Silchester at this time. At some point in the later first century, Silchester was redesignated the *civitas* capital of the Atrebates, with a forum and street system. The more substantial stone forum dated to the early second century. During the late second century the defences were constructed as an earth bank with two external ditches, and in the third century the rampart was supplemented with a substantial stone wall. The town continued to prosper into the fourth century before being abandoned during the fifth.

The rediscovery of ancient Silchester

Silchester was known to be a Roman town from the sixteenth century. A remarkably early plan of the remains was produced in 1741, and excavations began during the succeeding century. During the final decade of the nineteenth century substantial excavations were conducted, uncovering much of the urban plan and exploring the defences. From the 1970s to the present, modern excavations at the site have been directed by Professor Mike Fulford (Figure 50). These have provided detailed knowledge of site chronology and information about some of the main buildings.

The *oppidum*

This *oppidum* was called *Calleva*, a shortened form of which appears on some Iron Age coins. *Calleva* probably meant 'Place in the woods'

Figure 50 *Aerial photograph of Silchester under excavation in 2018. The area of the excavation is visible in the centre of the photograph and some of the streets of the Roman town are also showing as crop marks.* © https://www.gettyimages.co.uk/detail/news-photo/excavations-at-calleva-roman-town-silchester-hampshire-2018-news-photo/1447163415?adppopup=true.

in the Celtic language, referring to the earliest period of occupation since, as environmental work on archaeological deposits indicates, the tree cover was cleared swiftly. This *oppidum* probably originated as a meeting place for surrounding people during the first century BCE, and the first period of permanent occupation may have dated to *c.* 20 BCE. Some Iron Age coins of a king called Eppillus were struck with 'CALLE', an abbreviated version of *Calleva*. The king named probably ruled from this *oppidum*, but his coins predated the Claudian invasion by some time. Eppillus may have been succeeded by another king called Verica. The excavations indicate that a significant settlement developed here in the decades before the Roman invasion.

A circuit of defences named the 'Inner Earthwork' (Figure 48) defined the *oppidum*. Although there was also an outer series of earthworks, centuries of agriculture have left little trace, and these various banks and ditches require a practised eye to identify them. The Inner Earthwork contained a settlement comprising round buildings and at least some rectangular timber houses. The recent excavations in Insula IX uncovered these houses (Figure 49, A). Both this excavation and separate investigation of the layers of occupation beneath the Roman forum have revealed copious information about the *oppidum*, including evidence for large-scale importation of amphorae and fine ware pottery from the Continent. Unlike the other Iron Age *oppida* in southern Britain (Chichester, Colchester and Verulamium), Silchester was occupied by a substantial settled community. No traces of the *oppidum* are visible today, although there is some description of Iron Age Silchester on the information boards.

The early Roman settlement

Silchester was probably bypassed by the Roman military forces in 43 CE. Finds of military equipment during the recent excavations indicate that there were soldiers stationed here, but probably in relatively small numbers and housed in buildings in the *oppidum*. The settlement retained its Iron Age character into the early Roman period, with timber buildings, including some roundhouses. The recent excavations at the bathhouse indicate that the first phase of this building may date to the reign of the emperor Claudius (before 54 CE). This dating would make this bathhouse one of the earliest public buildings in Britain. The bathhouse was clearly in operation before the end of Nero's reign.

Indeed, this emperor probably played a significant role in the development of the early Roman settlement. Tiles with stamps bearing Nero's name, produced at a recently excavated tilery a few kilometres south of the town, have been found at Silchester. The most likely explanation for the tilery is that Nero favoured the ruler at Silchester for his support during the uprising led by Boudica (in 60 CE) and subsequently funded the construction of a monumental building (yet to be identified) at his capital. A substantial timber-built courtyard building at the centre of the developing town may have been the first in a sequence of fora. The amphitheatre to the east of the town was constructed at the same time. The temples in the eastern part of the town may have developed from a Late Iron Age ritual site or even a high-status burial of a ruler, as at Gosbecks (Colchester) and Folly Lane (Verulamium), but this is uncertain.

The amphitheatre

Although the highly impressive earthworks of the amphitheatre (Figure 49, B) are partly covered by trees, they effectively convey the scale of such structures, which were common in the towns of Roman Britain. This example has been very fully excavated, and more is known about the construction sequence here than at any of the urban amphitheatres in Britain. The first phase had a circular arena *c.* 43 metres in diameter. This was surrounded by a timber revetment entered through two opposing entrances, with an external seating bank.

When the amphitheatre was modified during the early second century, the arena was refashioned in the oval shape more typical of such structures. A new timber wall retained a massive seating bank that stood 6 metres above the arena floor. This bank was formed from earth and clay excavated from the arena. The modified structure could accommodate between 3,500 and 7,000 people, large enough to hold most of the town's population. During the third century, the arena wall was rebuilt in stone. Two stone recesses constructed to the east and west may have served as shrines or to house performers and the animals used in gladiatorial combat. Such displays were probably relatively rare and the amphitheatre's prime function was to hold community meetings and celebrate religious festivals.

The *civitas* capital

When its ruler died, the *oppidum* and its territory became part of the province of *Britannia*. It is unclear when this happened, although the construction of a new timber forum *c.* 78 CE may provide a hint. The laying out of the street grid may also date to this time. This new grid occasioned a complete reorganization of the layout of the *oppidum* as the town was established. Several buildings, including the bathhouse, lay on the earlier Iron Age alignment of tracks within the *oppidum*. By the time of the construction of the new streets, the Iron Age Inner Earthwork was out of use, and the settlement spread further to the east across the line of the earlier bank and ditch.

The new timber forum may have replaced an earlier predecessor. This building was, in turn, replaced by a masonry forum during the early second century. A grand courtyard building with substantial basilica, it underwent several stages of modification during its use. One famous find displayed in the Reading Museum is the Silchester Eagle. Probably once part of a large statue group sited in the forum, this bronze sculpture inspired Rosemary Sutcliff's 1954 novel *The Eagle of the Ninth*.

Perhaps because of flooding, the early bathhouse was demolished and replaced by a new one. Because of aerial photography, geophysical surveys and excavation campaigns since the late nineteenth century, the plan of Silchester is very well known. The locations of several additional public buildings and many stone houses are recorded, some with mosaic floors. Since these archaeological remains lie below the fields, however, they are not discussed further.

Walking the walls

Towards the end of the second century CE, a defensive circuit consisting of an earth bank with two external ditches was constructed. The area it enclosed was *c.* 43 hectares. Although this only coincided with the Iron Age Inner Earthwork along its south-western length, the new ramparts defined a polygonal area broadly comparable in shape to the earlier enclosure (but elongated to the east). The rampart stood *c.* 4 metres high, topped with a timber palisade. During the late third century, a masonry wall, mainly flint but with stone bonding courses, was added to the front of the earth rampart. This is one of the most impressive surviving Roman town walls in Britain. The best-preserved section, close to the south gate, stands at a height of just over 4 metres.

The east and west gates had double carriageways flanked by towers and may have been built prior to construction of the earthwork defences. In their initial form the north and south gates were probably of timber and only replaced in stone later. The south-east gate was also of timber in its initial form. The later Roman gates were all of stone. The north-east (amphitheatre) gate belongs only to the late-third-century stone wall phase of the defences and had no earlier predecessor, and the same is thought likely to be the case with the south-west gate.

This massive wall amazed medieval people, and at this time stories often attributed the monumental remains of Roman buildings to giants. A sixteenth-century account mentions a break in the walls to the south that the local people called 'Onion hole'. Local people suggested that this hole in the wall was the home of a giant of that name who once inhabited this place. Such local myths to explain monumental features have otherwise rarely come down to us.

I began my exploration at the site of the west gate, a double portal gateway uncovered by Victorian excavators (Figure 49, C). The road west from this gate took travellers towards Cirencester. From here,

I followed the top of the very substantial rampart around the northern circuit of the defences until reaching the north gate, which survives as a break in the rampart and wall (D). This gate gave access to a road running north to the Roman settlement at Dorchester on Thames. Walking further east brings you to the site of a smaller gate known as the Amphitheatre Gate (E). From this point, the remains of the rampart are within private gardens, but the location of the east gate itself is close to the farm track leading west from Church Lane, a public right of way (F). This gate gave access to the road running eastward towards London. The course of the town wall can be joined again by walking further south on Church Lane and following a footpath which leaves the course of the road just beyond the Church of St Mary the Virgin (G).

Beyond this point, the rampart, including the site of another small south-eastern gate, can be followed by walking outside its course to examine the masonry wall. You can also walk along the top of this section of the defences. Much of the southern section of the defensive circuit is remarkably well-preserved (H–H). A break in the rampart marks the site of the south gate, which was a single carriage gate (I). The road south from Silchester took travellers to Winchester and Chichester. Beyond this point, the defences run through woodland but are well-preserved as far as the location of the west gate (J–J). Traces of an external ditch are visible in this wooded area.

Beyond the walls

Several cemeteries lay beyond the rampart. Substantial geophysical survey work has located the likely location and extent of these burial grounds, but there is nothing to see on the ground, and there have been no excavations. Many inscriptions have been found during excavations, although these are mainly fragmentary. One well-preserved example commemorating Flavia Victorina was commissioned by her husband,

Titus Tammonius Vitalis. This tombstone was found in 1577 and presented to Lord Burleigh, Queen Elizabeth's Chancellor.

The end of Silchester

Information from excavations indicate that people were still living here during the late fourth century, and finds from the bathhouse suggest that it may still have been in use. Victorian excavations of a well in Insula IX produced an Ogham stone, now in Reading Museum. This inscription, which in the Celtic Irish language was known as 'ogham', reused part of a Roman column. Although this inscription cannot be entirely deciphered, it mentions a man called Tebicatos. The stone may have been deposited in the well when the neighbouring house was abandoned, perhaps during the early fifth century. After this time, there is little to indicate further occupation until the eleventh century, when there was a small medieval settlement, probably in the area close to the church. The walled area of the town was never substantially reoccupied.

Further reading

Iron Age and Roman Silchester are well-served by publications detailing recent excavations and research. Fulford (2021) provides an accessible account. A series of reports report the results of the excavations. These demonstrate several contrasting interpretations of the early phases of the site and include Fulford and Timby (2000), Fulford et al. (2018), Fulford et al. (2020) and Fulford (2022). Creighton and Fry (2016) address the town and its surroundings, including recent geophysical surveys. For the tale of Onion the giant, see Hingley (2008: 183–4). The Flavia Victorina tombstone is RIB 87. For relevant web links, see the website connected with this book.

17

Verulamium: Dwelling of the Very Greatest One

Introduction

Verulamium is one of Britain's most significant sites from Late Iron Age and Roman times. The extensive excavation of this site, much of which lies in open parkland and fields, has provided a detailed understanding of the Iron Age origins of the Roman town, and the archaeology can be explored on the ground as well as in the collections of the Verulamium Museum. Key features are the mosaics in the museum, the theatre, and the substantial town walls.

Main visible archaeological features with grading

	Star rating
Theatre	***
Townhouses and shops	**
Town walls	**
Museum	***

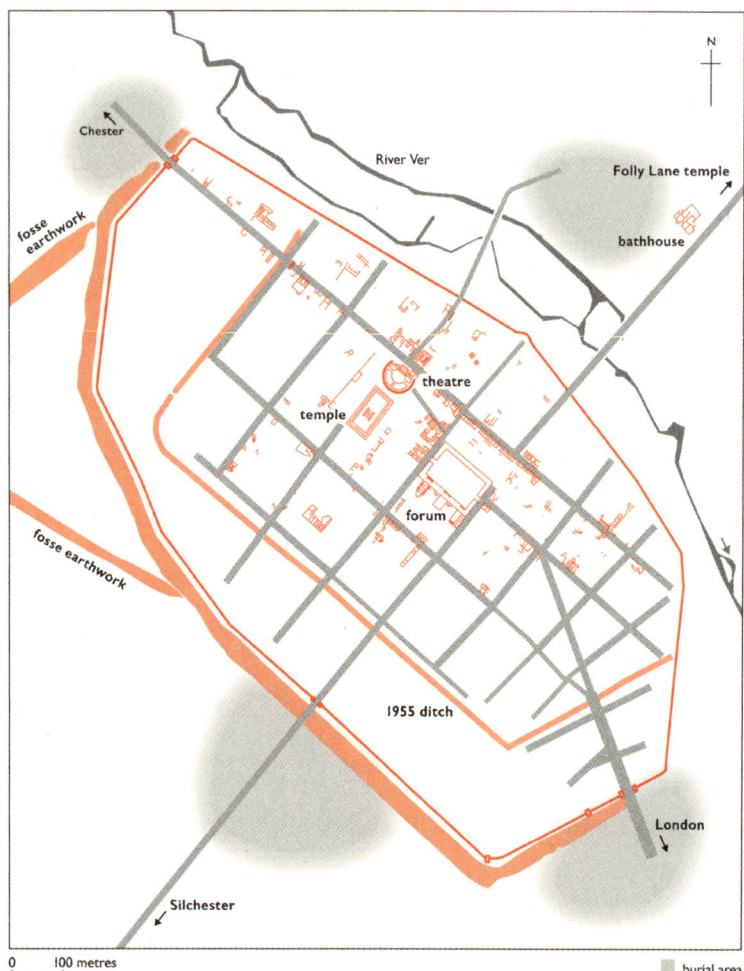

Figure 51 *Map of Roman Verulamium (after Wacher 1995: Figure 99, and Lockyear and Shlasko 2017: Figure 3). Drawn by Christina Unwin.*

Getting there

There is a public car park close to the Verulamium Museum. Roman Verulamium lies to the west of the city centre of St Albans, and it is a pleasant 20-minute walk from the cathedral to the museum, which is

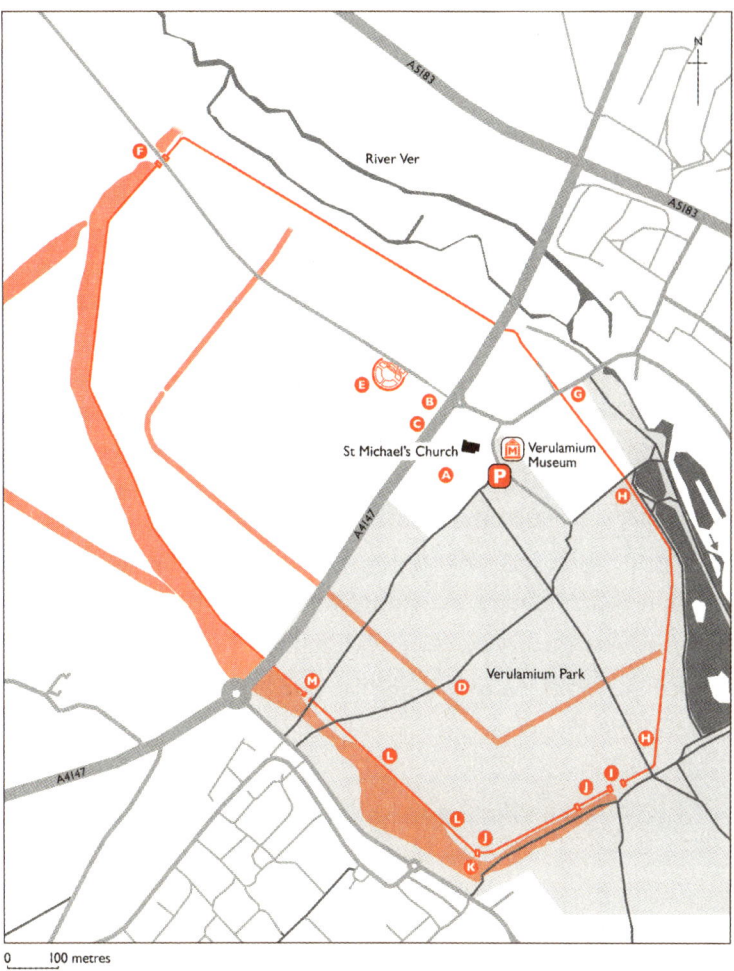

Figure 52 *Map of modern Verulamium with locations mentioned in the text marked. Drawn by Christina Unwin using information from Google Maps.*

inside the Roman walls. St Albans has a railway station and a bus station. Around half of the Roman town lies in Verulamium Park. The northern part of the site lies in the open fields of Gorhambury Estate, which permits public access to the theatre.

Exploring ancient Verulamium

It is best to explore Verulamium on foot. There is a cafe in Verulamium Park and plenty of places to eat and stay in St Albans. Walking gives access to the most significant remains, and much of the southern area of the town is in the park. There is a lot to see, and it took me 5 hours to explore all the accessible remains and visit the museum. There is an entrance fee to visit the Verulamium Museum and the Roman theatre.

Historical summary

During the later first century BCE, a significant Iron Age meeting place emerged alongside a marshy crossing place over the River Ver. During the early first century CE, this developed into an *oppidum* characterized by burial areas and at least one ritual enclosure. A series of earthworks (or dykes) on the hillslopes above the valley bottom defined this focus of activity. Evidence for a battle to the south-west of the river crossing could identify Verulamium as the location of the *oppidum* where, according to his account of the campaign in Britain in 54 BCE, Julius Caesar defeated Cassivellaunus, the leader of the resistance. Verulamium was also one of the two *oppida* controlled by the powerful Late Iron Age king Cunobelin during the decades before the Roman invasion.

When the emperor Claudius led his successful invasion of southern Britain in 43 CE, Verulamium may have surrendered peacefully to the Roman military. The evidence for this is the burial of a king who probably ruled from the *oppidum* during the conquest period before his death in *c.* 55. Verulamium swiftly developed into a significant town, with the first Roman-style buildings pre-dating the uprising of Boudica in 60. Tacitus tells us that when it was sacked by Boudica's followers, Verulamium was a *municipium*. This term means that this former *oppidum* was, in Roman terms, a town second in status only to the colony at Colchester.

Verulamium was quickly re-established in the wake of the uprising, and an ornate forum was built in *c.* 80. The street system and the first circuit of defences surrounding Verulamium may have originated from this time. The second-century town featured impressive public buildings, including a theatre and opulent houses with numerous mosaics. During the mid-third century, the Christian saint Alban was martyred here, an event that had a significant impact on the later history of the town. A substantial set of defences was constructed during the third century, enclosing an area larger than the earlier earthworks, and occupation continued until the early fifth century. During the late Roman period, or in the succeeding two centuries, a significant site of pilgrimage developed at the site of Alban's martyrdom. This eventually became the cathedral of the city of St Albans, less than 1 kilometre north-east of Verulamium.

The rediscovery of ancient Verulamium

The survival of the town walls and chance discoveries of Roman inscriptions fascinated the monks at the abbey of St Albans and prompted the earliest investigation of the buried remains in *c.* 1000 when Abbot Eadmar, having instructed men to dig for ruined temples, unearthed altars and statues. The remains of Verulamium were also described and surveyed by antiquaries during the sixteenth to eighteenth centuries. A new phase of interest in the site began after the discovery of the theatre in 1847 and its excavation under Kathleen Kenyon during the 1930s. Large-scale excavations directed by Mortimer Wheeler and Tessa Wheeler in the early 1930s uncovered information about the Iron Age *oppidum* and the Roman town. Sheppard Frere directed additional significant excavations in the

1950s. The most important discovery since is that of the Folly Lane burial, excavated by Rosalind Niblett in the 1990s. More recent work has included a substantial geophysical survey that has elucidated the layout of the town, its roads, buildings and defences.

The *oppidum*

Before the late first century BCE there is little to indicate activity at or around the crossing over the River Ver at Verulamium. There is a strong suspicion, however, that several of the *oppida* in southern Britain originated as meeting places for the peoples of the surrounding area before the construction of the dykes, and high-status burial and ritual spaces. The original name for the *oppidum* and Roman town may have been 'Verolamium', which probably means 'the dwelling of Verolamos'. This use of the personal name Verolamos – thought to mean 'very greatest one' – presumably references an early leader of the people associated with Verulamium.

It is informative that some Late Iron Age coins were struck with the abbreviated term 'VER', referring to the *oppidum*. These probably date to *c.* 20 BCE (below), and indicate that the significance of this location goes back before the date of the coins, despite the absence of any substantial archaeological discoveries that date to before the latter part of the first century BCE. One possibility is that Verulamium was the location of the *oppidum* of Cassivellaunus, which Julius Caesar overthrew in 54 BCE.

Metal detector finds from a hill about 1½ kilometres south-west of the river crossing, close to Prae Wood, included many Roman sling bullets. Although these bullets indicate a battle site, they cannot be dated more accurately than to the later first century BCE or first century CE. It is known from Caesar's narrative of his invasion of

Britain, however, that the *oppidum* of Cassivellaunus was located north of the Thames and was a defended place where people gathered at times of trouble. Caesar wrote that his forces overwhelmed this *oppidum*, thereby ending the conflict with the Britons, before sailing home to Rome with booty and captives. The extensive dyke system defining the river valley at Verulamium is not closely dated, and some of the linear banks and ditches could date to the time of Cassivellaunus. Where dating is available, however, they are later. It is unclear when this battle occurred and two other possible dates are considered in a footnote.[1]

Verulamium entered recorded history c. 20 BCE, linked to Tasciovanus, a king mentioned in classical texts. Coins of this ruler were struck to include his name and the abbreviation 'VER'. His successor, king Cunobelin, also had coins struck with the same abbreviation. Cunobelin, mentioned by several classical authors, was the most powerful leader in Britain in the years leading up to the Roman invasion. He was probably the king of the Catuvellauni, and we know that Verulamium became the capital of this people during the Roman period. The Catuvellauni were the most powerful of the pre-Roman peoples of southern Britain. Some of the coins of both Tasciovanus and Cunobelin included the abbreviated name of *Camulodunum*, indicating that these kings controlled both *oppida*. The death of Cunobelin appears to have been one of the factors leading to the invasion of Claudius in 43 CE.

---

[1] Another possible context for this battle is the Roman invasion of southern Britain under Claudius in 43. Indications that Verulamium submitted peacefully around this time (below) makes this date less likely, however. The third option is that the battle might have occurred in 60 when Boudica's followers sacked Verulamium. There is no record of a battle here at this time, meaning that Verulamium may well have been the *oppidum* mentioned by Caesar. Another possible location for Cassivellaunus' *oppidum* is at Colchester. In truth, we may never know the location of the *oppidum* stormed by Caesar's troops.

Dykes and rituals

Very little of the Late Iron Age *oppidum* is visible on the ground. Some of the Iron Age dykes still exist, but are mostly on private land. A substantial section of the Beech Bottom dyke can be visited (at NGR TL 157 093) by car. The dyke system surrounding Verulamium delineates the valley bottom, and appears less defensive than the dykes at Colchester and Silchester. Although there is little indication of contemporary settlement, there may have been several small farms on the hillslopes near the dykes. The most notable evidence from the *oppidum* is a series of burials, including a significant cemetery at King Harry Lane, just to the south-west of where the town was to develop. Although few people were living at Verulamium, the deceased from the surrounding territory were interred here. A ditched enclosure in the valley bottom under the site of the later forum has been partially excavated. Known as the 'Central Enclosure' (Figure 52, A), it has produced evidence for metalworking and coin production. The museum contains an informative display of finds indicating Late Iron Age activity.

The burial of an unknown king

Although there are some military finds, there is nothing directly to indicate that Roman forces attacked the community here in 43. Perhaps soldiers were accommodated in houses within the early settlement, as at Silchester. A highly significant discovery made during the 1990s suggests that the leader at Verulamium surrendered directly to Claudius and became a pro-Roman ruler.

In *c*. 55, a high-ranking individual was buried in a grand ceremony on the hillside north-east of the *oppidum*. This burial site, known as Folly Lane, was located outside the area shown on the maps, near St Albans City Hospital, and is believed have contained the remains of an Iron Age ruler. This king was probably a descendant of Cunobelin, potentially his son Adminius. He was cremated on a pyre with immense quantities of possessions, highlighting his elevated status as ruler. The remains from this cremation pyre fell into a large pit inside a substantial rectangular enclosure. The dating of the burial suggests that this unnamed king ruled his people for a decade following the Roman invasion.

During the late first century, a Romano-Celtic temple was built directly on top of the Folly Lane burial site. The enclosure around the burial became the *temenos* of this temple. Worship at the temple focused on the cult of the last king of Verulamium. The finds from Folly Lane are displayed and interpreted in Verulamium Museum.

The early Roman settlement

When this ruler died, the town and surrounding area were annexed to form part of the expanding province of *Britannia*. Initially, very little changed at the *oppidum*, although a forum may have been constructed before 60 CE when the followers of Boudica attacked the settlement during their uprising against Roman rule.

Verulamium was a highly significant settlement before its destruction. Although the early settlement in the valley probably included, at most, only a few hundred people, Tacitus states in his account of the uprising that Verulamium was a *municipium*. The title, which will have been granted to the community by the emperors Claudius or Nero, indicates the high standing of the dynasty ruling here. Granting this status to a community meant that its magistrates became Roman citizens. Verulamium was the only town in Britain that was designated as a *municipium*, and its high status may explain why the *oppidum* was targeted by Boudica's followers.

Like Colchester and London, at the time of the uprising the settlement had no defensive bank and ditch. Timber buildings within the developing settlement indicate people settling in the valley close to the Central Enclosure. These buildings included a range of shops built in the Roman manner (Figure 52, B). The location of this structure, consisting of a range of rooms fronted by a colonnade, is marked out for visitors to see. The shops were burnt down, probably in 60, and rebuilt later in the first century. Fragmentary walls found sealed in layers below the later forum may also indicate that Verulamium already had a forum before the uprising (A).

Although traces of burning have been found across the central area of the town, the burnt deposits are less extensive than in Colchester and London. A writing tablet from London indicates that by 62 a trader from Verulamium provided twenty loads of provisions to another trader based in London. The urban infrastructure at Verulamium may not have been re-established for over a decade, however.

The *municipium*

By the early 80s, the settlement had changed from an *oppidum* to a Roman town. It had a forum and a defensive circuit of banks and ditches. An inscription mentioning the provincial governor Agricola and the emperor Vespasian dates the construction of the substantial forum to 79–81. The museum displays the few fragments that survive from this inscription. Illustrating the high status of this urban community, this forum was one of the most ornate examples of such buildings in Britain. The forum lies under St Michael's Church and the surrounding area as far as the school playing fields. Some of the walls of the basilica (which is buried underneath) are marked out on the pavement in front of the museum.

The street system in the central area of Verulamium was probably created around this time. Several other structures, including a market hall, bathhouses and temples, are also believed to have been contemporary. A bank and ditch, referred to in the literature as the '1955 ditch', after its discovery by Sheppard Frere in that year, surrounded the early town (Figure 51). This substantial earthwork measures c. 3 metres deep and 6 metres wide. It enclosed an area of 48 hectares, including the early settlement's core. The excavations identified the course of this boundary, and a geophysical survey confirmed its path. An internal rampart would have accompanied the ditch. The marshy valley floor next to the River Ver comprised the north-western part of the defensive circuit. This ditched circuit significantly influenced the layout of the later town. Two triumphal arches were constructed during the third century at the points where Watling Street crossed the enclosure formed by the 1955 ditch.

Excavations have uncovered the sites of several public buildings, although these are not visible today, and the remains of several houses. The earlier buildings, as at other towns in Britain, were built of timber and earth. There is evidence that a serious fire, known to archaeologists as the 'Antonine Fire', engulfed much of the central area of Verulamium c. 150. Burnt deposits found during the excavations illustrate the extent of this fire, and the recent geophysical survey has provided additional indications of the conflagration. This fire may be one of the reasons that the wealthier townspeople began building their houses in stone. Many of the houses were constructed in masonry in the towns in Britain after this time, perhaps because of the fire risks posed by timber houses.

Townhouses

Two of the townhouses are displayed, and the museum also contains the impressive mosaics and wall plaster from several townhouses. These buildings and their fittings draw attention to the ruling elite of the urban settlement. Close to the early shops mentioned above, the foundations of part of a townhouse of second-century date are displayed, including the remains of a hypocaust and several rooms (Figure 52, C). This was one of many such buildings in the town. A modern building in Verulamium Park protects an ornate mosaic from another townhouse (D). Titled the 'Roman Hypocaust' in the publicity material in the museum, this townhouse and its mosaic were excavated by the Wheelers in 1931–2. The house had thirty rooms and a second storey. The fine mosaic displayed in the building onsite has a geometric design, and several of the rooms had underfloor heating systems. A second mosaic from this house, depicting the horned sea god Oceanus, can be seen in the museum.

The recent geophysical survey has produced remarkable results, revealing an extensive series of masonry buildings in the insula directly north of the theatre, between Watling Street and the town defences. One of these substantial courtyard structures is so large and architecturally complex that it has been described as a 'palace', perhaps broadly comparable to the 'governor's palace' at London. This building was evidently the home of a very rich family or an important official.

The quality and number of the mosaics from Verulamium indicate that this was a wealthy settlement. There is also copious information for trade and industry from the town. To balance the focus on the urban elite provided by the mosaics, the wall plaster, and the Roman Hypocaust in the park, the museum includes a detailed exploration of everyday activities within the town. These include carpentry, metalworking and potting.

The theatre

Verulamium is the only Roman town in Britain where the remains of an entire theatre can be inspected (Figure 52, E; Figure 53). Several other towns also had theatres, but the only other example on public display is the fragmentary remains of the theatre at Colchester. At Verulamium, the theatre was first uncovered in 1847 and its current appearance reflects Kenyon's excavations in 1934. The bank allowing visitors a good view over the theatre is Kenyon's excavation spoil heap. It was refurbished for modern performance use in 2014, and a Shakespearean play was staged the day that I visited. A temporary box office had been set up on the edge of the ancient monument.

The theatre was constructed *c*. 150 CE, then extended and altered later in the second century. It was a standard type of provincial, or Gallo-Roman, structure, with the seating bank nearly surrounding the orchestra (or arena), three entrances, and a stage to the north-east. The banking was earth and gravel, and masonry walls formed the supporting structure for the seating. Structures such as this theatre

Figure 53 *Photograph of the Roman theatre at Verulamium from the air.* © *https://www.gettyimages.co.uk/detail/news-photo/verulamium-roman-town-st-albans-hertfordshire-2015-aerial-news-photo/918903926?adppopup=true.*

are, in effect, halfway between the more conventional theatres of the Mediterranean and the amphitheatres that were common in the towns of Britain and Gaul. The structure at Verulamium, with an external diameter of *c.* 46 metres, is smaller than these urban amphitheatres. This theatre may have held *c.* 2,000 people and served a religious purpose.

A substantial Romano-Celtic temple, sited just to the south-east of the theatre, was a venue for religious meetings and events (Figure 51). As here at Verulamium, theatres in Britain and Gaul were usually directly connected with temples. Before the theatre was constructed, the area in front of the temple had been kept clear of buildings to serve as a meeting place. The burial enclosure on Folly Lane on the hill on the far side of the valley would also have been visible beyond the stage of the theatre (to the north-east). During the later first century, a Romano-Celtic temple was built within the Folly Lane enclosure to commemorate the unnamed king buried there. Just downhill from the Folly Hill temple was a substantial bathhouse constructed during the second century. The temple and its neighbouring theatre were evidently part of a more extensive religious complex that linked the town to the temple on the site of the burial of the last king to rule Verulamium.

The town defences

The town appears to have been partly defended by an additional earthwork known as the Fosse Earthwork, which is very poorly understood. Even its dating is completely uncertain. This earthwork, partly shown on Figures 51 and 52, lies north-west of the Roman town but is on private land and cannot be explored.

When it was built during the third century, the town wall followed a different course. Extensive drainage work was required to construct the defences above the River Ver to the north-east of the circuit. Until this time, the land alongside the river was marshland, which had to be drained and canalized before the wall could be built. The dating of the construction of this wall is based on a few old excavations and is far from definitive. The standard interpretation for this defensive line is that wall, bank and external ditch were conceived as a whole. At many other towns, however, an earthwork rampart pre-dated the insertion of a later stone wall, and this may also have been the case at Verulamium. The wall also had two external bastions (towers) at the south corner of the circuit. At many other towns, bastions were fourth-century additions to the walled circuits, but the bastions at Verulamium seem to have been constructed at the same time as the town wall. Although there are many uncertainties about these walls, the scale and extent of these defences certainly provide a dramatic indication of the significance of late Roman Verulamium.

Although the wall does not survive to its full height, it was at least 4 metres in elevation with a crenellated walkway along the top. It encloses an area of 81 hectares. The only traces of the wall visible today are a few stretches of flint and mortar core. The buried remains of the wall footings nevertheless indicate a facing of dressed flint with regular tile levelling courses. Behind the wall was a massive clay-and-gravel bank formed from material derived from an equally massive external ditch. Remarkably well-preserved to the south of the circuit, the bank and ditch form a much more impressive indication of the scale of these works than the few surviving fragments of the stone wall. The walled circuit had at least four gateways.

Around half of the circuit of the southern part of the town wall is in Verulamium Park. The remains of the walls to the north of the A4147 are on the private land of the Gorhambury Estate. The only place you can study the northern section of the wall may be reached by walking up the footpath which follows a metalled lane past the

Roman theatre, and on to the site of the Chester Gate (Figure 52, F). If you walk along the lane and then turn around to look back towards the theatre, the stone wall and external ditch is visible to the right (to the south-west), running for some distance up a rising hill. Slight traces of the defences are also evident in the meadow to the left, following a field boundary just this side of the course of the River Ver. Although nothing is visible on the ground, the remains of the Chester Gate have been uncovered during excavations. This gate was very similar to the London Gate described below. These two gates sat astride Watling Street, which ran from Chester to the west of Verulamium and London to Dover in the east.

The north-east gate was close to where Blacksmith's Lane joins St Michael's Street (G). This gateway may have been a simple single entrance, but nothing is visible onsite. Returning to Verulamium Park, you can walk along and explore much of the southern half of the defensive circuit. Some faint traces of the earthworks are visible running uphill alongside the lake, turning an angle to meet a surviving section of the core of the Roman wall (H–H). The wall turned another angle just south of this point, where it is possible to view the foundations of the London Gate (I). These clearly show the ground plan of twin portals for traffic and two additional passages to either side for pedestrians. This gateway was flanked externally by massive round-faced towers.

Beyond this point (J), the remains of the defensive bank and huge external ditch are visible by the side of the metalled path as it runs through woodland. One of the bastions from this wall section is visible but poorly preserved. The defences turn another corner, bringing you to the remains of a better-preserved bastion (K). Beyond this point, you can follow the substantial remains of the rampart and ditch through the woodland (L–L). There is no formal path along this section, and the ground is muddy. A slight earthwork marks the course of the defensive line past the site of the Silchester Gate, close to the field boundary (M). This gate was simpler in plan than the two gateways on Watling Street, with a single carriageway for traffic and pedestrian passageways to either side. To the north-west of the A4147 road, the remains of the earthwork of the town defences are visible in private ground.

The recent geophysical survey results show that large parts of the area defined by the later walls were open land, and the densest housing area lay within the boundaries of the 1955 ditch, which defined the early town. Additional areas of dense occupation lining Watling Street to the south-east and north-west of the 1955 ditched enclosure presumably originated as extramural settlements during the late first and second centuries. Much of the land in the periphery of the area enclosed by the third-century walls, especially to the south-west, was never built on. Why the third-century defences enclosed such a large area is unknown.

In the late Roman period, cemeteries were established beyond the Chester and London Gates. Several cemeteries lined the hillslope north-east of Verulamium, including one close to St Albans Abbey.

St Alban and the late town

Verulamium continued to flourish during the third century, and it has long been supposed that it declined during the fourth century. Because of more recent work, it now appears that many of the buildings and houses continued to be used well into the fourth century and perhaps beyond. A single event – the martyrdom of Alban – explains the prominence of Verulamium after the Roman period. This event was to assume considerable significance, as the modern city's name indicates.

Although we are uncertain about the dating of this event, the most likely times are during the persecutions of Christians under the emperors Decius in 249–51 CE or Valerian in 253–60. Alban's life and martyrdom are described in later, doubtlessly elaborated, hagiographies. The central element of these stories, however, is the arrival of a Christian priest in Verulamium who was given shelter by a local man called Alban at a time of persecution. Impressed by the devotion of his guest, Alban renounced his pagan beliefs. When the priest's safety came under threat, Alban dressed in his visitor's cloak and surrendered to the authorities in his place. Questioned by the judge, Alban declared himself a Christian, refused to undertake a pagan sacrifice, and was sentenced to a flogging. When he continued to refuse to reject his new beliefs, however, Alban was condemned to death and taken for execution to a nearby hill.

The cult of St Alban survived into post-Roman times, and anecdotal information has been used to suggest that the martyrdom occurred on the site where St Albans Cathedral stands today. A church was probably constructed at this location when the Roman empire became tolerant of Christianity during the fourth century. The town went into gradual decline, and the later settlement was established around the church on the site of the martyrdom of Alban.

Further reading

Niblett (2001) is a handy and accessible guide to the Iron Age *oppidum* and Roman town. The volume by Niblett and Thompson (2005) contains more detailed summaries of Iron Age and Roman Verulamium. Reid, Müller and Sabine (2022) discuss the possible battle site north-west of the *oppidum*. Breeze (2019) assesses the original meaning of the name Verulamium. Thorold (2023) provides a colourful guide to the Verulamium Museum and the archaeological site, including information on the geophysical survey. Hingley (2022) addresses the context of Verulamium in the Late Iron Age and during the Roman conquest. Lockyear and Shlasko (2017) give an overview of the geophysical survey undertaken across the town. Lockyear (2019) provides more information about the geophysical survey results, although these are yet to be fully published. Lambert (2010: 20-1) describes the early stages of St Alban's cult. For relevant web links, see the website connected with this book.

18

Winchester: Market of the Proud Ones

Introduction

Winchester is best known for its association with King Alfred and its grand medieval cathedral; its highly significant Iron Age and Roman past is less familiar to many visitors. Little of the archaeology of ancient Winchester is visible today and most of what we know about this early history is the result of archaeological excavations. What is known suggests that this important town has a pre-Roman origin.

You can follow the course of the Roman town defences on foot. Although substantially rebuilt in medieval times, the layout of the modern urban centre partly reflects the course of these defences and the six gateways that provided access to the Roman town. Winchester City Museum displays and interprets the city's history, including some impressive Roman finds.

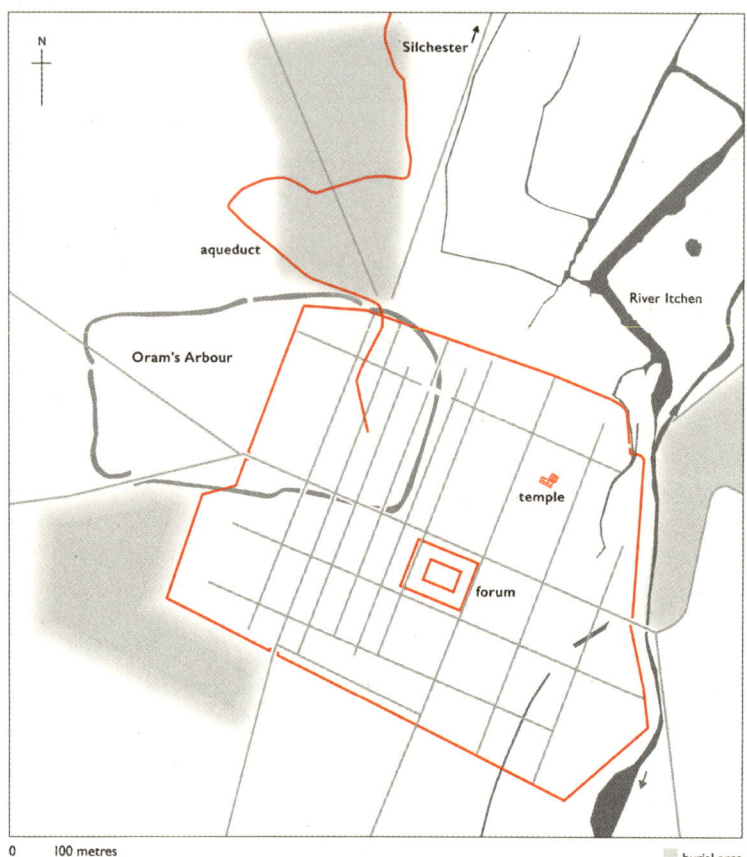

Figure 54 *Map of ancient Winchester. The Iron Age fort of Oram's Arbour to the north-west of the Roman town is marked in grey and Roman features are marked in red (after Wacher 1995: Figure 132, and Ford and Teague 2011: Figures 1.3 and 1.4b). Drawn by Christina Unwin.*

Main visible archaeological features with grading

	Star rating
Town walls	*
Museum	**

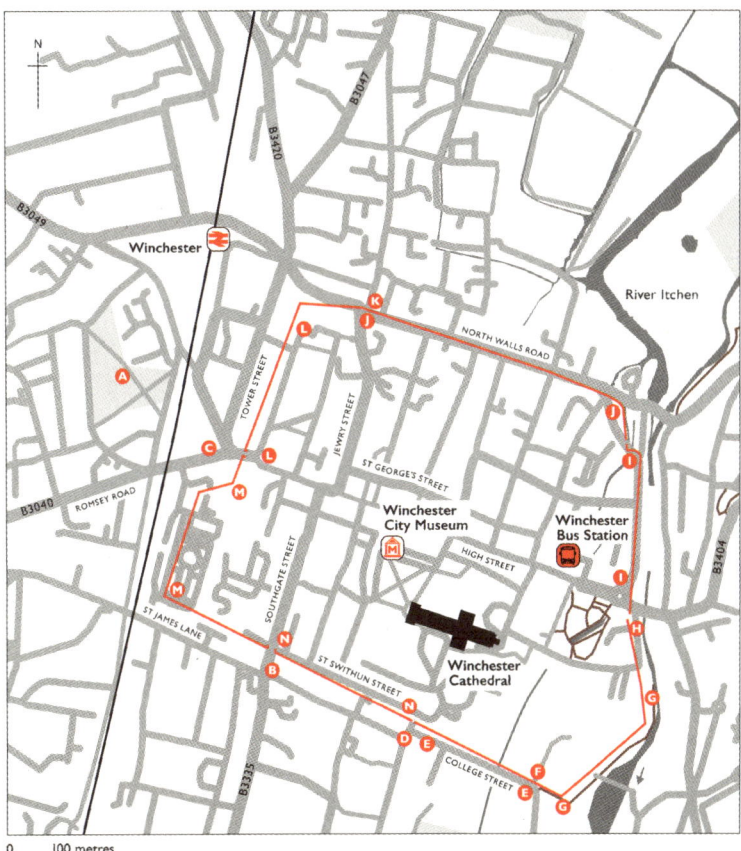

Figure 55 *Map of modern Winchester with locations mentioned in the text marked. Drawn by Christina Unwin using information from Google Maps.*

Getting there

Winchester is well-served by public transport and has a railway and bus station. There are several car parks, including a Park and Ride service, and a good range of places to eat, shop and stay in the city. Winchester is a pleasant place to explore on foot, and you can visit all the Iron Age and Roman sites this way.

Exploring ancient Winchester

The City Museum, close to the cathedral, contains a significant display of the Iron Age and Roman finds from Winchester and its surrounding area. Walking the circuit of the Roman and medieval walls provides an insight into the scale and importance of this town. Just to the north-west of the city centre, and partly within the area of the walls, is the site of an extensive Iron Age fort known as Oram's Arbour, now largely built over. It took me *c*. 3½ hours to visit the museum, walk the circuit of the walls, and walk up to the park at Oram's Arbour. Exploring the cathedral and other medieval features of the city would require at least another half day.

Historical summary

There is some doubt about the origins of the town, which was the *civitas* capital of a people known as the Belgae. The Iron Age fort at Oram's Arbour has been flattened and partly underlies the Roman town (Figure 54). Excavation of this defended hillslope enclosure indicates that it was occupied by a community in the Middle Iron Age (from *c*. 300 BCE) and may have been largely abandoned by the Late Iron Age (40 BCE). Since this river-crossing site remained significant until the establishment of the town, some occupation probably continued within and around this fort.

Winchester may have been the centre of one of the people ruled over by Togidubnus in the aftermath of the Roman conquest of southern Britain (see Chichester). The earliest Roman-period occupation dates to the 60s CE. One surprising discovery from the excavations is that during the mid-70s Winchester had earthwork defences. Only limited information is available about the street system and the monumental buildings, which date to the late first or early second century. The earth ramparts of the town, which defined an area of 58 hectares, were constructed during the late second or early third century, partly following the line of the earlier defences. That this is the third largest defensive circuit of a Roman town in Britain indicates the significance of Winchester.

There is little information about the town's late Roman history. Since late Roman burials were common in the extensive cemetery at Lankhills, north of the town, it seems that Winchester continued to be occupied into the early fifth century.

The rediscovery of Iron Age and Roman Winchester

Roman remains were discovered during the eighteenth and nineteenth centuries, although archaeological exploration did not commence until after the Second World War. Excavations during the 1950s located the Iron Age fort at Oram's Arbour, and during the following decade, the scale of research increased under the newly formed Winchester Excavation Committee. These excavations led to a far better understanding of the town. More recently excavation of Iron Age and Roman sites has continued in advance of urban redevelopment, providing further insights.

Iron Age Winchester

The substantially defended fort at Oram's Arbour, occupying a sloping area of ground close to a river crossing, indicates the significance of Winchester during the Iron Age (Figure 54). Oram was the name of the family that leased this open ground for grazing during the eighteenth century. The eastern half of the fort disappeared under the Roman town, but the western part remained open land until it became part of the urban area of Winchester in the modern era. An information board in the parkland at Oram's Arbour marks the last substantial remaining section of open ground overlying this Iron Age fort (Figure 55, A).

Since no traces of the fort survive, there is no hint on the ground of its scale. Enclosed by a ditch up to 4 metres deep and 10 metres wide, an equally substantial rampart lay inside the ditch. The ramparts enclosed an area of 20 hectares, comparable to some of the largest and most heavily defended hillforts in southern Britain (e.g. Hod Hill, Dorset). Although the exact course of the earthwork defences under the Roman town is unclear, the excavations have located four offset entrances through the ramparts. While the interior was occupied by farming communities living in roundhouses, excavations suggest that the density of occupation was not as great as some other hillforts in Dorset and Hampshire.

Although the excavations uncovered some earlier Iron Age occupation, the ramparts were Middle Iron Age in date (*c.* 300–40 BCE). The chronology of Oram's Arbour contrasts with many of the hillforts in southern Britain which were often constructed during the Late Bronze Age and Early Iron Age and refortified, sometimes in a more substantial manner, during the Middle Iron Age. The excavations also suggest that this fort continued to be occupied on a modest scale during the Late Iron Age (40 BCE to 43 CE). Its location on the hillslope above a river crossing resembles that of other Late Iron Age *oppida*. Unlike those places, however, very little amphora and other pottery imported from the Continent have been found here.

Winchester probably remained a highly significant meeting place during the Late Iron Age. If the Belgae, who had their *civitas* centre here in the Roman period, were one of the peoples under the control of Togidubnus, this royal connection might help explain the presence of the early Roman urban defences.

The early Roman town

There is no convincing evidence for a Roman fort. The Roman-period place name of the town, *Venta*, meant 'market' or 'meeting place' (as at Caerwent and Caistor). This name probably referred to the role of Oram's Arbour as an assembly point close to which the urban centre began to develop in the 60s CE. The town was to become the *civitas* capital of the Belgae, a people whose name may have meant 'proud ones'.

Early ramparts

One hint of possible involvement by the Roman military in establishing Winchester derives from the excavations of the town's defences undertaken by Martin Biddle in 1971. His team uncovered a timber gateway associated with an early series of ramparts (Figure 55, B), closely dateable to *c.* 70 CE by a coin found in a stratified context. Late-first-century towns rarely possessed defensive circuits, exceptions being the high-status sites at Colchester and Verulamium. The early timber gate at Winchester has been compared with those of several first-century Roman forts, suggesting a military presence. Since Britons had served in Roman auxiliary units for over two decades by the 70s, however, this early gate is far from conclusive evidence for a military garrison. A group of soldiers with experience in Roman fort construction may have returned to their home community at Winchester to help establish this initial phase of the town.

Houses and burials

The construction of the early ramparts probably indicates the date of the formal establishment of the town. There is also some indication that houses were built here during the 70s or slightly later in the century. Although people had probably been living on the site of the new town during the entire period since the Middle Iron Age, little closely dated occupation has been found. During the early Roman period, burials were also deposited in graves close to the northern entrance to the Oram's Arbour enclosure.

The *civitas* capital

There is little information on the early history of the town, and knowledge of the public buildings is slight. The street system probably dates to the late first or early second century. It is possible to reconstruct much of the network of streets from the fragmentary remains uncovered during excavation (Figure 54). Planning the town required substantial work to control and canalize the River Itchen. Much of the eastern part of Roman Winchester occupied a river floodplain requiring considerable drainage. The forum was probably just north-west of the medieval cathedral, although excavations have uncovered only limited parts of this building. Traces of a small temple have been found in the north-eastern part of the town, and some domestic buildings have also been excavated. The City Museum contains fragments of several mosaics, an interpretation of excavated townhouses, and a collection of other significant finds from the excavations.

From springs to the west of Winchester an aqueduct, or channel, supplied water to the north-western area of the town. There is no sign of this feature visible today. On the north side of Romsey Road, just uphill from the last shop in the road, there is a segment of a stone column incorporated into the flint and brick roadside wall – a rare trace of Roman archaeology (Figure 55, C; Figure 56). The City Museum displays additional fragments of Roman columns.

Figure 56 *Photograph of a Roman column built into a modern roadside wall in Winchester.* © *Richard Hingley.*

Walking the walls

A few traces of the Roman town defences survive, incorporated in the fragmentary remains of the medieval town wall. The new defensive line incorporated the southern and western boundaries of the earlier rampart, including the site of the earlier timber gateway (mentioned above). The new ramparts enclosed 58 hectares and were constructed during the late second century. Adding a stone wall to the front of the rampart during the early third century strengthened the defences, as did the addition of one, and probably more, external bastions during the fourth century. There may originally have been six gates providing access to the town. No traces of these gates survive today, and the little that is known derives from excavation. The medieval walls incorporated the substantial remains of their predecessors. During the early nineteenth century, however, their ruinous condition led to large-scale demolition, except to the south-east and east of the circuit.

The circuit of the walls makes an informative walk, although there is less to see than at several other towns. Kingsgate is probably on the site of one of the Roman south gates (Figure 55, D). The southern defences ran south-east from here, and traces of the wall survive built into later properties, as you can see by following along the left side of College Street (E–E). The best-preserved section of the town wall is the south-east corner. This inner face of this wall section is visible on private land from the gateway into the Pilgrim's School playing fields (F). These defences retain traces of the bank of the Roman rampart, but the wall was entirely rebuilt in medieval and later times (G–G). From just south-east of the school gateway, the lane on your left running alongside the River Itchen follows the outer face of the wall. Traces of the medieval wall survive in several places, possibly incorporating some Roman masonry. Elsewhere, the wall has been entirely rebuilt to provide modern property boundaries. Just to the south of where the east gate once lay is the only visible surviving section of Roman wall foundation (H). This is located in a recessed enclosure at the foot of a wall bounding a riverside property. A metal plaque on the wall provides a brief description.

Although nothing is visible today, traces of the Roman east gate were located during excavations. North of here, all traces of the defences are lost, but their course can be followed by walking up Eastgate Street (I–I), continuing onto Durngate Terrace, and turning left onto Easton Lane. The arrangement of the Roman and medieval defences was complicated at this point by the braided course of River Itchen, and there was formerly a gateway at Durngate which may also have had a Roman origin.

To the north, the defences have been entirely removed, although North Walls follows the line of the wall (J–J). A metal plaque at the junction with Hyde Street records the former location of the Roman north gate (K). From here, the line is lost but picked up again by Tower Street, which runs along the inner side of the western defences as far as the medieval West Gate (L–L). The medieval West Gate is on the site of the Roman west gate.

The Roman (and medieval) defences then turned a dog-leg before continuing through what is now the Peninsula Barracks, to the south-west corner (M–M). We have no idea why there was a dog-leg in this section. Although St James Lane follows the outside of the western section of the southern defences, no traces of the wall survive. The site of the south gate (B) is recorded by the appropriately named Southgate Street, just south of the junction of St Swithun Street. Continue walking down St Swithun Street to follow the inner line of the ramparts as far as Kingsgate (N–N).

Cemeteries

The town had extensive cemeteries outside the north, east, west and south-western gates. The best known is at Lankhills, to the north. Some of the burials from this cemetery have produced belt sets and distinctive brooches, indicating the presence of state officials, possibly including soldiers, at Winchester during the fourth century. Scientific analysis of the bones from these burials indicates that some of the population of Winchester had their origins in the Mediterranean Basin and Western Europe.

Further reading

The fullest accounts of Iron Age and Roman Winchester are Ottaway (2017) and Morris and Biddle (2023). This is supplemented by the recent account by Catling (2024). For Oram's Arbour, see Ford and Teague (2011). Wacher (1995: 291–301) remains a valuable account but is now somewhat dated. For relevant web links, see the website connected with this book.

19

Wroxeter: The Old Work

Introduction

Wroxeter was a *civitas* capital founded on a site that played a significant role in the Roman conquest of Britain. A fortress preceded the town, serving as a campaign base successively for at least two legions. When the fortress was decommissioned *c.* 90 CE, a town developed. The initial urban buildings were of timber and earth, and, in the 120s, the urban community constructed a substantial masonry forum. Wroxeter is an impressive site to visit because of the survival of a substantial section of masonry wall, once part of the bath basilica, known for centuries as the 'Old Work'. A defensive circuit was constructed around the town during the later second century. Wroxeter is a 'green field' site with few more modern buildings overlaying the Roman remains. It is looked after by English Heritage, which runs a small museum onsite.

Excavations have revealed the remains of several buildings, and extensive geophysical surveys have also provided considerable evidence for the layout of the urban settlement. A reconstructed

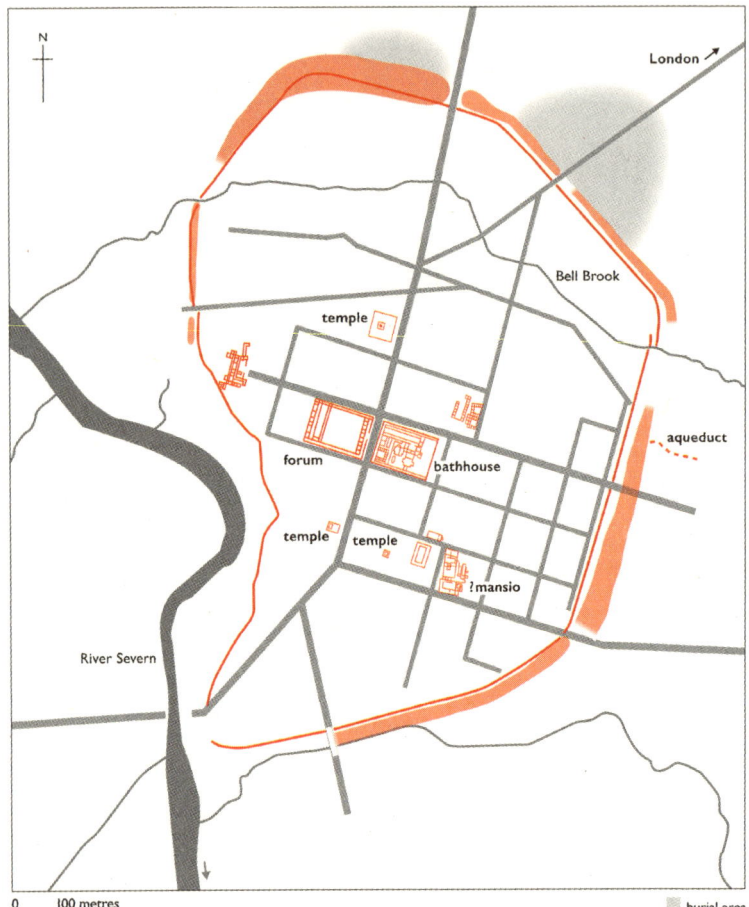

Figure 57 *Map of Roman Wroxeter (after Wacher 1995: Figure 165, White and Barker 1998: Figure 39, and White, Gaffney and Gaffney 2013: Figure 4.21). Drawn by Christina Unwin.*

townhouse provides a clear impression of the scale and appearance of an urban dwelling. Although the bath basilica ceased to be maintained c. 370 CE, new buildings on this site continued in use until around the middle of the fifth century. The town probably continued to be extensively occupied well into the fifth century.

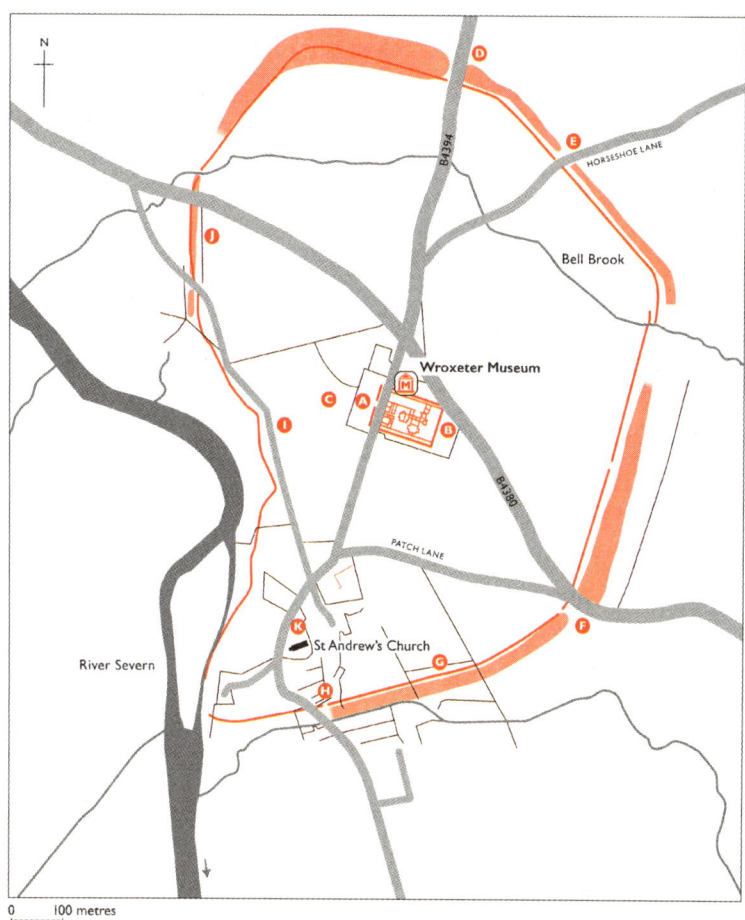

Figure 58 *Map of modern Wroxeter with locations mentioned in the text marked. Drawn by Christina Unwin using information from Google Maps and Newman and Pevsner 2006: 722.*

Main visible archaeological features with grading

	Star rating
Bathhouse	***
Market hall	***
Forum	*
Reconstructed townhouse	**
Urban defences	*
Museum	**

Getting there

Wroxeter can be reached by bicycle, car or bus, and the English Heritage website provides information on how to get there. The site is open every day of the week during the peak tourist season but only at weekends during the winter months. Check the opening times on the website before you visit.

Exploring Roman Wroxeter

The English Heritage site and museum has a car park and toilets. From here, the remains of the bathhouse, forum and reconstructed townhouse can be visited, which took me *c.* 2 hours. Several other places within the area of the Roman town are worth visiting on foot. At St Andrew's Church, two reused Roman columns help form the churchyard gateway. It is also possible to view the subtle remains of the urban earthwork defences at several locations by walking along minor roads close to the English Heritage site. Do take care walking or cycling along the minor roads. Many of the cars I met were driven at speed and did not expect to encounter any obstruction on these roads. My entire visit to Wroxeter took 4 hours.

There is a drinks machine at the English Heritage site, but as there are no shops or cafes near the Roman remains, do take refreshments with you when visiting.

Historical summary

The Roman military probably constructed a fort at Wroxeter, just south of the village, during the late 40s. By the late 50s this was replaced by a legionary fortress on the site later occupied by the town. Although the military decommissioned the fortress during the 90s, some veteran soldiers may have remained as part of the new urban community. Initially timber-built, the town was gradually redeveloped with several monumental masonry buildings including a forum, a monumental bathing complex and several temples (Figure 57). A circuit of defences enclosing an extensive area probably dates to the later second century. Substantial occupation continued into the fourth century, and Wroxeter was probably abandoned during the fifth century.

The rediscovery of Roman Wroxeter

The survival above ground of the very substantial remains of the 'Old Work' attracted the attention of antiquaries to Wroxeter from early times. The foundations of Roman buildings were located in the eighteenth century, and extensive excavations commenced during the mid-nineteenth century under the guidance of the antiquarian Thomas Wright. New excavations in the fields opposite (west of) the baths during the early and mid-twentieth century uncovered substantial areas of the remains. The work of Philip Barker from 1966 to 1990 revealed possible post-Roman occupation on the site of the bath basilica. The more recent work, managed by Vince Gaffney and

Roger White, involved a large-scale geophysical survey revealing information on the extent and layout of the military and urban phases. There has been little recent excavation, although a project in 2024 uncovered the remains of a mosaic depicting dolphins and fish. English Heritage's onsite museum has been recently refurbished and brought up to date to shed light on the people of Wroxeter.

The fortress

The geophysical survey of the site produced some evidence for Iron Age settlements, and the location of the Wrekin hillfort 6 kilometres to the east suggest that Wroxeter may have been a strategically significant location during the Roman conquest. The Roman military probably established the first fort somewhere close to Wroxeter during the late 40s, while campaigning in north Wales. The fortress, the headquarters of the Fourteenth Legion Gemina, was established in the late 50s. Located on a raised site above the floodplain of the River Severn to the west, with small brooks providing further protection to the north and south, the suitability of the setting can still be appreciated today. A ford over the River Severn lies just to the south-west of the site of the fortress. At some stage, the Fourteenth Legion was replaced by the Twentieth Legion as the fortress garrison.

Excavations have revealed the course of the rampart and some of the internal buildings. If you stand on the viewing platform just south of the baths, you can view the extent of the fortress, although no traces of its ramparts are visible. A civil settlement (or *canabae*) developed west of the fortress. The Twentieth Legion started to construct a bathhouse here at some point before the decommissioning of the fortress. This bathhouse was never completed, but much of the masonry of its walls was reused for the second-century forum.

The onsite museum displays the Roman military occupation of Wroxeter, including artefacts recovered during the excavation. The Shrewsbury Museum and Art Gallery also holds a substantial collection of finds from Wroxeter.

The early town

The town developed on the site of the vacated fortress after the legionary ramparts were demolished and flattened (Figure 57). The Roman-period name for the fortress and town was *Viriconium*, which may have meant 'Virico's place'. Although the origin of this name is unclear, from the dedicatory inscription in the forum the town is known to have been the *civitas* capital of a people called the Cornovii. It seems likely that the town retained aspects of its former military character, and its population included retired soldiers and their descendants. The excavations in the basilica of the forum uncovered a bronze diploma which dates to the 130s. This diploma records the discharge of Mansuetus, an auxiliary cavalryman originally belonging to a Germanic people known as the Treveri. Mansuetus presumably became a member of the urban community of Wroxeter on retirement.

The street system reused the roads of the fortress, and the area of the town extended beyond the limits of the flattened legionary ramparts. Excavation has produced traces of some early timber buildings and information about the trades and industries of the population. The museum display includes information on these aspects of urban life.

The capital of the Cornovii

The *civitas* capital at Wroxeter was one of the most extensive of Britain's Roman towns. The banks and ditches were constructed in the late second century to enclose an area of 78 hectares, the fourth largest area defined by urban defences in Britain. At least some of the land within the southern parts of this circuit was open ground, and Wroxeter, like all the Roman towns, probably had areas of open space and gardens. Unlike all the other towns described in this book, however, Wroxeter never seems to have been defined by a stone town wall. The defences remained in earthwork form.

Excavations and geophysical surveys have revealed much of the plan of Wroxeter. The sites of several temples and substantial buildings are known. This chapter focuses on the remains available for the visitor to explore.

The forum

The construction of the forum may have taken almost a decade. The buildings, completed c. 130, reused parts of an earlier unfinished legionary bathhouse (above). The imposing street facades of this forum were colonnaded, and the foundations of the east colonnade of the forum is the only part of the building visible to visitors (Figure 58, A). The bases of the columns are displayed at a depth below the modern ground surface, showing how much the ground level has built up at Wroxeter since the second century. The gap in the colonnade marks the entrance to the forum on the eastern side of the building, and over half of the monumental inscription from above this entrance survives, indicating a date of construction of 129–30 CE, during the reign of the emperor Hadrian. You can study a cast of this inscription in the museum. It is significant because it records that the *civitas* of the Cornovii erected the forum and dedicated it to the ruling emperor. On the far side of the building complex, behind the reconstructed townhouse (which lies over the remains of the forum courtyard), was the basilica. The other three sides of the courtyard, as you would expect, were lined with shops which were rented out to traders to provide income to the urban council.

The excavations revealed evidence of a substantial fire during the later second century that probably damaged much of the forum, destroying a pottery stall in the forum eastern portico. The forum was rebuilt after the fire and may have continued in use until the early fourth century.

The baths

Across the road from the forum to the east were the public baths (B). The Roman road, known as Watling Street, lies under the course of the modern north–south road at this location. The Old Work and the excavated foundations of the bathhouse form one of the most impressive examples of a monumental Roman building in Britain (Figure 59). This large and impressive bathhouse is an example of a building design found in many towns. The bathhouse complex filled an entire insula, consisting of the baths themselves, a basilican exercise hall, a latrine, two shops and a market hall. Building work to construct the baths commenced c. 120 CE and took about thirty years. A monumental portico surrounded the baths basilica. The extensive and, in places, exceptionally well-preserved remains of all these structures are well-displayed and interpreted by information boards.

The Old Work, which stands at a height of 7 metres, illustrates the complexity and scale of this building. This monumental fragment of masonry formed the wall and grand entrance between the southeastern part of the basilica and the main baths. Anyone entering the baths after exercising in the basilica would have passed through the double doorway. The basilica was a very substantial aisled hall, and round pink disks mark out the locations of the columns that formed the aisles. The Old Work was constructed of stonework separated by

Figure 59 Photograph of the centre of Roman Wroxeter, showing the bathhouse, including the Old Work in the foreground and the reconstructed townhouse beyond. © Richard Hingley.

neatly laid double rows of tile. On the south face, the upper part of the surviving wall features traces of three arches and projecting piers with the doorway under the central arch. This wide opening contained two sets of wooden doors. The regular rows of holes in the face of the Old Work were for the scaffolding used in the construction. When in use, all the internal walls of the bathhouse and basilica were faced with plaster which would have been decorated with painted scenes.

The original bath suite included the usual range of rooms: a cold room, warm room and hot steam room, while additional structures included a second smaller warm room, two hot dry rooms and a cold plunge pool. Several of the rooms had underfloor heating systems. An open-air pool lies to the south-west of the bathhouse. During the third century, some extra rooms were added to the west of the bathhouse. An aqueduct from Bell Brook brought water to a cistern north of the town, which supplied this substantial bathing complex via a buried channel. No trace of the aqueduct is visible today.

A portico separated the bathhouse from a latrine and two shops to the west. Just west of the latrine, two square rooms operated as shops or bars serving customers of the baths. South of the latrine are located the foundations of a courtyard building, a market hall (*macellum*) that was also accessible from the road to the west. In addition to the shops, the market hall had a second smaller latrine. Although several other towns in Britain are known from excavations to have had market buildings, the Wroxeter example is the only one that visitors can inspect.

A reconstructed house

In 2010, a townhouse was reconstructed to add to the visitor experience (Figure 58, C). This building is located within the area originally occupied by the forum. The reconstruction, which drew on the design of a late Roman building excavated at Wroxeter at a site a little to the south of the forum, took a team of builders six months to complete, and was featured in a Channel 4 television series, 'Rome Wasn't Built in a Day'. An L-shaped building with rooms around a courtyard, this building has a separate bathing suite heated by a furnace, and an underfloor hypocaust. The rooms are decorated with painted wall plaster, and the principal reception room also has a mosaic. The reconstruction includes a small corner shop which might have been occupied by a tenant of the owner of the house.

The town defences

During the late second century, a defensive circuit comprising a bank and ditch was constructed around the town. The lack of recent excavations limits our knowledge of these ramparts. It is known that the defences consisted of a bank with a clay-and-rubble core, topped with a timber palisade. Two ditches outside the bank provided additional protection.

Later, during the fourth century, the defences were strengthened by digging a substantial single ditch to replace the two earlier ditches, and by raising the height of the bank. The locations of seven gates, where the roads crossed the defences, can be inferred. Although the northern gatehouse was explored in the nineteenth century, there is no information available on the findings from that exploration. These gatehouses may have been constructed of timber or masonry.

In the past, it was assumed that a stone wall was added to the outer face of the earthen defences during the later Roman period, in parallel to developments at other Roman towns in Britain. However, recent re-evaluation of the excavated sections of the defences indicates that this was not the case for Wroxeter, and the reasons for the absence of a stone wall remain unclear. The nearest convenient source of stone was located

12 kilometres away, and it is possible that maintaining the earthen defences without constructing a stone-faced wall was judged simpler.

A visitor cannot see how substantial these earthwork defences, consisting of a rampart perhaps 6 metres in height with an equally massive external ditch, once were. Over the centuries, ploughing has removed almost all traces, and the earthworks all lie on private land. Although only very slight traces of these once-substantial earthworks are visible, several minor roads cross the course of the defences, enabling visitors to view their course. The Roman road that ran north of Wroxeter towards Whitchurch lay upon the route of the B4394. The course of the defences to either side of the location of the north gate is marked on both sides of this road by a chain-link fence (Figure 58, D). Traces of slight earthworks in the fields to the left (west) and right (east) indicate the course of the bank and ditch.

Another minor road, Horseshoe Lane (after the pub of that name), branches from the B4394 and follows the approximate course of the Roman road known as Watling Street. Horseshoe Lane crosses the line of the town defences by the site of the north-eastern gate (E). The field boundary that runs to Horseshoe Lane from the location described above (D) indicates the former course of the defences to the north-east. The earthwork traces of the ditch and rampart are more clearly visible in the field to the south-east as a broad hollow on the skyline.

The route from the English Heritage car park south-east down the B4380 (towards Buildwas and Ironbridge) takes you to the probable site of the south-eastern gate (F). The bank and ditch are not visible at this point. Walking west and then south-west down Patch Lane, past St Andrew's Church, takes you to the site of another section of the defences. The safest place to view the defences is from the car park of the Wroxeter Hotel, which lies immediately behind (east of) the church. From this location, you can see the defences in the fields to the east (G), which is the only unploughed section to survive. The old cottages south of the church and hotel lie on the line of the defences, which remain visible as a slight earthwork (H).

I also walked up the road that runs above the River Severn to the B4380, which follows the approximate line of the former defences. Limited excavations along this line have suggested that the break in the slope above the river just to the left (west) of the road is the approximate course of the rampart along at least part of this line (I). Walking along this lane also gives a prospect of the river valley to the left (west) and the location of the forum and bathhouse to the right (east). As you approach the B4380, the modern lane crosses the line of the town defences, which continues to the north. Slight earthworks in the triangular field to the right of the lane mark the course of the rampart and ditch (J). The Bell Brook also passes through the defences close to this point.

It is worth visiting St Andrew's Church while exploring the defences (K). The churchyard wall incorporates Roman building stones, and two columns with eroded capitals form the supports for the iron gate. The church contains some early medieval masonry, including a fragment of an eighth-century cross high in the south wall. The font was carved from a Roman column base.

The dead of Wroxeter

Several tombstones of soldiers from the military phases of Wroxeter's occupation have been discovered, and a cemetery was excavated in the nineteenth century to the north-east of the fortress. At many *civitas* capitals, cemeteries lined the roads leading from the main gates. A recent geophysical survey has identified a cemetery located alongside the roads running north from Wroxeter (see Figure 57). One tombstone commemorates a woman named Placida, who died at the age of 55, and a young man named Deuccus, who was probably her son.

Post-Roman Wroxeter

After the partial demolition of the bath basilica during the late fourth century the site was reused for a substantial timber-framed building that was probably occupied until the mid-fifth century. By the eighth century a Christian community was living here, as indicated by the fragment of Anglo-Saxon cross shaft at St Andrew's Church. It is possible that, as at Caerwent, an early monastery was established within the defences of the ruined town. It is not clear whether occupation at Wroxeter continued during the intervening centuries.

Further reading

Links for the English Heritage websites for Wroxeter are given in the website accompanying this book. The English Heritage guidebook (White 2023) provides an easily readable summary of the history and a detailed guide to the visible archaeology of the bathhouse, market building and forum. White and Barker (1998) includes a more detailed account of the town and references to the full excavation reports for the site. A detailed analysis of Wroxeter and its hinterland, giving the full results of the geophysical survey, is included in White, Gaffney and Gaffney (2013). The social history of the site and its excavators is considered by White (2022). Ellis and White (2003) address the defences. For the diploma naming Mansuetus, see RIB 2401.8, and RIB 295 for the inscription mentioning Placida and Deuccus. The original interpretation of the late- and post-Roman activity at the bath basilica suggested that the occupation continued for several centuries after the ending of Roman rule in Britain. A recent reassessment of the dating of these deposits through radiocarbon dating, however, suggests that the latest occupation ended by 450 (Roger White, personal communication). For other relevant web links, see the website connected with this book.

20

York and Demetrius of Tarsus

Introduction

The visible Roman remains in York derive from the military fortress north of the River Ouse (Figure 60). The medieval city wall south of the River Ouse is thought to have incorporated the defences of the Roman colony. Of this civil settlement, however, nothing else can be seen. As a result, this chapter focuses on the history of Roman York and provides a short description of the visible remains of the fortress. York was an important city, second only to London in significance. Several military generals, including two emperors, used York as their base of operations. The Yorkshire Museum houses a significant collection of Roman artefacts from the colony and the fortress.

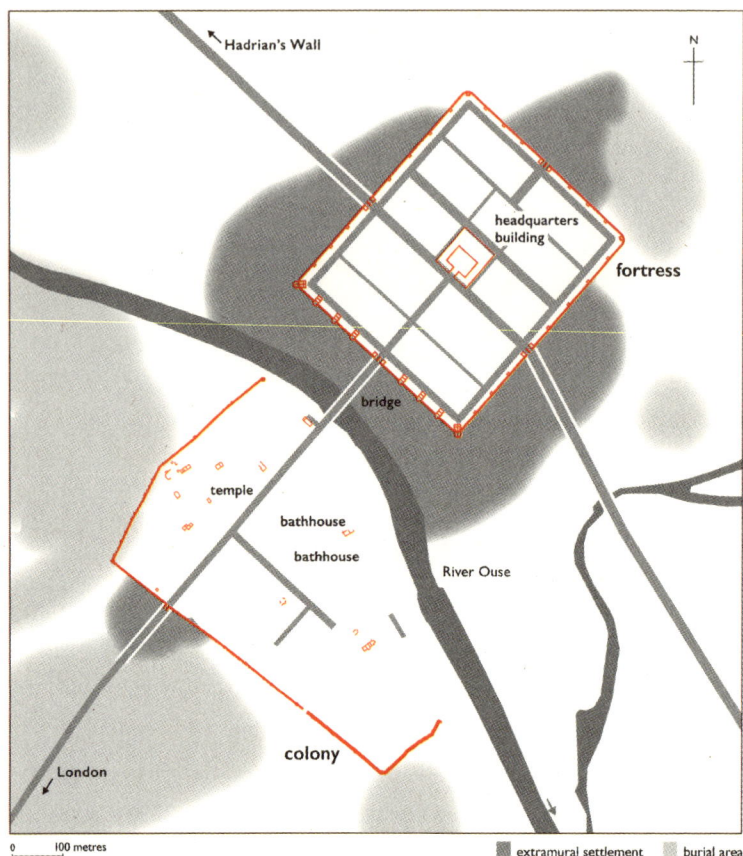

Figure 60 *Map of Roman York (from Ottaway 2011: Figures 13 and 44). Drawn by Christina Unwin.*

Main visible archaeological features with grading

	Star rating
Town defences	*
Museum	***

York and Demetrius of Tarsus

Figure 61 *Map of modern York with locations mentioned in the text marked. Drawn by Christina Unwin using information from Google Maps.*

Exploring Roman York

York is easiest to reach by train, being located on the main east coast line from London to Edinburgh. York Station, which is just a short walk from the city centre, was built just west of the medieval walls. If you plan to visit by car, it is advisable to use one of the Park and Ride services located on the outskirts of the city. York is also a popular destination for cyclists, though exploring the Roman remains by bike may be challenging. The Yorkshire Museum, situated north of the river, is within the area of the Roman fortress.

In addition to its Roman archaeology, York boasts many attractions, including the Jorvik Viking Centre and the impressive medieval minster. The city has numerous excellent cafes, restaurants and a variety of accommodation options. Exploring the town wall south of the River Ouse and visiting the Yorkshire Museum may take *c.* 3 hours. You should allow at least a day, however, to do justice to the surviving remains of the Roman fortress and the city's other historic sites.

Historical summary

The first Roman activities in this area may date back to the late 60s CE, as the military began to extend their control northwards across central Britain. In *c.* 70, a fortress for the Ninth Legion was established at this strategic location, near to both the Humber Estuary and a ford over the River Ouse. This bridge provided access for soldiers campaigning into territory further north. An extensive civil settlement developed around the fortress, extending to the south bank of the Ouse as well. A significant archaeological discovery from the south bank suggests that this area formed the base of operations for the provincial governor Agricola during the 80s.

By *c.* 120, the Sixth Legion had replaced the Ninth Legion at York. Excavations have revealed much of the fortress's ground plan and some fragments of military buildings. During the early third century, when the province of *Britannia* was divided into two, York became the capital of 'Lower Britain'. By the 230s, the civil settlement south of the River Ouse was granted the status of a colony. The fortress served as the military base for invasions of northern Britain under two emperors. York was the military headquarters of the emperor Septimius Severus during his violent invasion of northern Britain from 208 to 211 CE. A century later Constantine I (Constantine the Great) was proclaimed emperor in York.

Little is known about the colony, but it clearly featured a variety of monumental buildings and was surrounded by a wall. York's function as an occasional base for emperors during military campaigns suggests that there was an imperial palace within the colony. The occupation of the colony and fortress continued into the early fifth century, until the collapse of Roman rule in Britain.

The rediscovery of Roman York

York was recognized as a Roman centre in the late sixteenth century, and during the eighteenth century interest in the city's heritage grew. In the nineteenth century, significant remains were uncovered in the course of construction work in the city. The first systematic excavations revealing parts of the fortress then took place in the 1920s. More extensive excavations in the 1950s focused on the internal buildings of the fortress and one of the cemeteries. The establishment of the York Archaeological Trust in 1972 led to an increase in rescue excavations. While much of this work concentrated on the fortress, some excavations were conducted in the civil settlement south of the River Ouse. A recent project has explored the archaeological landscape buried beneath modern York, utilizing geophysical surveys to examine the streets and buildings of both the colony and the fortress.

The fortress

The fortress is located in a low-lying area prone to flooding, just north of a crossing over the River Ouse. In classical texts it is referred to as *Eboracum*, which may mean 'Place of the yew trees' in Celtic. This name probably reflects the environment of the site at the time the

Romans arrived. A bridge was located to the south of the fortress, probably replacing an earlier ford (Figure 61, A). This bridge was sited some distance south-east of the nineteenth-century Lendal Bridge, but we know little else about it.

Initially constructed from timber and turf, the fortress was rebuilt in masonry during the early second century. Fragmentary remains provide a glimpse into the impressive scale of the military headquarters building, on the site now occupied by York Minster. Visitors can explore these remains in the Undercroft of York Minster, along with various artefacts uncovered during excavations (B). A substantial column, once part of the north-eastern colonnade of the headquarters building, is displayed in Minster Yard (C), near the modern statue of Constantine. Standing at 7½ metres tall, this column indicates the immense size of the original building. Part of the cold room of the legionary bathhouse can also be viewed at the Roman Bath Public House (D).

The Yorkshire Museum gardens contain the remains of a section of the masonry fortress rampart, which includes the Multangular Tower and the Anglian Tower (E). The lower courses of the Multangular Tower, which formed the south-western corner of the fortress defences, dates to the third century (the upper part is medieval). The north-western and north-eastern sections of the Roman defensive circuit are buried beneath the substantial remains of the medieval city wall. The other visible remains of the Roman fortress defences are the foundations of the north-east corner and part of the curtain wall, including one of the interval towers (F). These can be viewed from the top of the medieval city wall near the Merchant Taylors' Hall. Archaeological excavations unearthed this section of the Roman defences, which had lain buried in the bank behind the medieval city wall. The south-eastern and south-western ramparts of the fortress were integrated into the area included in the medieval city and subsequently flattened.

The Roman fortress was rebuilt and reconstructed several times during the centuries and probably continued in use until the mid-fourth century. Towards the end of the century, it was abandoned, as soldiers were withdrawn from Britain to serve in conflicts overseas. Occupation may have continued on the site of the headquarters building, however. Finds from the excavations within the fortress are displayed in the Yorkshire Museum.

The colony

Although the colony to the south of the river was one of the highest-status urban settlements in Britain, no visible traces of this urban settlement survive. Our understanding of the buildings, streets and defences is hampered by York's urban infrastructure and the considerable depth at which the Roman deposits are buried. Many excavations have uncovered fragments of buildings, but even the course of the streets within the colony is uncertain. In addition, little is known about the structure and dating of the defensive circuit that defined the limits of the colony. The massive medieval city walls are thought to incorporate and bury the Roman defences, but even this is not known for sure. These medieval defences enclose an area of *c.* 27 hectares to the south of the Ouse. While this is a smaller area than many of the towns in this book, the extensive areas of civil settlement on the north bank, outside the boundaries of the fortress, probably also formed part of the colony.

An early Roman headquarters?

From the area to the south of the river, where the colony was to develop, the earliest finds date to the later first century. The occupation began on the south bank of the Ouse, close to the bridgehead.

Although little is known about this early settlement, one highly significant archaeological find may suggest that it played a significant role in the campaigns to conquer northern Britain under Agricola in the early 80s. In 1840, two bronze plaques were discovered during work on the old railway station, which lay just inside the medieval city wall (Figure 61, G). Unfortunately, we have no detailed information about the context in which these artefacts were found.

These plaques bore Greek votive inscriptions in the name of a man called Demetrius. One of the plaques honoured the gods of the governor's headquarters, and the other the two ancient Greek aquatic divinities, Oceanus and Thetys. A recent study argues that the Demetrius who dedicated these offerings may have been the Greek grammatician and explorer Demetrius of Tarsus. The Roman author Plutarch recorded that he met Demetrius at Delphi (Greece), probably in 83, when the grammatician was travelling home to Tarsus. Plutarch mentions that Demetrius was returning from a trip on the emperor's business, having been sent to explore islands lying off the coast of Britain. Demetrius had probably accompanied Agricola on campaign in the far north of Britain during the early 80s. The plaques were votive offerings that were probably offered to these divinities at the household shrine in Agricola's military headquarters. High-status Roman houses often included shrines to domestic gods.

The colony

The excavations south of the river demonstrate that a wealthy settlement developed during the second century. We know from an inscription found at Bordeaux (France) that York was a colony by c. 237, but this status may well have been awarded somewhat earlier. Septimius Severus led campaigns to the north of Hadrian's Wall during the early third century, dying at York in 211. He was succeeded by his two sons, one of whom, Caracalla, had his brother murdered. York was the campaign base for both Severus and his sons. Caracalla may have been responsible for dividing the province of Britain into two.

Since Severus spent four years campaigning in Britain, the emperor is likely to have required a winter base, including an imperial palace. The substantial foundations uncovered during the nineteenth century, close to where the Demetrius plaques were found, might indicate the location of such a complex (Figure 61, G). A century later, in 306, the emperor Constantius I visited Britain to campaign against rebellious peoples in the north, and once again York was his base. When Constantius died at York, he was succeeded by his son, Constantine I. Constantine is famous since he made Christianity the official religion of the Roman empire. This is why the modern bronze statue of this emperor is located outside the minster.

Traces of other buildings, including a range of wealthy late Roman dwellings, have been found across the area enclosed within the colony's walls. The most impressive mosaic from York, which depicts the four seasons, was uncovered in 1853 at Toft Green (H). This was lifted, and is now on display in the Yorkshire Museum. Little more is known about the colony, and even less is visible within the city. Traces of three buildings which may have been bathhouses have been found, potentially associated with private residences in each case. The locations of the forum and other significant public buildings are unknown.

The medieval city wall is believed to have incorporated the remains of the defences of the colony, which remain buried within it. Walking along the top of the city walls certainly provides a good view of the area within the former colony. We know nothing about the structure and dating of the Roman defences in this area. The alignment of the Roman road crossing the Ouse indicates that there was a south gate in the defences, sited near Micklegate Bar (I). It is also likely that there were Roman gateways in the east and west sides of the walled circuit. There is no evidence that the circuit of defences included a wall along the south bank of the Ouse, as the protection offered by the fortress to the north of the river was presumably considered sufficient.

Several altars and dedications found across the colony, including dedications to Mithras, Jupiter Optimus Maximus, Serapis and the *Deae Matres* (Divine Mothers), attest to the religious practices of the townspeople. Inscriptions record the names of several traders, and a stone sarcophagus (now lost) identified one of these tradespeople as Marcus Verecundius Diogenes. Originally from a *civitas* known as the *Bituriges Cubi*, with its capital at Bourges in central France, he had later settled in York. The inscription suggests that Diogenes served as a *sevir Augustalis*, taking a role in superintending the cult of the emperor. This suggests that there was a temple to the emperor in York. The sarcophagus of Diogenes' wife, Julia Fortunata, who originated from Sardinia, has also been found and is displayed in the Yorkshire Museum.

Extensive cemeteries surrounded the colony and fortress on both sides of the river. The scientific analysis of human bones from excavated burials has revealed detailed information about the diversity of York's population. There is an impressive display of tombstones, military and civil, in the Yorkshire Museum, which also contains a highly informative discussion of the diverse geographical origins of the people living here, including one individual who has become known as the 'Ivory Bangle Lady'. Interred in a stone coffin, this woman was buried with a rich array of offerings that included exotic ivory objects. The scientific analysis of her remains has proved particularly informative, suggesting that she had grown up away from York, possibly on the Continent, and was of 'mixed race' ancestry. The displays at the museum tell her story, together with that of other individuals from York.

Further reading

Ottaway (2011) provides a detailed account of the fortress and colony. Wacher (1995: 167–88) remains very useful for the discussion of the status and history of the colony. For the bronze tablets mentioning Demetrius (RIB 662 and 663), see Koon (2023). For the context of Demetrius' visit to Britain, see Hingley (2022: 162–3). The sarcophagi of Diogenes and Julia Fortunata are RIB 678 and 687. For the Ivory Bangle Lady, see Leach et al. (2009). For relevant web links, see the website connected with this book.

References

Online databases

RIB = Roman Inscriptions of Britain. Available online: https://romaninscriptionsofbritain.org/rib.

Vindolanda Tablets. Available online: https://romaninscriptionsofbritain.org/tabvindol.

Books, articles and websites

Bidwell, P. (2010). 'A survey of the Anglo-Saxon crypt at Hexham and its reused Roman stonework', *Archaeologia Aeliana* 5(39): 53–146.

Bird, S. and B. Cunliffe (2019). *The Essential Roman Baths. Revised edition.* London: Scala Arts & Heritage.

Bishop, M. C. (2005). 'A new Flavian Military Site at Roecliffe, North Yorkshire', *Britannia* 36: 135–223.

Bishop, M. C. and J. N. Dore (1988). *Corbridge: Excavations of the Roman fort and town, 1947–80.* London: Historic Buildings & Monuments Commission for England. Available online: https://archaeologydataservice.ac.uk/archives/view/eh_monographs_2014/contents.cfm?mono=1089071.

Blagg, T. F. C. (1984). 'Roman architectural ornament in Kent', *Archaeologia Cantiana* 100: 65–80.

Bogaers, J. E. (1979). 'King Cogidubnus at Chichester: Another reading of *RIB* 91', *Britannia* 10: 243–54.

Bowden, W. (2013a). 'The Urban Plan of *Venta Icenorum* and Its Relationship with the Boudican Revolt', *Britannia* 44: 145–69.

Bowden, M. (2013b). 'Townscape and identity at Caistor-by-Norwich', in H. Eckardt and S. Rippon (eds), *Living and Working in the Roman World: Essays in honour of Michael Fulford on his 65th birthday.* Portsmouth, RI: Journal of Roman Archaeology, Supplementary Series no. 95: 47–62.

Bowden, W. (2020). *Venta Icenorum: A brief history of Caistor Roman Town*. Norwich: Norfolk Archaeological Trust. Available online: https://caistorromanproject.org/news/venta-icenorum-a-brief-history-of-caistor-roman-town/.

Bowden, W. and D. J. Bescoby (2008). 'The Plan of Venta Icenorum (Caistor-by-Norwich): Interpreting a new geophysical survey', *Journal of Roman Archaeology* 21(1): 325–34.

Bowman, A. K. (1994). *Life and Letters on the Roman Frontier: Vindolanda and its people*. London: British Museum Press.

Breeze, A. (2019). 'Verolamium: "St Albans" and Old Irish *Ollam* "Poet"', *Classics Ireland* 26: 30–45.

Brewer, R. (2006). *Caerwent Roman Town*. Third edition. Cardiff: Cadw.

Buckley, R., N. C. Cooper and M. Morris (2021). *Life in Roman and Medieval Leicester*. Leicester: University of Leicester Archaeological Services.

Catling, C. (2024). 'Visualising Venta Belgarum', *The Past*, 3 April. Available online: https://the-past.com/feature/visualising-venta-belgarum-touring-prehistoric-roman-and-post-roman-winchester/.

Champion, T. (2007). 'Prehistoric Kent', in J. H. Williams (ed.), *The Archaeology of Kent to AD 800*. Woodbridge: Boydell Press, 67–134.

Cousins, E. H. (2020). *The Sanctuary at Bath in the Roman Empire*. Cambridge: Cambridge University Press.

Creighton, J. and R. Fry (2016). *Silchester: Changing Visions of a Roman Town*. London: Society for the Promotion of Roman Studies.

Crummy, P. (2003). 'Colchester's Roman Town Wall', in P. Wilson (ed.), 44–52.

Crummy, P (2008). 'The Roman circus at Colchester', *Britannia* 39: 15–32.

Cunliffe, B. W. and P. Davenport (1995). *The Temple of Sulis Minerva at Bath* (2 vols). Oxford: Oxford University Committee for Archaeology.

Davenport, P. (2021). *Roman Bath: A new history and archaeology of Aquae Sulis*. Stroud: History Press.

Dawkes, G. and D. Hart (2017). 'Chichester *Thermae* reconsidered', *Sussex Archaeological Collections* 155: 43–66.

Eckardt, H. and G. Müldner (2016). 'Mobility, Migration, and Diaspora in Roman Britain', in M. Millett, L. Revell and A. Moore (eds), 203–22.

Ellis, P. and R. White (eds) (2003). *Wroxeter Archaeology: Excavation and research on the defences and in the town*. Transactions of the Shropshire Archaeological and History Society 78. Available online: https://archaeologydataservice.ac.uk/library/browse/issue.xhtml?recordId=1079792&recordType=Journal.

Ferraby, R. and M. Millett (2020). *Isurium Brigantium: An archaeological survey of Roman Aldborough*. London: Society of Antiquaries of London. Available online: https://library.oapen.org/handle/20.500.12657/37741.

Ford, B. M. and S. Teague (2011). *Winchester: A city in the making*. Oxford: Oxford Archaeology.

Frere, S. S. (1971). 'The Forum and Baths at Caistor by Norwich', *Britannia* 2: 1–26.

Fulford, M. (2021). *Silchester Revealed*. Oxford: Windgather.

Fulford, M. (2022). *The Emperor Nero's Pottery and Tilery at Little London, Pamber, by Silchester, Hampshire: The Excavations of 2017*. London: Society for the Promotion of Roman Studies.

Fulford, M., A. Clarke, E. Durham and N. Pankhurst (2018). *Late Iron Age Calleva: The pre-conquest occupation at Silchester Insula IX*. London: Society for the Promotion of Roman Studies.

Fulford, M., A. Clarke, E. Durham and N. Pankhurst (2020). *Silchester Insula IX: The Claudio-Neronian occupation of the Iron Age Oppidum*. London: Society for the Promotion of Roman Studies.

Fulford, M. and J. Timby (2000). *Late Iron Age and Roman Silchester: Excavations on the Site of the Forum-Basilica 1977, 1980–86*. London: Society for the Promotion of Roman Studies.

Fulford, M. and N. Holbrook (eds) (2015). *The Towns of Roman Britain: The contribution of commercial archaeology since 1990*. Oxford: Oxbow. Available online: https://archaeologydataservice.ac.uk/library/browse/issue.xhtml?recordId=1161493&recordType-onographSeries.

Garland, N. (2020). 'The origins of British *oppida*: Understanding transformation in Iron Age practice and society', *Oxford Journal of Archaeology* 39(1): 107–25.

Gascogne, A. and D. Radford (eds) (2013). *Colchester: Fortress of the War God*. Oxford: Oxbow. Available online: https://library.oapen.org/handle/20.500.12657/54106.

Green, T. (2012). *Britons and Anglo-Saxon Lincolnshire*. Lincoln: History of Lincolnshire Committee.

Guest, P. (2022). 'The Forum-Basilica at Caerwent (Venta Silurum): A History of the Roman Silures', *Britannia* 53: 227–67.

Hart, J. (2021). 'Two thousand years of development in Gloucester's Greater Blackfriars Area', *Cotswold Archaeology*. Available online: https://cotswoldarchaeology.co.uk/two-thousand-years-of-development-in-gloucesters-greater-blackfriars-area/.

Hart, J. (2022). 'All along the watchtower: New discoveries along the line of Gloucester's Roman defences', *Cotswold Archaeology*. Available online: https://cotswoldarchaeology.co.uk/all-along-the-watchtower-new-discoveries-along-the-line-of-gloucesters-roman-defences/.

Hilts, C. (2022). 'Caistor St Edmund: Excavating a Roman aqueduct in Roman Norfolk', *The Past*, 31 October. Available online: https://the-past.com/feature/caistor-st-edmund-excavating-an-aqueduct-in-roman-norfolk/.

Hilts, C. and W. Bowden (2021). 'The "Priest's House"; Excavating an enigmatic Roman structure at Caistor St Edmund', *The Past*, 25 October. Available online: https://the-past.com/feature/the-priests-house-excavating-an-enigmatic-roman-structure-at-caistor-st-edmund/.

Hingley, R. (2008). *The Recovery of Roman Britain*. Oxford: Oxford University Press.

Hingley, R. (2018). *Londinium: A biography*. London: Bloomsbury.

Hingley, R. (2019). 'Assessing How Representation of the Roman Past Impacts Public Perceptions of the Province of Britain', *Public Archaeology* 18(4): 241–60.

Hingley, R. (2022). *Conquering the Ocean: The Roman Invasion of Britain*. New York: Oxford University Press.

Hingley, R., K. Sharpe and T. Yarrow (2025). *Ancient Identities in Britain: Exploring Heritage in the Making*. London: UCL Press.

Hingley, R. and C. Unwin (2005). *Boudica: Iron Age Warrior Queen*. London: Bloomsbury.

Historic Towns Trust (2021). *An Historical Map of Canterbury: From Roman Times to 1907*. London: The Historic Towns Trust.

Hodgson, N. (2015). *Roman Corbridge: Fort, Town and Museum*. London: English Heritage.

Holbrook, N. (2008a). *Excavations and Observations in Roman Cirencester 1998–2007*. Cirencester Excavations VI. Cirencester: Cotswold Archaeology. Available online: https://cotswoldarchaeology.co.uk/wp-content/uploads/2011/06/Excavations-and-Observations-in-Roman-Cirencester-1998-2007_Part01.pdf.

Holbrook, N. (2008b). 'Cirencester and the Cotswolds: The early Roman evolution of a town and rural landscape', *Journal of Roman Archaeology* 21: 303–23.

Hurst, H. (2020). *Gloucester: The Roman Forum and post-Roman sequence at the city centre*. Gloucester: Gloucester Archaeological Publications.

Johns, C. and T. W. Potter (1985). 'The Canterbury Late Roman Treasure', *Antiquaries Journal* 65: 312–52.

Jones, M. J. (2002). *Roman Lincoln*. Stroud: Tempus.

Jones, M. J., D. Stocker and A. Vince (2003). *The City by the Pool: Assessing the Archaeology of Lincoln*. Oxford: Oxbow. Available online: https://www.jstor.org/stable/j.ctv2p7j5sw.

Koon, K. (2023). 'Demetrius of Tarsus in Two Greek Votive Tablets from York', *Archaeological Journal* 180(1): 82–103.

La Trobe-Bateman, E. and R. Niblett (2016). *Bath: An Archaeological Assessment*. Oxford: Oxbow.

Lambert, M. (2010). *Christians and Pagans: The Conversion of Britain from Alban to Bede.* London: Yale University Press.

Leach, S., H. Eckardt, C. Chenery, G. Müldner and M. Lewis (2009). 'A Lady of York', *Antiquity* 84: 131–45.

Lockyear, K. (2019). 'Where Finding Nothing Is Interesting', in J. Bonsall (ed.), *New Global Perspectives on Archaeological Prospection.* Oxford: Archaeopress, 157–60.

Lockyear, K. and E. Shlasko (2017). 'Under the Park: Recent geophysical surveys at Verulamium (St Albans, Hertfordshire, England)', *Archaeological Prospection* 24(1): 17–36.

Magilton, J. (2003). 'The Defences of Roman Chichester', in P. Wilson (ed.), 156–67.

Manley, H., P. Cheetham, D. Stewart and M. Russell (2024). 'A Source of Confusion: New archaeological evidence from the Dorchester aqueduct', *Britannia* 55: 83–97.

Mattingly, D. (2006). *An Imperial Possession: Britain in the Roman Empire, 54 BC–AD 409.* London: Allen Lane.

Millett, M. (2007). 'Roman Kent', in J. H. Williams (ed.), 135–86.

Millett, M. and R. Ferraby (2016). *Aldborough Roman Site and Town.* London: English Heritage.

Millett, M., L. Revell and A. Moore (eds) (2016). *The Oxford Handbook of Roman Britain.* Oxford: Oxford University Press.

Moore, T. (2020). *A Biography of Power: Research and excavations at the Iron Age oppidum of Bagendon, Gloucestershire.* Oxford: Archaeopress.

Morris, F. M. and M. Biddle (2023). *Venta Belgarum: Prehistoric, Roman and Post-Roman Winchester, Volume 1: Excavations.* Oxford: Archaeopress.

Morris, M (2022). 'Leicester and Roman Africa', *The Past*, 8 June. Available online: https://the-past.com/feature/leicester-and-roman-africa-exploring-ancient-multiculturalism-in-the-midlands/.

Museum of London Archaeology (2011). *Londinium: A new map and guide to Roman London.* London: Museum of London Archaeology.

Newman, J. and N. Pevsner (2006). *The Buildings of England, Shropshire.* London: Yale University Press.

Niblett, R. (2001). *The Roman City of St Albans.* Stroud: The History Press.

Niblett, R. and I. Thompson (2005). *Albans Buried Towns: An assessment of St Albans' archaeology up to AD1600.* Oxford: Oxbow.

Ottaway, P. (2011). *Roman York.* Revised edition. Stroud: Batsford/English Heritage.

Ottaway, P. (2017). *Swithun's 'City of Happiness and Good Fortune'.* Oxford: Oxbow.

Perring, D. (2022). *London in the Roman World*. Oxford: Oxford University Press.
Putnam, B. (2007). *Roman Dorset*. Revised edition. Stroud: History Press.
Reid, J., R. Müller and S. Klein (2022). 'The Windridge Farm *Glandes* Revisited: Clues to conquest', *Britannia* 53: 323–46.
Revell, L. (2016). 'Urban monumentality in Roman Britain', in M. Millett, L. Revell and A. Moore (eds), 767–89.
Rippon, S. and N. Holbrook (2021). *Roman and Medieval Exeter and their Hinterlands: From* Isca *to* Excester. Oxford: Oxbow. Available online: http://openresearchlibrary.org/viewer/91c84bd0-b9c1-408a-80ee-7a4b6cea8aaf/1.
Rivet, A. L. F. and C. Smith (1979). *The Place-Names of Roman Britain*. London: Routledge.
Rogers, A. (2016). 'The development of towns', in M. Millett, L. Revell and A. Moore (eds), 741–65.
Salvatore, J. P. (2024). *Exeter: A Roman Legionary Fortress and* Civitas *Capital*. Oxford: Archaeopress.
Simmonds, A., N. Márquez-Grant and L. Loe (2008). *Life and Death in a Roman City: Excavation of a Roman cemetery with mass grave at 120–122 London Road, Gloucester*. Oxford: Oxford Archaeological Unit.
Sparey-Green, C. (2002). 'Where are the Christians? Late Roman Cemeteries in Britain', in M. Carver (ed.), *The Cross Goes North*. Woodbridge: Boydell and Brewer, 93–107.
Sparey-Green, C. (2021). 'Bigbury Camp and its associated earthworks', *Archaeologia Cantiana* 143: 31–58.
Speed, G. (2023). 'A Thermae and Aqueduct in Roman Leicester: Recent discoveries at Jewry Wall Museum and the Raw Dykes', *Transactions of the Leicestershire Archaeological and Historical Society* 97: 41–74.
Thorold, D. (2023). *Roman Verulamium: Museum Guide*. St Albans: St Albans Council.
Tibbs, A. (2024). *A Short Guide to Roman London*. Stroud: Amberley.
Tomlin, R. S. O. (2018). *Britannia Romana: Roman Inscriptions and Roman Britain*. Oxford: Oxbow.
Wacher, J. (1995). *The Towns of Roman Britain*. Second edition. London: Routledge.
Walton, C. and J. Kenny (2022). 'A festival of finds: celebrating Chichester's Roman past', *The Past*, 5 May. Available online: https://the-past.com/feature/a-festival-of-finds-celebrating-chichesters-roman-past/.
Weekes, J. (in preparation). 'Durovernum Cantiacorum . . . Cantwaraburh . . . Canterbury', *The Historic Atlas of Canterbury*. London: Historic Towns Trust and Canterbury Archaeological Trust.
Welch, M. (2007). 'Anglo-Saxon Kent to AD 800', in J. H. Williams (ed.), 187–248.

White, G. M. (1934). 'The Chichester Amphitheatre: Preliminary excavations', *Antiquaries Journal* 16(2): 149–59.

White, R. H. (2023). *Wroxeter Roman City*. Revised edition. London: English Heritage.

White, R. H. (2022). *Wroxeter: Ashes under Uricon*. Oxford: Archaeopress.

White, R. H. and P. Barker (1998). *Wroxeter: Life & Death of a Roman City*. Stroud: Tempus.

White, R. H., C. Gaffney and V. L. Gaffney (2013). *Wroxeter, the Cornovii and the Urban Process: Final Report of the Wroxeter Hinterland Project, 1994–1997. Volume 2: Characterizing the City*. Oxford: Archaeopress.

Williams, J. H. (ed.) (2007). *The Archaeology of Kent to AD 800*. Woodbridge: Boydell Press.

Wilson, P. (ed.) (2003). *The Archaeology of Roman Towns*. Oxford: Oxbow.

Index

Note: Towns explored in this book are given in bold type

Adminius (Iron Age noble), 259
aerial photography, 65, 68, 69, 70, 71, 125, 126, 147, 239, 247
Agricola, Gnaeus Julius (provincial governor), 260, 302, 306
Aldborough (*Isurium*), 11, 20, 23–35, 205
   Aldborough museum, 23, 24, 26, 27, 31, 33
   amphitheatre, 24, 29, 30, 31
   bridge, 24, 29, 33, 34
   burial/cemetery, 24, 33–4
   defences/town walls, 24, 26, 27, 30–2
   forum, 24, 26, 29–30, 32, 35
   fort (Roecliffe), 23, 26, 27, 28, 35
   mosaic/townhouse, 20, 23, 24, 32–3, 34
Allectus (usurper emperor), 222, 236–7
altar, 32, 44, 60, 64, 133, 255, 308
amphitheatre, 9, 13, 14, 15, 99, 158, 246, 264
   Aldborough, 24, 29, 30, 31
   Caistor St Edmund, 66, 70
   Chichester, 89, 90, 99, 101
   Cirencester, 99, 103, 104, 105, 106, 113

   Dorchester, 99, 149, 150, 152, 153, 154, 156–8
   London, 99, 218, 220, 221, 222, 226, 227, 228, 237
   Silchester, 99, 113, 158, 239, 240, 242, 246–7, 248, 249
Aquae Sulis, see Bath
aqueduct, 14, 168, 192, 278, 293
   Corbridge, 138, 140, 144, 145
   Dorchester, 153, 158–9, 162
   Leicester, 184, 192, 196
   Lincoln, 198, 207, 212–3
Ashby, Thomas, 54, 58
Atkinson, Donald, 68, 70, 71
Atrebates (Iron Age people/Roman *civitas*), 5, 239, 243
August (Switzerland), 133

Bagendon (Iron Age *oppidum*), see Cirencester
Balkerne Gate, see Colchester
Barker, Philip, 287
bastion, see tower
Bath (*Aquae Sulis*), 4, 8, 12, 13, 15, 16, 20, 37–49, 80, 81, 96, 110, 111, 194
   baths and temple of Sulis Minerva/Museum, 12, 15,

37, 38, 39, 40, 41, 42–4, 46,
        47, 48, 49, 194
    Sacred Spring, 41, 42–5, 48,
        96, 194
    burial/cemetery
        tombstones, 41, 42, 44–5, 47
    Cross Bath Springs, 45
    defences/town walls, 16, 37, 38,
        40, 46–7
    extramural settlement, 37, 38, 47
    King Bladud (legendary
        founder), 20, 48, 49
    pilgrims/visitors, 45
    baths/bathhouse
        military, 167, 168, 288, 304
        private, 17, 161, 307
        London, Billingsgate, 17, 220,
            234–5
        public, 8, 9, 14, 15, 17, 54, 60, 68,
            70, 80, 82, 109, 130, 158,
            161, 168, 178, 201, 207,
            212, 213, 215, 225, 227,
            242, 243, 245, 247, 250,
            261, 264, 304, 307
        Bath, 15, 37, 38, 39, 40, 41,
            42–5, 46, 47, 48, 49, 194
        Chichester, at the Novium
            Museum, 89, 90, 96, 101
        Leicester, Jewry Wall, 14, 184,
            186, 190–2, 196
        Wroxeter, Old Work, 14, 284,
            286, 287, 288, 290, 291–3,
            296, 297
Bede (early medieval author), 86
Belgae (Iron Age people/Roman
        civitas), 274, 276, 277
Biddle, Martin, 277
Bigbury Camp (Iron Age hillfort),
        see Chichester
Billingsgate bathhouse, *see* London
Bitterne, 98

Bladud, King, *see* Bath
Bloomberg letters, 225, 260
Bordeaux (France), 306
Boroughbridge, 25, 26, 31, 34
Boudica (Iron Age warrior leader),
    16, 65, 68, 73, 94, 122, 126,
    128, 129–30, 134, 222, 224,
    225, 246, 254, 257, 259
Brewer, Richard, 54
bridge (Roman), 24, 29, 30, 31, 33, 34,
    71, 81, 139, 140, 148, 167,
    171, 192, 205, 218, 222,
    226, 233, 237, 302, 303, 304
Brigantes (Iron Age people/Roman
    civitas), 23, 29
Britannia (province of), 19, 129, 141,
    225, 247, 259, 302
    Britannia Prima, 110, 115
    Britannia Secunda, 214, 302
British Museum, 60, 204, 226, 230
Brough on Humber (Roman town), 4
buildings (*see also* amphitheatre,
    bathhouse, forum, house,
    temple, etc.), 2, 6, 20, 23, 27,
    40, 41, 42, 45, 47, 48, 55, 56,
    60, 64, 66, 68, 73, 86, 96,
    117, 121, 137, 140, 142, 141,
    147, 148, 154, 161, 174, 176,
    178, 218, 221, 222, 223, 238,
    243, 247, 248, 254, 256, 262,
    267, 278, 283, 284, 288, 303,
    305, 307
industrial, 10, 135
military, 6, 17, 108, 122, 142, 143,
    144, 145–6, 168, 176,
    228–9, 288, 302
public 6, 8, 9, 13–15, 32, 55, 70,
    78, 80, 81, 107, 109, 122,
    130, 136, 144–5, 156, 158,
    159, 163, 166, 168, 187,
    189, 210, 226, 227, 228,

237, 245, 247, 255, 260,
    261, 262–3, 274, 278, 287,
    290–3, 303, 307
  shops, 9, 17, 28, 51, 54, 56, 58–9
  Corbridge, 17, 140, 143, 144,
    146
  Verulamium, 17, 251, 260, 262
  Wroxeter, 291, 293
burial/cemetery, Iron Age, 6, 79, 92,
    93, 103, 106, 108, 121, 123,
    124–5, 128, 154, 155, 246,
    254, 256, 258–9, 264
  Colchester, Lexden Tumulus, 121,
    124–5
  Verulamium, Folly Lane, 108,
    246, 256, 258–9, 264
  Verulamium, King Harry Lane,
    258
burial/cemetery, Roman, 18, 19, 24,
    33–4, 47, 60, 64, 72, 76, 85,
    90, 100, 104, 115, 118, 122,
    135, 136, 138, 147, 150,
    162, 172, 174, 176, 181,
    184, 193, 202, 213, 218,
    226, 230–1, 238, 240,
    249–50, 252, 267, 275, 278,
    281, 284, 296, 300, 303, 308
  cremation, 18, 60, 115, 259
  inhumation, 18, 115, 162, 181
  mausoleum, 18, 33, 60, 230
    Caerwent (?), 60
    London, St Bride (?), 220, 231
  tombstone, 18, 41, 42, 44–5, 47,
    72, 108, 115, 127, 147, 148,
    156, 172, 173, 176, 177,
    181, 202, 203, 204, 213–14,
    226, 249–50, 296, 308
  tower tomb, Corbridge, 138, 147,
    148
burial/cemetery, early medieval, 72,
    195

Cadw, 52, 53, 58
Caerleon (Roman fortress), 54, 55,
    57, 61, 166
Caerwent (*Venta Silurum*), 8, 11, 14,
    15, 17, 51–64, 68, 110, 277,
    297
  defences/town walls, 52, 54, 55,
    60–2, 63
  forum, 14, 51, 52, 54, 55, 56–8,
    64
  mausoleum (?), 60
  Roman finds in St Tathan's
    Church, 59–60
  shops, 51, 54, 56, 58–9
  temple, 15, 51, 52, 54, 55, 56, 58,
    60, 62
  townhouse, 51, 52, 54, 56, 58–9,
    60, 61
Caesar, Julius (Roman dictator), 79,
    254, 256–7
**Caistor St Edmund (*Venta
    Icenorum*)**, 8, 11, 13, 16,
    55, 65–73, 277
  amphitheatre, 66, 70
  burial/cemetery, 72
  defences/town walls, 16, 65, 66,
    67, 69, 70–1, 73
  forum, 66, 67, 68, 69, 70, 73
  temple, 66, 68, 69, 70, 73
Camulodunum, see Colchester
Camulos (deity), 4, 123
Cantaci (Iron Age people/Roman
    civitas), 78
Canterbury (*Durovernum*), 6, 7, 15,
    17, 19, 75–87, 188, 230
  burial/cemetery, 76, 85
  Canterbury Roman Museum, 75,
    77, 79, 81–2, 86
  defences/town walls, 75, 76, 78,
    82–5
  oppidum, 6, 7, 75, 77, 78–9, 80

Bigbury Camp (hillfort), 75, 76, 79, 87
  Bridge Helmet, 79
  sacred focus (temple, theatre), 76, 79–80, 81
  townhouse/mosaic, at Canterbury Roman Museum, 75, 81–2
Caracalla (Roman emperor), 306–7
Carausius (Roman usurper emperor), 222, 237
Carlisle (Roman town), 4, 140, 141
Carmarthen (Roman town), 4
Cassivellanus (Iron Age leader), 254, 256, 257
Catuvellauni (Iron Age people/ Roman *civitas*), 5, 108, 257
causewayed enclosure (Neolithic), 153, 154
cemetries, *see* burial
Chedworth Roman Villa, 106
Chester (fortress), 203, 266
Chichester (*Noviomagus*), 7, 20, 89–101, 108, 243, 245, 249, 274
  amphitheatre, 89, 90, 99, 101
  bathhouse at the Novium Museum, 89, 90, 96, 101
  burial/cemetery, 90, 100
  defences/town walls, 90, 91, 97–9
  Fishbourne Roman Palace, 89, 90, 91, 92, 93–4, 95, 98
  Novium Museum, 89, 90, 91, 93, 95, 96, 101
  oppidum, 7, 90, 92, 93–4, 95, 100
  dykes, 92, 93, 101
  North Bersted Iron Age burial, 93
  temple of Neptune and Minerva, 94, 96
  Togidubnus inscription, 89, 90, 92, 93–5, 96, 100, 101

Chi-Rho symbol, 86
Christianity, 19, 35, 86, 115, 136, 162, 215, 255, 267–8, 297, 307
  churches, Roman (?)
  Colchester, Butt Road, 15, 19, 118, 119, 136
  Lincoln, St Paul in the Bail, 19, 35, 215
circus, *see* Colchester
Circus Maximus (Rome, Italy), 135
Cirencester (*Corinium*), 6, 10, 19, 99, 103–16, 248
  amphitheatre, 99, 103, 104, 105, 106, 113
  burial/cemetery, 104, 106, 108, 115
  Tar Barrow, 103, 108
  tombstones, 108, 115
  Corinium Museum, 10, 103, 104, 105, 106, 108, 109, 113–14, 115
  defences/town walls, 104, 106, 110–12, 113, 115
  fort (Roman) (?), 103, 106, 108
  forum, 104, 109
  Jupiter Column, 109–10, 115
  mosaic, 107, 113–14
  oppidum at Bagendon, 6, 103, 106, 107, 108
City Wall at Vine Street, *see* London
civitas capital, 2, 3, 4, 7–8, 11, 12, 13, 14, 16, 23, 26, 29–37, 51, 55–64, 65, 69–73, 75, 78, 80–7, 89, 96–101, 103, 107, 109–16, 137, 149, 158–62, 163, 168–72, 183, 186, 188–96, 226, 239, 243, 247–50, 274, 276, 277, 278–81, 283, 289–97, 308
civitas/civitates, 3, 14, 57, 128, 133, 290, 308

Claudius (Roman emperor), 121, 122, 126–7, 133, 135, 136, 186, 245, 254, 257, 258, 259
coin production (Iron Age), 79, 107, 188, 258
Colchester (*Camulodunum*), 6, 7, 11, 13, 14, 15, 16, 21, 80, 117–36, 201, 202, 217, 223, 224, 225, 255, 257, 260, 277
   burial/cemetery, 118, 122, 124, 125, 135
   Castle Museum, 120, 122, 123, 124, 127, 128, 130, 133, 135, 136
   church (?), Butt Road, 15, 19, 118, 119, 136
   circus, 14, 118, 120, 121, 122, 123, 134–5
   defences/town walls, 16, 118, 119, 121–12, 128, 130–2
     Balkerne Gate, 121, 128–9, 131, 132
   Fenwick Hoard, 130
   fortress, 6, 13, 17, 121, 122, 126–7, 128, 203
   mosaic, Firstsite Art Museum, 120, 135
   oppidum, 6, 121, 123–5, 127, 136, 242, 245, 246, 257, 258
     dykes, 6, 107, 121, 122, 123–4, 125
     Gosbecks, 80, 120, 121–2, 124, 125–6, 127, 128, 129, 131, 134, 246
     Lexden Tumulus, 121, 124–5
   temple of Claudius, 15, 43, 44, 81, 118, 120, 121, 122, 128, 129–30, 131, 132–4, 226
   theatre (in colony), 118, 120, 134, 263
colony, 2–3, 6–7, 8, 11, 13, 16, 17, 37, 62, 121–2, 127–36, 173, 175, 176, 177–81, 197, 200, 201, 204–15, 224, 228, 255, 296, 299, 302–3, 305–9
column, 32, 43, 57, 59, 109, 110, 115, 175, 178, 198, 211, 236, 250, 278, 279, 286, 290, 291, 296, 304
Constantine the Great (Roman emperor), 302–3, 304, 307
Constantius I (Roman emperor), 237, 307
Corbridge (*Coria*), 8, 11, 17, 137–48
   aqueduct, 138, 140, 144, 145
   bridge, 138, 140, 148
   burial/cemetery, 147
     tower tomb (mausoleum), 138, 147, 148
   Corbridge Museum, 137, 139, 140, 143, 144, 147
   defences/town walls (?), 138, 143, 147
   fort, 11, 137, 141, 142–3, 144
   fountain, 138, 140, 143, 144, 147
   granary, 140, 143–4, 146
   Iron Age settlement, 137, 142
   military compound, 146
   shops, 17, 140, 143, 144, 146
Corieltauvi (Iron Age people/Roman *civitas*), 183, 186, 187
Corinium Museum, *see* Cirencester
Corinthian capitals, 43, 57, 81, 109
Cornovii (Iron Age people/Roman *civitas*), 289, 290
Council of Arles (AD 314), 19, 115
Crummy, Philip, 123
Cunliffe, Barry, 40, 48, 93
Cunobelin (Iron Age king), 117, 121, 122, 123, 125, 126, 136, 254, 257, 259
curse (lead), 10, 72, 42, 43, 45, 183, 186, 189, 194–5

Deae Matres (deities), 32, 308
Decius (Roman emperor), 268
defences/town walls, 1, 9, 16–17, 20
   Aldborough, 24, 26, 27, 30–2
   Bath, 16, 37, 38, 40, 46–7
   Caerwent, 52, 54, 55, 60–2, 63
   Caistor St Edmund, 16, 65, 66, 67, 69, 70–1, 73
   Canterbury, 75, 76, 78, 82–5
   Chichester, 90, 91, 97–9
   Cirencester, 104, 106, 110–12, 113, 115
   Colchester, 16, 118, 119, 121–2, 128, 130–2
   Corbridge (?), 138, 143, 147
   Dorchester, 150, 151, 152, 159–60
   Exeter, 16, 163, 164, 165, 166, 168–71
   Gloucester, 16, 173, 174, 175, 176, 178–80
   Leicester, 183, 184, 185, 187, 188, 192–3, 195
   Lincoln, 6, 16, 168, 179, 197, 198, 200, 204–10, 213
   London, 20, 218, 220, 222, 229, 231–4, 237–8
   Silchester, 110, 239, 240, 242, 243, 248–9
   Verulamium, 16, 251, 253, 255, 260, 256, 261, 262, 264–7
   Winchester, 20, 271, 272, 274, 275, 276, 277, 279–81
   Wroxeter, 16, 284, 286, 287, 290, 294–6, 297
   York, 299, 300, 305, 307–8
Dere Street (Roman road), 29, 141, 147, 148
Devil's Arrows (Neolithic standing stones), 27
Dobunni (Iron Age people/ Roman *civitas*), 103, 108, 109

Domitian (Roman emperor), 177, 201, 204
Dorchester (*Durnovaria*), 11, 149–62
   amphitheatre, Maumbury Rings, 99, 149, 150, 152, 153, 154, 156–8
   aqueduct, 153, 158–9, 162
   burial/cemetery, 150, 155, 156, 162
      Poundbury cemetery, 162
      tombstone, 156
   defences/town walls, 149, 150, 152, 159–60
   Dorset Museum, Dorchester, 151, 152, 162
   fort (?), 153, 156
   Maiden Castle hillfort, 149, 152, 153, 154–5, 156, 162
   Roman temple, 155, 162
   Poundbury Fort (Iron Age), 152, 153, 154, 155, 156, 159, 162
   Town House, 17, 149, 152, 154, 160–2
Dorchester on Thames (Roman small town), 249
Dorset Museum, *see* Dorchester
Down, Alec, 93
Dumnonii (Iron Age people/Roman *civitas*), 163, 168
Durotriges (Iron Age people/ Roman *civitas*), 149, 153
dyke (Iron Age earthwork defences), 6, 187
   Bagendon (Cirencester), 6, 106, 107
   Chichester, 92, 93, 101
   Colchester, 6, 107, 121, 122, 123–4, 125
   Silchester (Inner Earthworks), 6, 244–5, 247, 248
   Verulamium, 6, 254, 256, 257, 258

Index

English Heritage, 23, 26, 27, 31, 113, 137, 140, 141, 143, 146, 147, 148, 154, 242, 283, 286, 287, 288, 295, 297
enslaved people, 10, 114, 183, 195, 224, 228
   Fortunata (London), 228
   slave's quarters, Leicester, 10, 194
Eppillus (Iron Age leader), 244
Exeter (*Isca*), 8, 11, 12, 16, 163–72
   Catacombs (nineteenth-century), 171
   burial/cemetery, 172
   defences/town walls, 16, 163, 164, 165, 166, 168–71
   fortress, 11, 164, 166, 167, 168, 172
   forum, 163, 164, 166, 168
   Royal Albert Memorial Museum, 163, 164, 165, 166, 171
   extramural settlement, 17–18, 26, 33, 37, 38, 47, 60, 85, 100, 115, 136, 171–2, 179, 180–1, 205, 267

Fishbourne Roman Palace, *see* Chichester
Folly Lane burial/temple, *see* Verulamium
fort (Roman), 11, 13, 40, 41–2, 84, 153, 156, 184, 188, 204, 225, 226, 277, 287, 288
   Aldborough, Roecliffe, 23, 26, 27, 28, 35
   Cirencester (?), 103, 106, 108
   Colchester, Gosbecks, 126
   Corbridge, 11, 137, 141, 142–3, 144
   Dorchester (?), 153, 156
   Leicester (?), 184, 188
   London, Cripplegate, 220, 229–30, 231, 232, 234

fort/hillfort (Iron Age), 11, 152, 153, 276, 288
   Bigbury Camp, Canterbury, 75, 76, 79, 87
   Maiden Castle, Dorchester, 149, 152, 153, 154–5, 156, 162
   Oram's Arbour, Winchester, 272, 274, 275–6, 277, 278, 281
   Poundbury, Dorchester, 152, 153, 154, 155, 156, 159, 162
fortress (Roman), 6, 11, 17, 54, 55, 57, 61, 156
   Colchester, 6, 13, 17, 121, 122, 126–7, 128, 203
   Exeter, 11, 164, 166, 167, 168, 172
   Gloucester, 6, 17, 55, 121, 173, 176, 177, 178
   Lincoln, 6, 197, 201, 202, 203–4, 205, 207, 211
   Wroxeter, 8, 11, 283, 287, 288, 289, 296
   York, 11, 57, 203, 299, 300, 302, 303, 304, 305, 308, 309
forum, 7, 13–14, 15–16, 37, 45, 81, 96, 130, 133, 158, 278, 307
   Aldborough, 24, 26, 29–30, 32, 35
   Caerwent, 14, 51, 52, 54, 55, 56–8, 64
   Caistor St Edmund, 66, 67, 68, 69, 70, 73
   Cirencester, 104, 109
   Exeter, 163, 164, 166, 168
   Gloucester, 174, 178, 181
   Leicester, 184, 189–90
   Lincoln, 197, 198, 200, 201, 211–12, 215
   London, 218, 220, 222, 225, 226, 228–9, 233, 237
   Silchester, 240, 243, 245, 247
   Verulamium, 252, 255, 258, 259, 260

Wroxeter, 283, 284, 286, 287, 288, 289, 290–1, 293, 294, 296, 297
Fortunata (enslaved woman), *see* London
Fosse Way (Roman road), 188, 264
fountain, 201, 212, 213
   Corbridge, 138, 140, 143, 144, 147
   Leicester (*septizonium*), 189
Frere, Sheppard, 255–6, 261
Fulford, Mike, 243

Gaffney, Vince, 287
gate/gateway/gatehouse (on town walls), 17, 30, 31, 33, 46–7, 60, 61–4, 68, 71, 72, 82, 83–5, 86, 97–9, 110–12, 113, 115, 131–2, 159–60, 166, 169–71, 172, 179–80, 181, 192–3, 197, 201, 205–11, 213, 223, 229, 230, 231–4, 248–9, 266–7, 277, 279, 280–1, 294, 295–6, 307
   Caerwent, south gate, 62, 63
   Canterbury, Quening Gate, 84
   Colchester, Balkerne Gate, 121, 128–9, 131, 132
   Lincoln, Newport Arch, 97, 200, 205–7
Gaul, 42, 57, 80, 226, 264
geophysical survey, 23, 27, 30, 31, 32, 33, 34, 55, 60, 62, 65, 69, 72, 73, 108, 125, 141, 143, 147, 239, 247, 249, 250, 256, 261, 262, 267, 269, 283, 288, 290, 296, 297, 303
German settlers/travelers, 72, 45, 86, 289
Glanum (Provence, France), 147
Gloucester (*Glevum*), 6, 11, 16, 17, 18, 62, 122, 169, 173–81, 201

   burial/cemetery, 174, 176, 181
   tombstone, 177, 181
   defences/town walls, 16, 173, 174, 175, 176, 178–80
   fortress, 6, 17, 55, 121, 173, 176, 177, 178
   forum, 174, 178, 181
   Museum of Gloucester, 18, 173, 174, 176, 177, 178, 180
   statue of Nerva, 175, 178
Gosbecks, *see* Colchester

Hadrian (Roman emperor), 290
Hadrian's Wall, 137, 140, 141, 306
henge (Neolithic), 149, 153, 154, 157
hillfort, *see* fort/hillfort (Iron Age)
houses, Iron Age, 11, 78, 93, 155, 188, 245, 276
houses, Roman, 9, 12, 13, 15, 17, 18, 28, 32, 33, 41, 45, 47, 70, 80, 81, 96, 106, 109, 115, 131, 140, 143, 146, 155, 159, 176, 177, 180, 181, 193, 194, 201, 212, 230, 250, 258, 267, 277–8, 306
   palace, 9, 89, 90, 91, 92, 93, 94, 95, 98, 227, 236–7, 262, 303, 307
   timber houses, 10, 17, 28, 54, 55, 59, 67, 69, 72, 78, 81, 95, 96, 109, 114, 122, 128, 130, 156, 161, 188, 194, 213, 215, 224, 227, 235, 245, 260, 261, 283, 287, 297, 289
   townhouse, 17, 45, 113, 114, 135, 158, 171, 213, 228, 235, 247, 255, 278
   Aldborough, 20, 23, 24, 32–3, 34
   Caerwent, 51, 52, 54, 56, 58–9, 60, 61
   Canterbury, 75, 81–2

Dorchester, 17, 149, 152, 154, 160-2
Leicester, Vine Street, 10, 183, 186, 189, 194-5, 196
Verulamium, 251, 261-2
Wroxeter (reconstruction), 17, 283-4, 286, 290, 292, 293-4
houses, early medieval, 86
Housesteads (Roman fort), 143
Hudd, Alfred, 54, 58
hypocaust, 9, 17, 59, 194, 213, 262
Bath, Great Baths, 43
Billingsgate bathhouse (London), 234
Canterbury townhouse, 81-2
Chichester bathhouse, 96
Dorchester townhouse, 161
Leicester bathhouse, 192
Verulamium townhouse, 262
Wroxeter reconstructed house, 294

Iceni (Iron Age people/Roman *civitas*), 65, 73, 129
industry, 9, 10, 18, 33, 72, 80, 96, 114, 125, 135, 147, 159, 194, 228, 237, 245-6, 262

Jewry Wall, *see* Leicester
Jupiter
Jupiter Column, Cirencester, 109-10, 115
Jupiter Dolichenus (deity), 147
Jupiter Optimus Maximus (deity), 32, 308

Kenyon, Kathleen, 191, 255, 263

Lawson, Andrew, 27
legions/legionaries, 6, 11, 13, 16, 54, 57, 61, 77, 127, 130, 137, 141, 146, 156, 201, 228, 283
Second Legion Adiutrix, 203, 204
Second Augusta, 156, 163, 166, 167, 168, 236
Third Legion Cyrenaica, 195
Sixth Legion Victrix, 28, 57, 146, 177, 178, 195, 302
Ninth Legion Hispana, 28, 197, 201, 202, 203, 204, 205, 302
Fourteenth Legion Gemina, 288
Twentieth Legion Valeria Victrix, 121-2, 127, 146, 173, 175, 176, 178, 177, 195, 288
Twenty-Second Legion Second Primigenia, 204
Leicester (*Ratae*), 10, 11, 12, 183-96
aqueduct, 184, 192, 196
bathhouse, Jewry Wall, 14, 184, 186, 190-2, 196
burial/cemetery, 184, 193
Cherry Orchard Mosaic, 194
defences/town walls, 183, 184, 185, 187, 188, 192-3, 195
fort (?), 184, 188
forum, 184, 189-90
fountain (*septizonium*), 189
Jewry Wall Museum, 184, 185, 186, 188, 190, 191, 192, 193
macellum/market hall, 184, 190
oppidum, 186, 187-8
townhouse, Vine Street, 10, 183, 186, 189, 194-5, 196
Lexden Tumulus, *see* Colchester
Lincoln (*Lindum*), 6, 11, 12, 19, 35, 115, 197-215
aqueduct/water supply, 14, 198, 204, 207, 211, 212-13
Roaring Meg (spring), 212
Brayford Pool, 202, 205

burial/cemetery
  tombstone, 204, 213–4
church (?), St Paul in the Bail, 19, 35, 215
defences/town walls, 6, 16, 168, 179, 197, 198, 200, 204–10, 213
  Newport Arch, 97, 200, 205–7
fortress, 6, 197, 201, 202, 203–4, 205, 207, 211
forum, 197, 198, 200, 201, 211–2, 215
Mint Wall, 211
Iron Age finds, 200, 201, 202, 203, 215
Witham Shield, 202
Lincoln Museum, 197, 199, 200, 202, 204, 213
mosaics, 213
Lower City, 197, 200, 203, 205, 209–11, 213
Upper City, 197, 200, 205–9, 211, 213
London (*Londinium*), 2, 7, 8, 9, 12, 17, 18, 19, 20, 83, 99, 110, 115, 122, 131, 170, 203, 217–38, 249, 260, 262, 266, 299, 301
  amphitheatre, 99, 218, 220, 221, 222, 226, 227, 228, 237
  Billingsgate bathhouse, 17, 220, 234–5
  Bloomberg letters, 225, 260
  bridge, 218, 222, 226, 233, 237
  burial/cemetery, 18, 218, 226, 230–1
    mausoleum (?), St Brides, 220, 231
  Classicianus, Gaius Julius Alpinus (provincial procurator), 226

defences/town walls, 20, 218, 220, 222, 229, 231–4, 237–8
  City Wall at Vine Street, 20, 232, 237
  fort, Cripplegate, 220, 229–30, 231, 232, 234
Fortunata (enslaved woman), 228
forum, 218, 220, 222, 225, 226, 228–9, 233, 237
'governor's palace', 218, 226, 262
'imperial palace' (?), 218, 236–7
London Museum, 18, 19, 217, 220, 221, 229
London Mithraeum, 15, 20, 218, 220, 221, 235–6
Lud, King (legendary founder of London, 20, 223

macellum/market hall
  Leicester, 184, 190
  Wroxeter, 286, 293
Maiden Castle hillfort, *see* Dorchester
Mainz (Germany), 204
Mars Ocelus (deity), 60, 64
Maumbury Rings amphitheatre, *see* Dorchester
Mediterranean, 18, 92, 133, 264, 281
Mercury (divinity), 30, 111
Merida (Spain), 135
Milan (Italy), 135
Minerva (deity) (*see also* Sulis Minerva), 37, 43, 94, 96, 155
Mithras (divinity), 136, 189, 235–6, 308
mosaic floor, 9, 17, 20, 43, 57, 58, 59, 60, 95, 107, 120, 161, 162, 171, 193, 194, 213, 230, 247, 251, 255, 261, 262, 278, 288, 294, 307

Aldborough, 20, 23, 32-3, 34
Canterbury Museum, 81-2
Cirencester, Corinium Museum, 113-14
Colchester, Firstsite Art Museum, 135
Leicester, Cherry Orchard Mosaic, 194
Verulamium Museum and 'Roman Hypocaust', 261, 262
municipium (*also see* Verulamium), 7, 254, 259, 260-8
Museum of Gloucester, *see* Gloucester
Museum of Wales, 54

Narbonensis (southern Gaul), 57
Neptune (divinity), 72, 94, 96
Nero (Roman emperor), 95, 108, 122, 128, 243, 245, 246, 259
Nerva (Roman emperor), 175, 177, 178
Newport Arch, *see* Lincoln
Niblett, Rosalind, 256
North Africa, 189, 196
Norwich Castle Museum, 67
Novium Museum, *see* Chichester

Ocenus (deity), 262, 306
Ogham stone, *see* Silchester
oppidum, 5-6, 7, 10, 13, 188, 245, 254, 256, 257, 276
  Bagendon, 6, 103, 106, 107, 108
  Canterbury, 6, 7, 75, 77, 78-9, 80
  Chichester, 7, 90, 92, 93-4, 95, 100
  Colchester, 6, 121, 123-5, 127, 136, 242, 245, 246, 257, 258
  Leicester, 186, 187-8
  Silchester, 6, 7, 11, 95, 239, 242, 243-5, 247
  Verulamium, 6, 7, 107, 108, 242, 245, 254, 255, 256-9, 260, 268
Oram's Arbour fort, *see* Winchester

Paulinus, Tiberius Claudius (Roman official), 57, 59-60
people/'tribes' (of Britain), 2, 5, 7, 8, 9, 94, 128, 155, 222, 225, 256, 257, 276, 307
  Atrebates, 5, 239, 243
  Belgae, 274, 276, 277
  Brigantes, 23, 29
  Cantaci, 78
  Catuvellauni, 5, 108, 257
  Corieltauvi, 183, 186, 187
  Cornovii, 289, 290
  Dobunni, 103, 108, 109
  Dumnonii, 163, 168
  Durotriges, 149, 153
  Iceni, 65, 73, 129
  Regni, 89, 92, 94
  Silures, 51, 55
  Trinovantes, 5, 123, 129
Plutarch (Roman author), 306
population, figures for Roman towns, 12
Poundbury Fort (Iron Age), *see* Dorchester
provincial governor, 5, 16, 29, 42, 115, 204, 226, 227, 262, 306
  Agricola, Gnaeus Julius, 260, 302, 306
  Septimus, Lucius, 110
provincial procurator, 5, 29, 225, 227
  Classicianus, Gaius Julius Alpinus (provincial procurator), 226

Reading Museum, 242, 247, 250
Regni (Iron Age people/Roman *civitas*), 89, 92, 94

Index

Rhineland (Germany), 110
Richborough Roman fort and town, 84
river, 12–13, 65, 242
   Avon, 37
   Churn, 108, 109
   Colne/Roman, 123, 132
   Exe, 163, 166, 167, 169, 170, 171
   Frome, 149, 156, 160
   Great Stour, 79, 80, 81, 82, 83, 85
   Itchen, 274, 275, 276, 278, 280
   Lavant, 98
   Ouse, 299, 302, 303, 305, 306, 308
   Severn, 181, 288, 296
   Soar, 186, 187, 188, 193
   Tas, 65, 71, 72
   Thames, 220, 221, 222, 224, 227, 231, 234
   Till, 202
   Tyne, 140, 142, 148
   Ure, 26, 28, 29, 34
   Ver, 254, 256, 257, 261, 265, 266
   Walbrook, 235
   Witham, 197, 201, 202, 203, 205, 210
Roecliff Roman fort, *see* Aldborough
Roman citizen, 2, 6, 7, 34, 94, 127, 178, 204, 259
Rome (city of), 57, 95, 100, 127, 135, 171, 177–8, 189, 257
Royal Albert Memorial Museum, *see* Exeter

St Alban (martyr), *see* Verulamium
St Albans, 252–3, 254, 255, 258
   St Albans Abbey/Cathedral, 255, 267, 268
St Augustine (Christian saint), 86
Septimus, Lucius (provincial governor of *Britannia Prima*), 110

Serapis (deity), 308
Severus, Septimius (Roman emperor), 143, 302, 306–7
Shakespeare, William, 123, 263
Silchester (*Calleva*), 7, 11, 12, 80, 97, 108, 239–50
   amphitheatre, 99, 113, 158, 239, 240, 242, 246–7, 248, 249
   burial/cemetery, 240, 246, 249–50
   tombstone, 249–50
   defences/ town walls, 110, 239, 240, 242, 243, 248–9
   forum, 240, 243, 245, 247
   Ogham stone, 250
   Onion (giant)/Onion hole, 248, 250
   oppidum, 6, 7, 11, 95, 239, 242, 243–5, 247
   Inner Earthworks, 6, 244–5, 247, 248
   Silchester Eagle, 247
Silures (Iron Age people/Roman *civitas*), 51, 55
slaves, *see* enslaved people
sling bullets (Roman), 256
small towns, 4
Sol Invictus (deity), 147
spring, 14, 37, 144, 158, 212, 242, 278
   Roaring Meg, Lincoln, 212
   Sacred Spring at Bath, 41, 42–5, 48, 96, 194
Stanegate (Roman road), 141, 142, 143, 144, 145, 146
statue, 13, 15, 30, 43, 57, 110, 111, 144, 175, 178, 191, 211, 247, 255, 304, 307
street systems (of towns), 13, 14, 26, 37, 68, 69, 70, 73, 78, 80, 89, 107, 131, 158, 166, 188,

Index

204, 243, 255, 261, 274, 278, 289
Sutcliff, Rosemary, 247
Sulis (deity), 4, 37, 41, 42, 43, 44
Sulis Minerva (deity), 16, 37, 40, 41, 42–3, 46, 96

Tacitus (Roman author), 6, 7, 16, 94, 127, 128, 129, 134, 224, 225, 254, 259
Tar Barrow, *see* Cirencester
Tarragona (Spain), 133
Tasciovanus (Iron Age king), 257
taxation, 5, 168
temple, 15, 19, 37, 45, 80, 109, 126, 130, 136, 147, 189, 201, 226, 235, 246, 255, 261, 264, 278, 287, 290, 308
  classical temple, 15, 78, 80, 81, 87, 212, 226, 236–7
  Bath, temple of Sulis Minerva, 12, 15, 37, 38, 39, 40, 41, 42–4, 46, 47, 48, 49, 194
  Colchester, temple of Claudius, 15, 43, 44, 81, 118, 120, 121, 122, 128, 129–30, 131, 132–4, 226
  Chichester, temple of Neptune and Minerva, 94, 96
  London Mithraeum, 15, 20, 218, 220, 221, 235–6
  Romano-Celtic temple, 15, 32, 66, 68, 69, 70, 73, 230, 259, 264
  Caerwent, 15, 51, 52, 54, 55, 56, 58–9, 60, 62
  Maiden Castle, Dorchester, 155, 162
theatre, 9, 15, 40, 45, 80, 109, 126, 189, 263, 264
  Canterbury, 76, 78, 79, 80, 81

Colchester, 118, 120, 134, 263
Verulamium, 80, 251, 252, 253, 254, 255, 262–4, 266
Theodosius (Roman emperor), 222, 237
Thetys (deity), 306
Thrace (Roman province), 127, 177
Togidubnus, Tiberius Claudius (Iron Age 'friendly' ruler), 9, 20, 89, 90, 92–3, 94, 95, 96, 100, 101, 243, 274, 276
tombstones, *see* burial
tower/bastion/internal tower (on wall circuit), 17, 26, 31, 54, 67, 71, 82, 83, 97, 98, 110, 111, 131, 132, 169, 179, 205, 209, 215, 229, 265, 279
  Caerwent (tower/bastion), 61, 62–3
  Canterbury (internal tower), 84
  Cirencester (tower/bastion), 112
  London, Vine Street (tower/bastion), 237–8
  Verulamium (tower/bastion), 266
Tower of London, 232
townhouse, *see* houses
town walls, *see* defences
trade, 14, 28, 29, 78, 96, 181, 217, 221–2, 223, 224, 225, 226, 228, 230, 231, 237, 260, 262, 291, 308
Treveri (Iron Age people/Roman *civitas* on the Continent), 289
tribes, *see* peoples
Trinovantes (Iron Age people/Roman *civitas*), 5, 123, 129

Valerian (Roman emperor), 268
Verica (Iron Age king), 255

Verulamium, 2, 7, 15, 20, 80, 107, 108, 188, 203, 225, 246, 251–69, 277
  burial/cemetery, 252, 254, 256, 258, 259, 264, 267
  Folly Lane burial and temple, 108, 246, 256, 258–9, 264
  defences/town walls, 16, 251, 252, 255, 256, 260, 261, 262, 264–7
  forum, 252, 255, 258, 259, 260
  oppidum, 6, 7, 107, 108, 242, 245, 254, 255, 256–9, 260, 268
  Beech Bottom dyke, 258
  shops, 17, 251, 260, 262
  St Alban (martyr), 19, 255, 267–8
  theatre, 80, 251, 252, 253, 254, 255, 262–4, 266
  townhouse/mosaic, 251, 261–2
  Verulamium Museum, 10, 251, 252, 254, 258, 259, 260, 261, 262, 269
  Verulamium Park, 253, 254, 262, 265, 266
Vindolanda Tablets, 28, 142, 148

Watling Street (Roman road), 83, 84, 261, 262, 266, 267, 291, 295
wetlands, 12, 188, 197, 201, 202, 204, 205
Wheeler, Mortimer, 122, 154, 255
Wheeler, Tessa, 154, 255
White, Roger, 288
Winchester (*Venta Belgarum*), 11, 18, 20, 55, 68, 188, 249, 271–81
  burial/cemetery, 272, 277, 281
    Lankhills cemetery, 275, 281
  defences/town walls, 20, 271, 272, 274, 275, 276, 277, 279–81

Oram's Arbour (Iron Age fort), 272, 274, 275–6, 277, 278, 281
  Winchester City Museum, 271, 272, 273, 274, 278
Wood, John (the Elder), 48
Wroxeter (*Viriconium*), 8, 11, 19, 168, 283–97
  bathhouse, Old Work, 14, 284, 286, 287, 288, 290, 291–3, 296, 297
  burial/cemetery, 284, 296
    tombstone, 296
  defences, 16, 284, 286, 287, 290, 294–6, 297
  fortress, 8, 11, 283, 287, 288, 289, 296
  forum, 283, 284, 286, 287, 288, 289, 290–1, 293, 294, 296, 297
  latrine, 291, 293
  macellum/market hall, 286, 293
  shops, 291, 293
  townhouse (reconstruction), 17, 283–4, 286, 290, 292, 293–4

York (*Eboracum*), 7, 8, 11, 19, 115, 141, 299–309
  burial/cemetery, 300, 303, 308
    tombstone, 308
  defences/town walls, 299, 300, 305, 307–8
  Demetrius of Tarsus, 306, 307, 309
  fortress, 11, 57, 203, 299, 300, 302, 303, 304, 305, 308, 309
  'Ivory Bangle Lady', 308, 309
  York Archaeological Trust, 303
  Yorkshire Museum, York, 18, 19, 299, 301, 302, 304, 305, 307, 308
York Minster, 302, 304, 307